Hubert Ashton Holden

Foliorum Silvula, Part the Second

Being select passages for translation into Latin lyric and iambic verse. Third Edition

Hubert Ashton Holden

Foliorum Silvula, Part the Second
Being select passages for translation into Latin lyric and iambic verse. Third Edition

ISBN/EAN: 9783744795371

Printed in Europe, USA, Canada, Australia, Japan

Cover: Foto ©Thomas Meinert / pixelio.de

More available books at **www.hansebooks.com**

Foliorum Silvula

PART THE SECOND

BEING SELECT PASSAGES FOR TRANSLATION
INTO LATIN LYRIC AND IAMBIC VERSE

EDITED WITH NOTES BY THE REVEREND
HUBERT ASHTON HOLDEN LL.D.
HEAD MASTER OF IPSWICH SCHOOL
LATE FELLOW AND ASSISTANT TUTOR OF TRINITY COLLEGE
CAMBRIDGE
EDITOR OF ARISTOPHANES ETC.

Third Edition

CAMBRIDGE
DEIGHTON BELL AND CO
LONDON BELL AND DALDY
1864

INDEX OF EXAMINATIONS

CAMBRIDGE

University Scholarships, 114, 157, 58, 166, 224, 303, 304, 376, 416, 419, 442
Bell University Scholarships, 185, 253, 311
Chancellor's Medals, 93, 114, 128, 239, 268, 401, 402, 413, 421, 422, 475
Classical Tripos, 22, 34, 47, 54, 99, 109, 176, 177, 247, 273, 277, 298, 301, 350, 405, 407, 435, 487
Trinity College Fellowships, 36, 51, 53, 67, 84, 88, 153, 160, 175, 200, 214, 251, 269, 270, 302, 334, 361, 364, 400, 486
Downing College Fellowships, 146

Trinity College Scholarships, 133, 149, 180, 258, 271
Magdalene College Scholarships, 86, 426
St Peter's College, 143, 222, 240
Caius College, 57
Corpus Christi College, 150
King's College, 224, 360
Christ's College, 119, 138, 210
St John's College, 11, 29, 66, 87, 144, 206, 281, 306, 313, 363, 365, 427, 430, 519
Magdalene College, 96, 420, 433
Trinity College, 278, 280
Emmanuel College, 205

OXFORD

Ireland University Scholarships, 141, 164, 266, 295
Hertford University Scholarships, 115, 116
Lusby Scholarships, 276, 287

Balliol College Scholarships, 158
Exeter College ,, 239
Corpus Christi College ,, 73, 190, 263
Oriel College ,, 178, 199
Trinity College ,, 183

TRINITY COLLEGE, DUBLIN, 170, 253, 254, 321, 429, 438, 444, 479, 481

INDEX OF AUTHORS

WITH REFERENCES TO THE SECTIONS

A

ADDISON, JOSEPH, 23, 87, 246
Æschylus, 406
Akenside, Mark, 149, 241, 326
Alcæus, 413
Amelia, Princess, 82
Amos, 6
Aristoteles, 400
Arnold, Matthew, 203

B

Bacchylides, 28, 93
Bacon, Francis Lord, 477
Barbauld, Anna Lætitia, 170, 171
Barnard, E. W. 340
Barry Cornwall, 312, 324, 386
Beattie, James, 251, 272, 321
Beaumont and Fletcher, 22, 95
Blackburne, T. 509
Bowles, Caroline (Mrs Southey), 318, 338
Bowles, William Lisle, 482
Browne, W. 445
Bryant, W. C. 254, 350, 363
Burns, Robert, 52, 73, 210, 249, 365, 366, 455
Byron, Lord, 18, 72, 161, 162, 163, 185, 252, 263

C

Campbell, Thomas, 97, 294, 300, 457, 458
Carew, T. 37, 50, 80, 215, 216, 315, 381, 435
Carlyle, J. D. 182
Coleridge, Hartley, 431

Coleridge, S. T. 132, 145
Collins, W. 332, 344, 345, 375, 399, 471, 472, 473
Collins —, 466
Congreve, William, 248
Constable, Henry, 117
Cotton, Charles, 461
Cornish, George, 56
Cowley, Abraham, 16, 55, 150, 151, 160, 193, 194, 195, 196, 197, 316, 317, 335, 354, 359, 360, 434, 470, 510
Cowper, William, 374
Croft, Sir Thomas, 446
Croly, George, 166, 261
Cumberland, Richard, 15, 16, 17, 18, 19

D

Daniel, Samuel, 122, 123, 232, 233, 378, 463
Darwin, Erasmus, 159
D'Avenant, Sir William, 36
Davies, Sir John, 142
Dekker, 124
Denham, Sir John, 156
De Vere, Aubrey, 34
Donne, Dr John, 311, 460
Drummond, W. 66, 118, 119, 120, 121, 207
Dryden, John, 51, 53, 54, 235, 236, 323, 427, 442
Duncombe, W. 488

E

Ecclesiasticus, 355
Edwards, Richard, 593
Elizabeth, Charlotte, 475

Index of Authors

Euripides, 27, 92, 418, 419, 420, 421, 422, 423, 424
Ezekiel, 493

F
Ferrer, Miss, 376
Fletcher, John, 201, 437, 464, 469
Fletcher, Phineas, 8
Fosbery, T. V. 436

G
Grahame, James, Marquis of Montrose, 330
Grant, Dr, 69
Gray, Thomas, 11, 183, 239, 333, 334, 382, 383, 397, 398, 456, 467
Greene, Robert, 384

H
Habington, William, 202, 277, 281, 393, 394, 468, 508
Habakkuk, 492
Hagthorpe, 473
Hagthorpe, J. 476
Hamilton, W. 364
Hastings, Warren, 45
Heber, Reginald, 5, 265, 320, 379
Hemans, Felicia, 179, 276, 287, 288, 289, 346, 438
Herbert, George, 490
Herbert, Hon. William, 352, 380
Herrick, Robert, 1, 2, 32, 83, 140, 181, 209, 213, 224, 231, 270, 342
Hodgson, Francis, 86
Hood, Thomas, 157, 357, 430
Hughes, John, 389, 390

J
Isaiah, 494, 495, 496, 497
Jeremiah, 286, 501, 502, 503, 504
Jones, Sir William, 459
Jonson, Ben, 30, 267, 10, 11, 12, 13

K
Keats, John, 31, 377
Keble, John, 63, 77, 84, 184, 217, 230, 244, 298, 479
Kepler, John, 311
King, Henry, 75, 76, 274
Kingsley, Charles, 70
Knight, Gally, 26

L
Landor, W. S. 46, 71
Logan, John, 186, 187, 188, 189
Lovelace, Richard, 262
Lyra Apostolica, 85, 93, 136, 192, 331
Lyte, Henry F. 291
Lyttelton, George Lord, 506, 507

M
Macaulay, Lord, 177
Marvell, Andrew, 218, 362, 447, 478
Massinger, Philip, 138, 14
Melinno, 408
Merrick, James, 153
Milman, H. H. 303, 304
Milnes, R. Monckton, 64, 89
Milton, John, 112, 113, 114, 115, 116, 146, 180, 256, 371, 372, 373
Moir, D. M. 204
Montgomery, James, 155, 234, 395, 396
Montrose, Marquis of, *vide* J. Grahame
Moore, Thomas, 74, 154, 200, 237, 238, 250, 257, 260, 337, 449
More, Henry, 62
Moschus, 94
Moses, 499, 500, 505

N
Nairn, Lady, 325
Nash, T. 90

O
Otway, Thomas, 60

P
Parnell, Thomas, 144, 273
Peacham, Henry, 41
Philemon, 25
Philips, Ambrose, 329
Pindarus, 401, 402, 403, 404, 405, 409, 410, 411
Pope, Alexander, 3, 65, 273, 319, 511
Praed, W. M. 441
Prior, M. 292
Procter, Adelaide, A. 285
Procter, Bryan Walter, 312, 324, 386

Q

Quarles Francis, 223
Queen Elizabeth, 29

R

Raleigh, Sir Walter, 343
Rickards, Samuel, 293
Rogers, Samuel, 190, 295

S

Samuel, 498
Scadlock, J. 174
Schiller, J. F. 227, 228, 229
Scott, Sir Walter, 10, 15, 19, 58, 96, 141, 147, 172, 173, 253, 269, 336
Sedley, Sir C. 279
Selden, John, 33
Shakespeare, W. 14, 47, 88, 109, 110, 111, 512, 513, 514, 1, 2, 3, 5, 6, 7, 8, 9, 20
Shelley, P. B. 4, 44, 57, 143, 158, 164, 183, 191, 198, 247, 258, 259, 275, 356, 439, 450, 451, 480, 481
Shenstone, William, 177
Shirley, James, 206, 361
Sidney, Sir Philip, 105
Sigourney, Lydia H. 214
Solomon, 355
Sophocles, 407, 414, 415, 416, 417
Southey, Robert, 148, 167, 268, 297, 310, 341, 491
Southwell, Robert, 38, 39, 40
Spencer, W. R. 21, 78
Spenser, Edmund, 106, 107, 108, 264
Stanley, Thomas, 176, 226
Steele, Sir Richard, 329
Stevens, G. A. 489
Suckling, Sir J. 59
Surrey, Earl of, 219
Synesius, 425

T

Tannahill, Robert, 220
Tennyson, Alfred, 67, 99, 205, 208, 305, 306, 307, 370, 429
Theobald, 61
Theocritus, 412
Thompson, William, 48
Thomson, James, 369, 443
Tollet, Elizabeth, 280
Trench, R. C. 35, 484, 485, 486, 487
Trevor, George, 12

V

Vaughan, Henry, 242, 243, 283, 284, 309, 314, 339, 349, 353, 387, 388, 391, 392, 432, 433, 452, 453, 462

W

Walker, William Sidney, 221
Waller, Edmund, 266, 313
Warton, Joseph, 302
Warton, Thomas, 347, 348, 448
Watts, Isaac, 483
White, H. K. 133, 134, 135, 322, 367, 368
Wither, G. 454
Wordsworth, William, 9, 13, 17, 24, 43, 125, 126, 127, 128, 129, 130, 178, 199, 211, 212, 255, 271, 282, 301, 327, 452
Wotton, Sir Henry, 308
Wrangham, Francis, 68, 139, 465, 474
Anonymous and uncertain, 7, 20, 42, 49, 79, 81, 91, 100, 101, 102, 103, 104, 131, 137, 152, 165, 168, 169, 222, 225, 240, 245, 290, 296, 299, 318, 328, 351, 358, 385, 426, 428, 440, 444

COMPARATIVE TABLE OF SECTIONS IN SECOND AND THIRD EDITIONS

[* In part only. † Part I. *Ed.* 3]

2d Ed.	3d Ed.	2d Ed.	3d Ed.	2d Ed.	3d Ed.
1	3	46	265*	82	435*
3	5	47	42	83	69
7	7	48	41	85	70
9	8	49	228—9*	86	71
10	9	50	43	87	72
11	10	51	44	91	74
12	11	52	144†	92	75
14	335*	55	46	94	77
15	22	56	47	95	78
16	23	57	118†	96	153†
17	24	58	48	97	79
18	4	59	50†	93	94
19	13	60	103	99	114
24	14	61	50	100	95
25	62†	62	51	101	115
26	16	63	52	102	130
27	350†	64	53	105	132
29	17	65	96	106	129
30	18	66	54	107	113
34	19	67	55	108	125
35	31	68	56	109	452†
36	510*	70	58	110	141
37	29	71	59	111	142
38	491*	72	60	112	118
39	30	73	61	114	144
40	35	74	62	115	145
41	36	75	63	116	146
42	37	76	64	118	134
44	39*	77	65	119	147
45	34	79	209	120	133*

Comparative Table of Sections

2d Ed.	3d Ed.	2d Ed.	3d Ed.	2d Ed.	3d Ed.
121	86	176	188	237	297
122	87	177	189	238	298
123	88	178	190	239	486†
124	99	179	236	240	299
125—6	328	181	200	241	300
127	148	182	201	242	301
128	149	183	239	243	492†
129	150	184	199	244	302
130	152	185	365†	245	303
131	153	186	240	246	304
133—4	430	187	241	247	307
135	154	188	242*	248	308
136	155	190	245	249	306
137	470†	191—2	459	250	310
138	102	194	244	251	402
139	158	195	248	252	251
140	159	196	641†	253	311
141	164	197	641†	254	486
142	161	198—9	462	255	488†
143	166	204	247	256	312
144	167	206	206	257	313
145	168	207	393	258	314
146	169	208	250	259	323
147	170	209	382*	260	324
148	171	210	257	261	359
149	312†	211	258	262	360
150	175	213	264	263	361
152	176	214	440†	264	354
153	177	215	441†	265	193—5*
155	178	216	267	266	363
156	179	217	437†	267	224
157	401†	218	268	269	352
158	180	219	269	270	484
159	181	220	270	271	485
160	182	221	271	272—3	436
161	183	222	272	274	365
162	184	223	273	275	614†
163	119	225	274	276	368
164	487	226	495†	278	369
165	211	227	296	279	613†
166	232	228	275	280	370
167	469—470†	229	276	283	373
168	248†	230	519†	284	367
169	185	231	277	285	374
170	385†	232	278	286	375
171	162	233	279	287	616†
172	197†	234	280	288	376
174	186	235	344	289	382
175	187	236	345	290	377

2d Ed.	3d Ed.	2d Ed.	3d Ed.	2d Ed.	3d Ed.
291	379	311	460	329	463
293	383	312	421	330	196*
294	551†	313	356	331	197*
295	471	314	439	332	469
296	450	315	464	333	437
297	453	316	418	334	143
298	100—1	317	414	335	400
299	639†	318	401	336	520†
300	442	319	495	337	413
303	501*	322	505	339	93
304	441	323	494	340	130†
305	448	324	501*	343	509
306	449	325	502	344	628†
307	364	326	503	346	3
308	456	327	504	347	1
310	452	328	500		

ADDITIONS AND CORRECTIONS

PART I

PAGE	NO.				
6	19	*for* SIR W. SCOTT *lege* J. BUNYAN			
36	123,	*add author's name*,			G. GASCOIGNE
97	273,	,,	,,	,,	R. BURNS
131	349,	,,	,,	,,	F. HEMANS
172	436,	,,	,,	,,	,,
280	621,	,,	,,	,,	W. C. BRYANT
322	708,	,,	,,	,,	F. HEMANS
324	714,	,,	,,	,,	J. DRYDEN
352	784,	,,	,,	,,	F. HEMANS
360	824,	,,	,,	,,	W. WORDSWORTH
373	831,	,,	,,	,,	J. DYER
427	941,	,,	,,	,,	A. TENNYSON
454	990,	,,	,,	,,	S. T. COLERIDGE
480	1034,	,,	,,	,,	E. FAIRFAX

PART II

23	69, *add author's name*, DR GRANT: l. 2, *lege* now thy tyrant reign: l. 3, *for* merry *lege* mystic: l. 5, *for* bowl *lege* bowls: l. 6, *for* merry *lege* happy	
123	292, *add author's name*, M. PRIOR	
215	449, ,, ,, ,, H. TAYLOR	

PASSAGES FOR TRANSLATION

INTO LATIN LYRIC VERSE

1

LYRICS FOR LEGACIES

GOLD I've none, for use or show,
neither silver to bestow
at my death; but thus much know,

that each lyric here shall be
of my love a legacy,
left to all posterity.

Gentle friends, then do but please
to accept such coins as these,
as my last remembrances.

R. HERRICK

2

A CANTICLE TO APOLLO

PLAY, Phœbus, on thy lute,
and we will sit all mute;
by listening to thy lyre,
that sets all ears on fire.

Hark! hark! the God does play;
and as he leads the way
through heaven, the very spheres,
as men, turn all to ears.

R. HERRICK

3

MUSIC

MUSIC the fiercest grief can charm,
and fate's severest rage disarm;
music can soften pain to ease,
and make despair and madness please:
our joys below it can improve,
and antedate the bliss above.

A. POPE

4

MUSIC, when soft voices die,
vibrates in the memory—
odours, when sweet violets sicken,
live within the sense they quicken.

Rose leaves, when the rose is dead,
are heap'd for the beloved's bed;
and so thy thoughts, when thou art gone,
love itself shall slumber on.

P. B. SHELLEY

5

EVENING HYMN

GOD that madest earth and heaven,
darkness and light!
who the day for toil hast given,
for rest the night!
may Thine Angel Guards defend us,
slumber sweet Thy mercy send us,
holy dreams and hopes attend us,
this livelong night!

R. HEBER

6

A LAMENT FOR ISRAEL

HEAR ye this word which I take up against you,
even a lamentation, O house of Israel.
The virgin of Israel is fallen; she shall no more rise:
she is forsaken upon her land; there is none to raise
her up.

Wailing shall be in all the streets;
and they shall say in all the high-ways, Alas! alas!
and they shall call the husbandman to mourning,
and such as are skilful of lamentation to wailing.

AMOS

7

A SIMILE

I SAW a falling leaf soon strew
the soil to which it owed its birth;
I saw a bright star falling too,
but never reach the quiet earth.

Such is the lowly portion blest,
  such is ambition's foiled endeavour;
the falling leaf is soon at rest,
  while stars that fall fall on for ever.

8   *JOYS AS WINGED DREAMS FLY FAST*

BUT, ah! what liveth long in happiness?
  grief of a heavy nature steady lies,
and cannot be remov'd for weightiness;
  but joy of lighter presence eas'ly flies,
and seldom comes, and soon away will go:
some secret power here all things orders so,
that for a sunshine day follows an age of woe.
P. FLETCHER

9   *AN OLD MAN'S REFLECTIONS*

MY eyes are dim with childish tears,
  my heart is idly stirr'd,
for the same sound is in my ears
  which in those days I heard.

Thus fares it still in our decay;
  and yet the wiser mind
mourns less for what time takes away,
  than what he leaves behind.
W. WORDSWORTH

10   *MAJOR BELLENDEN'S SONG*

AND what though winter will pinch severe
  through locks of grey and a cloak that's old,
yet keep up thy heart, bold cavalier,
  for a cup of sack shall fence the cold.
For time will rust the brightest blade,
  and years will break the strongest bow;
was never wight so starkly made,
  but time and years would overthrow.
SIR W. SCOTT

11   *GRATITUDE*

WHAT is grandeur, what is power?
  heavier toil, superior pain.
what the bright reward we gain?
  the grateful memory of the good.

Sweet is the breath of vernal shower,
the bee's collected treasures sweet,
sweet music's melting fall, but sweeter yet
the still small voice of gratitude.

T. GRAY

12

O, WEEP not for the gathered rose!
   O mourn not for the friend that dies!
In beauty's breast the flower blows—
   the soul is happy in the skies.

Weep not for these! but weep for them,
   the unloved, the friendless, the unknown—
the flowers that wither on the stem,
   the living that must live alone!

G. TREVOR

13

THE DEATH OF THE GOOD

A POWER is passing from the earth
   to breathless Nature's dark abyss;
but when the great and good depart,
what is it more than this,

that man, who is from GOD sent forth,
doth yet again to GOD return?
Such ebb and flow must ever be;
then wherefore should we mourn?

W. WORDSWORTH

14

SERENADE

HARK! hark! the lark at heaven's gate sings,
   and Phœbus 'gins arise,
his steeds to water at those springs
   on chaliced flowers that lies;
and winking Mary-buds begin
   to ope their golden eyes;
with everything that pretty bin:
   my lady sweet, arise;
     arise, arise.

W. SHAKESPEARE

15 *TO A LADY, WITH FLOWERS FROM A ROMAN WALL.*

TAKE these flowers, which purple waving
    on the ruined rampart grew,
where, the sons of freedom braving,
    Rome's imperial standards flew.

Warriors from the breach of danger
    pluck no longer laurels there;
they but yield the passing stranger
    wild-flower wreaths for Beauty's hair.
SIR W. SCOTT

16 *THE RESURRECTION*

BEGIN the song, and strike the living lyre;
    lo, how the years to come, a numerous and well-
        fitted quire,
all hand in hand do decently advance
and to my song with smooth and equal measures dance.

Whilst the dance last, how long soe'er it be,
my music's voice shall bear it company;
    till all gentle notes be drowned
    in the last trumpet's dreadful sound.
A. COWLEY

17 *THE RAINBOW*

MY heart leaps up when I behold
    a rainbow in the sky!
so was it when my life began,
so is it, now I am a man,
so shall be it, when I grow old,
    or let me die!
The Child is father of the Man,
and I could wish my days to be
bound each to each by natural piety.
W. WORDSWORTH

18

    —'TIS sweet to hear
at midnight on the blue and moonlit deep
the song and oar of Adria's gondolier,
    by distance mellowed, o'er the waters sweep;

'tis sweet to see the evening star appear;
  'tis sweet to listen as the night-winds creep
from leaf to leaf; 'tis sweet to view on high
  the rainbow, based on ocean, span the sky.

LORD BYRON

19   *LITTLE IS BEST*

HE that is down need fear no fall,
  he that is low no pride;
he that is humble ever shall
  have God to be his guide.

Fulness to such a burthen is
  that go on pilgrimage;
here little, and hereafter bliss,
  is best from age to age.

SIR W. SCOTT

20   *THE PATH OF DUTY*

NOT once or twice in our rough island story
  the path of duty was the way to glory:
he that walks it, only thirsting
for the right, and learns to deaden
love of self, before his journey closes
he shall find the stubborn thistle bursting
into glossy purples, which outredden
all voluptuous garden-roses.

21   *VISIONS OF DEPARTED JOYS*

WHEN midnight o'er the moonless skies
  her pall of transient death has spread,
when mortals sleep, when spectres rise,
  and none are wakeful but the dead;
no bloodless shape my way pursues,
no sheeted ghost my couch annoys,
visions more sad my fancy views,—
visions of long-departed joys.

W. R. SPENSER

THE DYING MAIDEN'S SONG

L AY a garland on my hearse of the dismal yew;
maidens, willow-branches bear; say I died true.
My love was false, but I was firm from my hour of birth;
upon my buried body lie lightly, gentle earth!
BEAUMONT AND FLETCHER

HUMILITY

M Y fortune might I form at will,
my canvas Zephyrs soft should fill
with gentle breath, lest ruder gales
crack the main-yard or burst the sails:
by winds that temperately blow
the barque should pass secure and slow,
nor scare me leaning on her side:
but smoothly cleave the unruffled tide.
J. ADDISON

A SLUMBER did my spirit seal;
I had no human fears:
she seemed a thing that could not feel
the touch of earthly years.

No motion has she now, no force;
she neither hears nor sees;
rolled round in earth's diurnal course
with rocks, and stones, and trees!
W. WORDSWORTH

THE VANITY OF TEARS

Εἰ τὰ δάκρυ' ἡμῖν τῶν κακῶν ἦν φάρμακον,
ἀεί θ' ὁ κλαύσας τοῦ πονεῖν ἐπαύετο,
ἠλλαττόμεσθ' ἂν δάκρυα δόντες χρυσίον·
νῦν δ' οὐ προσέχει τὰ πράγματ' οὐδ' ἀποβλέπει
εἰς ταῦτα, δέσποτ', ἀλλὰ τὴν αὐτὴν ὁδόν,
ἐάν τε κλαίῃς ἄν τε μή, πορεύσεται.
Τί οὖν ποιεῖς πλέον; οὐδέν· ἡ λύπη δ' ἔχει,
ὥσπερ τὸ δένδρον τοῦτο καρπὸν, τὸ δάκρυον.
PHILEMON

26   *CHARITY*

O H, golden link connecting man with man,
    celestial charity! oh, rarely seen
since lust of rule and thirst of gold began
   unhallowed reign—whenc'er thy look serene
sheds placid influence, how the softened mien
and softened heart consenting own thy sway!
   thus rifted ice, enchained by winter keen,
thawed by the sun, in rivers rolls away,
and glads the parched waste and sparkles to the day.
                              GALLY KNIGHT

27   *A WISH*

Κείσθω δόρυ μοι μίτον ἀμφιπλέκειν
ἀράχναις, μετὰ δ' ἡσυχίας πολιῷ
γήρᾳ συνοικοίην·
ἀείδοιμι δὲ στεφάνοις κάρα
πόλιον στεφανώσας,
Θρηίκιον πέλταν πρὸς Ἀθάνας
περικίοσιν ἀγκρεμάσας θαλάμοις,
δέλτων τ' ἀναπτύσσοιμι γῆρυν,
ἃν σόφοι κλέονται.
                              EVRIPIDES

28   *CHEERFULNESS*

Εἷς ὅρος, μία δὲ βροτοῖς ἐστὶν εὐτυχίας ὁδός,
θυμὸν εἴτις ἔχων ἀπενθῆ δύναται διατελεῖν βίον·
οἷς δὲ μέριμνα μὲν ἀμφιπολεῖ φρενί,
τὸ δὲ παρ' ἀμάρ τε καὶ νύκτα μελλόντων χάριν
ἑὸν ἰάπτεται κέαρ, ἄκαρπον ἔχει πόνον·
τί γὰρ ἐλαφρὸν ἔτ' ἐστὶν ἄπρηκτ' ὀδυρόμενον δονεῖν
καρδίαν;
                              BACCHYLIDES

29   *TO FORTUNE*

O H, Fortune, how thy restless wavering state
    hath fraught with cares my troubled wit!
witness this present prison, whither fate
   could bear me, and the joys I quit:

thou causedest the guilty to be losed
from bands wherein are innocents inclosed,
  causing the guiltless to be strait reserved
  and freeing those that death had well deserved.
But by her envy can be nothing wrought,
so God send to my foes all they have thought.
QUEEN ELIZABETH

30   THE GOOD LIFE LONG LIFE

IT is not growing like a tree
  in bulk, doth make Man better be;
or standing long an oak, three hundred year,
to fall a log at last, dry, bald and sere:
    a lily of a day
    is fairer far in May,
although it fall and die that night —
it was the plant and flower of Light.
In small proportions we just beauties see;
and in short measures life may perfect be.
B. JONSON

31   ON A GRECIAN URN

WHO are these coming to the sacrifice?
  to what green altar, O mysterious priest,
lead'st thou that heifer lowing at the skies,
  and all her silken flanks with garlands drest?
what little town by river or sea-shore,
  or mountain-built with peaceful citadel,
    is emptied of its folk, this pious morn?
and, little town, thy streets for evermore
  will silent be; and not a soul to tell,
    why thou art desolate, can e'er return.
J. KEATS

32   GOOD PRECEPTS

IN all thy need, be thou possest
  still with a well-prepared breast;
nor let thy shackles make thee sad;
thou canst but have, what others had.
And this for comfort thou must know,
times that are ill wont still be so:

Clouds will not ever pour down rain:
a sullen day will clear again:
first peals of thunder we must hear,
then lutes and harps shall stroke the ear.
R. HERRICK

33   *TO MR WILLIAM BROWNE*

SO much a stranger my severer Muse
    is not to love-strains or a shepherd's reed,
but that she knows some rites of Phœbus' dues,
    of Pan, of Pallas and her sister's meed.
Read and commend she durst these tuned essays
    of him that loves her (she hath ever found
her studies as one circle). Next she prays
    his readers be with rose and myrtle crowned!
no willow touch them! As his bays are free
    from wrong of bolts, so may their chaplets be!
J. SELDEN

34   *MIDNIGHT SOUNDS*

AGAIN those sounds sweep on
    crushing the air to sweetness;
they came and they are gone;
again my dreams desert me;
    I sit once more alone.

When from some doomed city
    her gods depart, such sound
of mixed reproof and pity,
    in refluent airs half drowned,
is heard at night among the crowds,
    by kneelers on the ground.
A. DE VERE

35   *LIFE THROUGH DEATH*

A DEW-DROP, falling on the wild sea-wave,
    exclaimed in fear—'I perish in this grave:'
but in a shell received, that drop of dew
unto a pearl of marvellous beauty grew;
and, happy now, the grace did magnify
which thrust it forth, as it had feared, to die;—

until again, 'I perish quite,' it said,
torn by rude diver from its ocean bed:
O unbelieving!—so it came to gleam,
chief jewel in a Monarch's diadem.
R. C. TRENCH

36 *SONG*

THE lark now leaves his watery nest,
    and climbing shakes his dewy wings;
he takes his window for the east,
    and, to implore your light, he sings,
awake, awake, the moon will never rise,
till she can dress her beauty at your eyes.

The merchant bows unto the seaman's star,
    the ploughman from the sun his season takes;
but still the lover wonders what they are,
    that look for day before his mistress wakes:
awake, awake, break through your veils of lawn,
then draw your curtains and begin the dawn.
SIR W. D'AVENANT

37 *THE TRUE BEAUTY*

HE that loves a rosy cheek
    or a coral lip admires,
or from star-like eyes doth seek
    fuel to maintain his fires;
as old Time makes these decay,
so his flames must waste away.

But a smooth and steadfast mind,
    gentle thoughts, and calm desires,
hearts with equal love combined,
    kindle never-dying fires:—
where these are not, I despise
lovely cheeks or lips or eyes.
T. CAREW

38 *CONTENT AND RICH*

MY conscience is my crown,
    contented thoughts my rest:
my heart is happy in itself,
    my bliss is in my breast.

Enough I reckon wealth:
a mean, the surest lot,
that lies too high for base contempt,
too low for envy's shot.

My wishes are but few,
all easy to fulfil,
I make the limits of my power
the bounds unto my will.

39 I feel no care for coin,
well-doing is my wealth;
my mind to me an empire is,
while grace affordeth health.

I clip high climbing thoughts,
the wings of swelling pride;
their fall is worst, that from the height
of greatest honours slide.

Sith sails of largest size
the storm doth soonest tear;
I bear so low and small a sail
as freeth me from fear.

40 I envy not their hap,
whom favour doth advance;
I take no pleasure in their pain,
that have less happy chance.

No change of Fortune's calms
can cast my comforts down:
when Fortune smiles, I smile to think
how quickly she will frown.

And when in froward mood
she proves an angry foe,
small gain I found to let her come,
less loss to let her go.

       R. SOUTHWELL.

41   *HVMILIBVS DAT GRATIAM*

THE mountains huge, that seem to check the sky,
 and all the world with greatness over-peer,
with heath or moss for most part barren lie;
 when valleys low doth kindly Phœbus cheer,
and with his heat in hedge and grove begets
the virgin primrose or sweet violets.

So God oft-times denies unto the great
    the gifts of nature or his heavenly grace,
and those that high in honour's chair are set
    do feel their wants: when men of meaner place,
although they lack the others' golden spring,
    perhaps are blest above the richest king.
H. PEACHAM

42   TO THE VIOLET

CHILD of the Spring! thou charming flower,
    no longer in confinement lie;
arise to light, thy form discover,
    rival the azure of the sky!

The rains are gone, the storms are o'er,
    winter retires to make thee way:
come then, thou sweetly-blooming flower,
    come, beauteous stranger, come away!

The sun is dressed in beaming smiles,
    to give thy beauties to the day;
young zephyrs wait with gentlest wiles
    to fan thy bosom, as they play.

43   TO THE CLYDE

LORD of the vale! astounding Flood;
    the dullest leaf in this thick wood
quakes—conscious of thy power;
the caves reply with hollow moan;
and vibrates to his central stone
    yon time-cemented Tower!

And yet how fair the rural scene!
for thou, O Clyde, hast ever been
    beneficent as strong;
pleased in refreshing dews to steep
the little trembling flowers that peep
    thy shelving rocks among.
W. WORDSWORTH

44   THE WORLD'S WANDERERS

TELL me, thou Star, whose wings of light
    speed thee in thy fiery flight,
in what cavern of the night
    will thy pinions close now?

Tell me, Moon, thou pale and grey
pilgrim of heaven's homeless way,
in what depth of night or day
    seekest thou repose now?

Weary Wind, who wanderest
like the world's rejected guest,
hast thou still some secret nest
    on the tree or billow?

P. B. SHELLEY

45   CONTENTMENT

SHORT is our span; then why engage
    in schemes, for which man's transient age
was ne'er by fate design'd?
Why slight the gift of Nature's hand?
What wanderer from his native land
    e'er left himself behind?

For me, O Shore, I only claim
to merit, not to seek for, fame:
    the good and just to please,
a state above the fear of want,
domestic love,—Heaven's choicest grant—
    health, leisure, peace and ease.

WARREN HASTINGS

46   AGAINST REGRET

WHY, why repine, my pensive friend,
    at pleasures slipt away?
Some the stern Fates will never lend,
    and all refuse to stay.

I see the rainbow in the sky,
    the dew upon the grass,
I see them, and I ask not why
    they glimmer or they pass.

With folded arms I linger not
    to call them back; 'twere vain;
in this or in some other spot
    I know they'll shine again.

W. S. LANDOR

47 *INFLUENCE OF MUSIC*

ORPHEUS with his lute made trees,
  and the mountain-tops that freeze,
bow themselves, when he did sing:
to his music plants and flowers
ever sprung; as sun and showers
  there had made a lasting spring.

Everything that heard him play,
even the billows of the sea,
  hung their heads, and then lay by.
In sweet music is such art;
killing care and grief of heart
  fall asleep, or hearing die.

W. SHAKESPEARE

48 *TO A SKYLARK*

FEATHERED lyric! warbling high,
  sweetly gaining on the sky,
opening with thy matin lay
(nature's hymn!) the eye of day,
teach my soul, on early wing,
thus to soar and thus to sing.

While the bloom of orient light
gilds thee in thy tuneful flight,
may the day-spring from on high,
seen by faith's religious eye,
cheer me with his vital ray,
promise of eternal day!

W. THOMPSON

49 *THE WORLD*

WHETHER men do laugh or weep,
  whether they do wake or sleep,
whether they feel heat or cold,
whether they be young or old;
  there is underneath the sun
  nothing in true earnest done.

All our pride is but a jest,
none are worst and none are best:
grief and joy, and hope and fear,
play their pageants everywhere;
  vain opinion all doth sway,
  and the world is but a play.

50   THE PRIMROSE

ASK me why I send you here
   this firstling of the infant year;
ask me why I send to you
this primrose all bepearled with dew;
I straight will whisper in your ears,
the sweets of love are washed with tears.

Ask me why this flower doth show
so yellow, green, and sickly too;
ask me why the stalk is weak,
and bending, yet it doth not break;
I must tell you these discover
what doubts and fears are in a lover.
                              T. CAREW

51   SONG TO BRITANNIA

FAIREST isle, all isles excelling,
   seat of pleasures and of loves;
Venus here will choose her dwelling,
  and forsake her Cyprian groves.

Cupid from his favourite nation
  care and envy will remove,
jealousy, that poisons passion,
  and despair, that dies for love.

Gentle murmurs, sweet complaining,
  sighs that blow the fire of love;
soft repulses, kind disdaining,
  shall be all the pains you prove.
                              J. DRYDEN

52   *THE INJURED LOVER*

HAD I a cave on some wild distant shore,
where the winds howl to the waves' dashing roar,
there would I weep my woes,
there seek my lost repose,
till grief my eyes should close,
    ne'er to wake more.

Falsest of womankind, canst thou declare
all thy fond-plighted vows—fleeting as air?
to thy new lover hie,
laugh o'er thy perjury,
then in thy bosom try
    what peace is there!
                                R. BURNS

53   *TO A FAIR YOUNG LADY, GOING OUT OF THE TOWN
              IN SPRING*

ASK not the cause why sullen Spring
    so long delays her flowers to bear;
why warbling birds forget to sing,
    and winter storms invert the year:
Chloris is gone, and fate provides
to make it Spring, where she resides.

Chloris is gone, the cruel fair;
    she cast not back a pitying eye:
but left her lover in despair,
    to sigh, to languish, and to die:
ah, how can those fair eyes endure
to give the wounds they will not cure!
                                J. DRYDEN

54   *THE FOLLY OF MAKING TROUBLES.*

AH, fading joy, how quickly art thou past!
    yet we thy ruin haste:
as if the cares of human life were few,
    we seek out new:
and follow fate, which would too fast pursue.

See, how on every bough the birds express
　　in their sweet notes their happiness:
　　they all enjoy and nothing spare;
but on their mother Nature lay their care:
why then should man, the lord of all below,
　　such troubles choose to know,
as none of all his subjects undergo?

　　　　　　　　　　　　　　J. DRYDEN

55　　　　　　　　SONG

THE merry waves dance up and down and play,
　　sport is granted to the sea:
birds are the queristers of th' empty air,
　　sport is never wanting there,
the ground doth smile at the spring's flowery birth,
　　sport is granted to the earth:
the fire its cheering flame on high doth rear,
　　sport is never wanting there:
if all the elements, the earth, the sea,
　　air and fire, so merry be;
why is man's mirth so seldom and so small,
　　who is compounded of them all?

　　　　　　　　　　　　　　A. COWLEY

56　　　　　　TO THE REDBREAST

UNHEARD in summer's flaring ray,
　　pour forth thy notes, sweet singer,
wooing the stillness of the autumn day:
　　bid it a moment linger,
　　　　nor fly
too soon from winter's scowling eye.

The blackbird's song at eventide,
　　and hers, who gay ascends
filling the heavens far and wide,
　　are sweet: but none so blends,
　　　　as thine,
with calm decay and peace divine.

　　　　　　　　　　　　　　H. CORNISH

57   *SONG OF PROSERPINE WHILE GATHERING FLOWERS ON THE PLAIN OF ENNA*

SACRED Goddess, Mother Earth,
    thou from whose immortal bosom
gods and men and beasts have birth,
    leaf and blade, and bud and blossom,
breathe thine influence most divine
on thine own child, Proserpine.

If with mists of evening dew
    thou dost nourish these young flowers
till they grow, in scent and hue,
    fairest children of the hours,
breathe thine influence most divine
on thine own child, Proserpine.
P. B. SHELLEY

58   *TRUE LOVE*

TRUE love's the gift which God has given
    to man alone beneath the heaven,
it is not fantasy's hot fire,
whose wishes soon as granted fly;
it liveth not in fierce desire,
    with dead desire it doth not die;
it is the secret sympathy,
    the silver link, the silver tie,
which heart to heart, and mind to mind,
in body and in soul combined.
SIR W. SCOTT

59   *TO A DESPONDING LOVER*

WHY so pale and wan, fond lover?
    prythee why so pale?
will, if looking well can't move her,
    looking ill prevail?
    prythee why so pale?

Why so dull and mute, young sinner?
    prythee why so mute?
will, when speaking well can't win her,
    saying nothing do't?
    prythee why so mute?

quit, quit for shame! this will not move,
    this cannot take her;
if of herself she will not love,
    nothing can make her:—
    let who will take her.

SIR J. SUCKLING

60   THE ENCHANTMENT

I DID but look and love awhile,
    'twas but for half an hour;
then to resist I had no will,
    and now I have no power.

To sigh and wish is all my case;
    sighs which do heat impart,
enough to melt the coldest ice,
    yet cannot warm your heart.

O! would your pity give my heart
    one corner of your breast;
'twould learn of yours the winning art,
    and quickly steal the rest.

T. OTWAY

61   THE TYRANT LOVE

OFT on the troubled ocean's face
    loud stormy winds arise;
the murmuring surges swell apace,
    and clouds obscure the skies.

But when the tempest's rage is o'er,
    soft breezes smoothe the main;
the billows cease to lash the shore,
    and all is calm again.

Not so in fond and amorous souls
    if tyrant love once reigns,
there one eternal tempest rolls
    and yields unceasing pains.

THEOBALD

62 THE BEAUTY OF VIRTUE

ALL earthly charms, however dear,
howe'er they please the eye or ear,
    will quickly fade and fly;
of earthly glory faint the blaze,
and soon the transitory rays
    in endless darkness die.

The nobler beauties of the just
shall never moulder in the dust
    or know a sad decay;
their honours time and death defy,
and round the throne of heaven on high
    beam everlasting day.

H. MORE

63 THE EARTH'S BOUNTY

THE Earth that in her genial breast
makes for the down a kindly nest,
where wafted by the warm south-west
    it floats at pleasure,
yields, thankful, of her very best,
    to nurse her treasure:

true to her trust, tree, herb or reed,
she renders for each scattered seed,
and to her Lord with duteous heed
    gives large increase:
thus year by year she works unfeed,
    and will not cease.

J. KEBLE

64

SHE had left all on earth for him,
her home of wealth, her name of pride,
and now his lamp of love was dim,
and, sad to tell, she had not died.

She watched the crimson sun's decline,
from some lone rock that fronts the sea,—
'I would, O burning heart of mine,
there were an ocean-rest for thee.

'The thoughtful moon awaits her turn,
the stars compose their choral crown,
but those soft lights can never burn,
till once the fiery sun is down.'
R. M. MILNES

65   THE PRAYER OF ORPHEUS

BY the streams that ever flow,
  by the fragrant winds that blow
    o'er the Elysian flowers;
by those happy souls who dwell
  in yellow meads of asphodel
    or amaranthine bowers;
by the heroes' armed shades,
glittering through the gloomy glades;
by the youths that died for love,
wandering in the myrtle grove,
restore, restore Eurydice to life:
oh take the husband, or return the wife!
A. POPE

66   THE STUDY OF NATURE BRINGS NOT HAPPINESS

NOR can it bliss you bring
  hid Nature's depths to know,
why matter changeth, whence each form doth spring;
nor that your fame should range,
  and after-worlds it blow
from Tanais to Nile, from Nile to Gange:
and these have not the power
  to free the mind from fears,
  nor hideous horror can allay one hour,
when Death in steel doth glance,
  in sickness lurk or years,
and wakes the soul from out her mortal trance.
W. DRUMMOND

67   ENID'S SONG

TURN, Fortune, turn thy wheel and lower the proud:
  turn thy wild wheel thro' sunshine, storm and cloud;
thy wheel and thee we neither love nor hate.

Turn, Fortune, turn thy wheel with smile or frown;
with that wild wheel we go not up or down;
our hoard is little, but our hearts are great.

Smile and we smile, the lords of many lands;
frown and we smile, the lords of our own hands:
for man is man and master of his fate.

Turn, turn thy wheel above the staring crowd;
thy wheel and thou are shadows in the cloud;
thy wheel and thee we neither love nor hate.
A. TENNYSON

68 *TO THE CICADA*

CICADA! thou who, tipsy with the dews
   of weeping skies, on the tall poplar-tree,
perch'd swayingly, thyself dost still amuse,
   and the hush'd grove, with thy sweet minstrelsy

after long tedious winters, when the sun
   through the brief summer speeds his whirling ray,
with thy shrill chiding, as he hastens on,
   check his too rapid wheels and urge delay.

The brightest day that dawns on mortal eyes,
   hurries—ah! fleetly hurries to its close—
ne'er long enough to rapture are his joys,
   ever too long to anguish are her woes.
F. WRANGHAM

69 *DRINKING SONG*

CARE, thou canker of all joys!
   see the tyrant's reign is o'er;
fill the merry bowl, my boys,
   join the bacchanalian roar;

o'er the merry midnight bowl,
   O! how merry will we be,
day was made for vulgar souls,
   night, my boys, for you and me.

Seize the villain, plunge him in,
   see! the hated miscreant dies;
mirth, with all thy train come in,
   banish sorrow, tears and sighs.

70   *ELIZABETH'S SONG*

OH! that we two were maying
  over the fragrant leas;
like children with young flowers playing
down the stream of the rich spring breeze.

Oh! that we two sat dreaming
on the sward of some sheep-trimmed down;
watching the white mist streaming,
from river and mead and town.

Oh! that we two lay sleeping
under the church-yard sod;
with our limbs at rest in the quiet earth's breast,
and our souls at home with God!
C. KINGSLEY

71   *TRANQUILLITY*

RETIRE, and timely, from the world, if ever
  thou hopest tranquil days:
its gaudy jewels from thy bosom sever,
  despise its pomp and praise.
The purest star that looks into the stream
  its slightest ripple shakes,
and Peace, where'er its fierce splendours gleam,
  her brooding nest forsakes.
The quiet planets roll with even motion
  in the still skies alone;
o'er Ocean they dance joyously, but Ocean
  they find no rest upon.
W. S. LANDOR

72   *WE'LL GO NO MORE A ROVING*

SO, we'll go no more a roving
  so late into the night,
though the heart be still as loving,
  and the moon be still as bright.

For the sword outwears its sheath,
  and the heart wears out the breast,
and lips must pause to breathe,
  and love itself have rest.

Though the night was made for loving
  and the day returns too soon,
yet we'll go no more a roving
  by the light of the moon.
LORD BYRON

73 ON CHLORIS BEING ILL

CAN I cease to care?
  can I cease to languish,
while my darling fair
  is on the couch of anguish?

Every hope is fled,
  every fear is terror;
slumber even I dread,
  every dream is horror.

Hear me, Pow'rs divine!
  O, in pity hear me!
take aught else of mine,
  but my Chloris spare me!
R. BURNS

74 HOME

I'VE roamed through many a weary round,
  I've wandered east and west,
pleasure in every clime I've found,
  but sought in vain for rest.

While glory sighs for other spheres,
  I feel that one's too wide,
and think the home, which love endears,
  worth all the world beside.

The needle thus, too rudely moved,
  wanders unconscious where;
till having found the place it loved,
  it trembling settles there.
T. MOORE

75 GRIEF AND BEAUTY

DRY those fair, those crystal eyes,
  which like growing fountains rise
to drown their banks. Grief's sullen brooks
would better flow in furrowed looks:

thy lovely face was never meant
to be the shore of discontent.
Then clear those waterish stars again,
which else portend a lasting rain;
lest the clouds which settle there
prolong my winter all the year:
and the example others make,
in love with sorrow for thy sake.

H. KING

76   AGAINST DESIRE OF LONG LIFE

ILL-BUSIED man! why should'st thou take such care
to lengthen out thy life's short kalendar?
when every spectacle thou look'st upon,
presents and acts thy execution:
   each drooping season and each flower doth cry,
   'Fool! as I fade and wither thou must die.'

The beating of thy pulse, when thou art well,
is just the tolling of thy passing bell:
night is thy hearse, whose sable canopy
covers alike deceased day and thee,
and all those weeping dews, which nightly fall,
are but the tears shed for thy funeral.

H. KING

77   THE BLESSING OF SYMPATHY

THE low sweet tones of Nature's lyre
   no more on listless ears expire,
nor vainly smiles along the shady way
   the primrose in her vernal nest,
   nor unlamented sink to rest
sweet roses one by one, nor autumn leaves decay.

   There's not a star the heaven can show,
   there's not a cottage hearth below,
but feeds with solace kind the willing soul—
   men love us or they need our love;
   freely they own, or heedless prove
the curse of lawless hearts, the joy of self-control.

J. KEBLE

78   TO A LADY

TOO late I've stayed, forgive the crime;
  unheeded flew the hours:
how noiseless falls the foot of Time,
  that only treads on flowers!

What eye with clear account remarks
  the ebbings of the glass,
when all its sands are diamond sparks,
  that dazzle as they pass?

Ah, who to sober measurement
  Time's happy fleetness brings,
when birds of Paradise have lent
  their plumage for his wings!
                          W. R. SPENCER

79

SHE sighs—like winds at eve,
  like lovers' tongues that grieve,
like tones—oh! never to be heard again,
like voices from the sea
where the sea-maids be,
like aught of pleasure with a touch of pain.

A more melodious tune
never beneath the moon
was uttered, since the Delphian girls were young,
and the chaste Dian, bright
with beauty and delight,
lay listening on the mountains, while they sung.

80   EPITAPH ON THE LADY MARY VILLIERS

THE lady Mary Villiers lies
  under this stone; with weeping eyes
the parents that first gave her birth,
and their sad friends, laid her in earth:
if any of them (reader) were
known unto thee, shed a tear;
or if thyself possess a gem,
as dear to thee, as this to them;

> though a stranger to this place,
> bewail in theirs thine own hard case;
> for thou perhaps at thy return
> may'st find thy darling in an urn.
>
> T. CAREW

81   *WOLFRAM'S SONG IN TANNHAUSER*

> OH! from your sacred seats look down,
>   angels and ministers of good;
> with sanctity our spirits crown,
> and crush the vices of the blood!
>
> Open our hearts and set them free
> that heavenly light may enter in;
> and from this fair society
> obliterate the taint of sin.
>
> Thee, holy Love, I bid arise
> propitious to my votive lay;
> shine thou upon our darken'd eyes,
> and lead us on the perfect way.

82   *GAIETY*

> UNTHINKING, idle, wild and young,
>   I laughed and danced and talked and sung;
> and fond of health, of freedom vain,
> dream'd not of sorrow, care or pain;
> concluding in those hours of glee,
> that all the world was made for me.
>
> But when the hour of trial came,
> and sickness shook this trembling frame;
> when folly's gay pursuits were o'er,
> and I could dance and sing no more—
> it then occurr'd how sad 'twould be,
> were this world only made for me.
>
> PRINCESS AMELIA

83   *A HYMN TO THE MUSES*

> O, YOU the Virgins nine,
>   that do our souls incline
> to noble discipline,
> nod to this vow of mine:

come then and now inspire
my viol and my lyre
with your eternal fire,
and make me one entire
composer in your quire.
Then I'll your altars strew
with roses sweet and new;
and ever live a true
acknowledger of you.
R. HERRICK

84   *BALAAM*

O FOR a sculptor's hand
that thou might'st take thy stand,
thy wild hair floating on the eastern breeze,
thy tranced yet open gaze
fixed on the desert haze,
as one who deep in heaven some airy pageant sees.

In outline dim and vast
their fearful shadows cast
the giant forms of empires on their way
to ruin; one by one
they tower and they are gone,
yet in the Prophet's soul the dreams of avarice stay.
J. KEBLE

85   *CAUTION TO ENGLAND*

TYRE of the West, and glorying in the name
more than in Faith's pure fame!
O trust not crafty fort nor rock renowned
earned upon hostile ground;
wielding Trade's master-keys, at thy proud will
to lock or loose its waters, England! trust not still.

Dread thine own power! since haughty Babel's prime
high towers have been man's crime:
since her hoar age, when the huge moat lay bare,
strongholds have been man's snare.
Thy nest is in the crags; ah, refuge frail!
mad council in its hour, or traitors will prevail.
LYRA APOSTOLICA

86   *EMBLEM OF DEATH*

THE fallen leaf repeats the mournful tale
  of beauty faded and retiring joy;
some golden reliques float on every gale,
and nature's death comes hastening to destroy.

Brief is that death;—and is not ours the same?
the mystic voice, that wakes the new-born year,
with mightier sound shall from the dust reclaim
the friend we mourn in chilly sorrow here.

O, as the Spring adorned with flowers will rise,
so may their virtues bear a deathless bloom,
and spread and brighten in serener skies,
saved through the silent winter of the tomb.
                                    F. HODGSON

87   *HYMN*

HOW are thy servants blest, O Lord,
  how sure is their defence;
eternal Wisdom is their guide,
  their help Omnipotence.

In distant lands and realms remote,
  supported by Thy care,
through burning climes I passed unhurt,
  and breathed in tainted air.

Thy mercy sweetened every soil,
  made every region please;
the hoary Alpine hills it warmed,
  and smoothed the Tyrrhene seas.
                                    J. ADDISON

88   *UNDER THE GREENWOOD TREE*

UNDER the greenwood tree
  who loves to lie with me,
and tune his merry note
unto the sweet bird's throat,
come hither, come hither, come hither;
here shall we see no enemy,
but winter and rough weather.

Who doth ambition shun,
and loves to lie in the sun,
seeking the food he eats,
and pleased with what he gets,
come hither, come hither, come hither;
here shall he see no enemy,
but winter and rough weather.

W. SHAKESPEARE

89   *A PARABLE*

EVERY mortal, small or great,
   his subtle cobweb weaves;
and seated there within elate
   himself a King believes,
and drives his little feelers out
to strike whoever dares to doubt.

And when, at last, the besom strong
   sweeps all the work away,
it seems an outrage and a wrong
   unheard of till to-day;
as if that stroke had downward hurled
the noblest palace in the world.

R. M. MILNES

90   *ON THE DEPARTURE OF SUMMER*

FAIR summer droops, droop men and beasts
   therefore,
so fair a summer look for never more:
all good things vanish less than in a day,
peace, plenty, pleasure, suddenly decay.
Go not yet away, bright soul of the sad year;
the earth is hell when thou leavest to appear.

What, shall those flowers that decked thy garland erst,
upon thy grave be wastefully dispersed?
O trees consume your sap in sorrow's source,
streams turn to tears your tributary course.
Go not yet hence, bright soul of the sad year;
the earth is hell when thou leavest to appear.

T. NASH

91   *GUARDIAN ANGELS*

WHERE the angelic hosts adore Thee,
    Thou o'er earth and heav'n dost reign,
at Thy word they rose before Thee,
    and Thy breath doth them sustain.
From high angels Thee attending,
    Thou dost faithful guardians send;
in mysterious ways descending,
    may they keep us to the end:
keep us, else with wiles deceiving
    the persuader of all ill,
round his deadly meshes weaving,
    the lost soul will rend and kill.

92   *TO PEACE*

Εἰρήνα βαθύπλουτε καὶ
καλλίστα μακάρων θεῶν,
ζῆλός μοι σέθεν, ὡς χρονίζεις,
δέδοικα δὲ μὴ πρὶν πόνοις
ὑπερβάλῃ με γῆρας,
πρὶν σὰν χαρίεσσαν προσιδεῖν ὥραν
καὶ καλλιχόρους ἀοιδὰς
φιλοστεφάνους τε κώμους.
ἴθι μοι, πότνια, πόλιν
τάνδ᾽ ἐχθρὰν στάσιν εἴργ᾽ ἀπ᾽ οἴκων
τὰν μαινομέναν τ᾽ ἔριν,
θηκτῷ τερπομέναν σιδήρῳ.

                                    EVRIPIDES

93   *THE BLESSINGS OF PEACE*

Τίκτει δέ τε θνατοῖσιν Εἰράνα μεγάλα
πλοῦτον καὶ μελιγλώσσων ἀοιδᾶν ἄνθεα,
δαιδαλέων τ᾽ ἐπὶ βωμῶν θεοῖσιν αἴθεσθαι βοῶν
ξανθᾷ φλογὶ μῆρα τανυτρίχων τε μήλων,
γυμνασίων τε νέοις αὐλῶν τε καὶ κώμων μέλειν.
ἐν δὲ σιδαροδετοῖς πόρπαξιν αἰθᾶν
ἀραχνᾶν ἱστοὶ πέλονται·
ἔγχεά τε λογχωτὰ ξίφεά τ᾽ ἀμφάκεα δάμναται εὐρώς·

χαλκεᾶν δ' οὐκ ἔστι σαλπίγγων κτύπος·
οὐδὲ συλᾶται μελίφρων ὕπνος ἀπὸ γλεφάρων,
ἁμὸν ὃς θάλπει κέαρ.
συμποσίων δ' ἐρατῶν βρίθοντ' ἀγυιαὶ παιδικοί θ' ὕμ-
νοι φλέγονται.

BACCHYLIDES

94 THE CONTRAST

Τὰν ἅλα τὰν γλαυκὰν ὅταν ὤνεμος ἀτρέμα βάλλῃ,
τὰν φρένα τὰν δειλὰν ἐρεθίζομαι, οὐδ' ἔτι μοι γᾶ
ἐντὶ φίλα, ποθίει δὲ πολὺ πλέον ἅ με γαλάνα.
ἀλλ' ὅταν ἀχήσῃ πολιὸς βυθός, ἁ δὲ θάλασσα
κύρτον ἐπαφρίζῃ, τὰ δὲ κύματα μακρὰ μεμύκῃ,
ἐς χθόνα παπταίνω καὶ δένδρεα, τὰν δ' ἅλα φεύγω,
γᾶ δέ μοι ἀσπαστά, χἀ δάσκιος εἴαδεν ὕλα,
ἔνθα καί, ἢν πνεύσῃ πολὺς ὤνεμος, ἁ πίτυς ᾄδει.
ἦ κακὸν ὁ γριπεὺς ζώει βίον, ᾧ δόμος ἁ ναῦς,
καὶ πόνος ἐντὶ θάλασσα καὶ ἰχθύες ἁ πλάνος ἄγρα.
αὐτὰρ ἐμοὶ γλυκὺς ὕπνος ὑπὸ πλατάνῳ βαθυφύλλῳ,
καὶ παγᾶς φίλ' ἐμοὶ τᾶς ἐγγύθεν ἄχον ἀκούειν,
ἃ τέρπει ψοφέοισα τὸν ἄγριον, οὐχὶ ταράσσει.

MOSCHVS

95 PAN

SING his praises that doth keep
our flocks from harm,
Pan, the father of our sheep:
and arm in arm
tread we softly in a round,
whilst the hollow neighbouring ground
fills the music with her sound.

Pan, O great god Pan, to thee
thus do we sing!
thou that keep'st us chaste and free
as the young spring;
ever be thy honour spoke,
from that place the Morn is broke
to that place Day doth unyoke!

BEAUMONT AND FLETCHER

96   THE POET'S OBSEQUIES

CALL it not vain:—they do not err,
    who say, that, when the poet dies,
mute Nature mourns her worshipper,
    and celebrates his obsequies;
who say, tall cliff and cavern lone
for the departed bard make moan;
that mountains weep in crystal rill;
that flowers in tears of balm distil;
through his loved groves that breezes sigh,
and oaks in deeper groan reply;
and rivers teach their rushing wave
to murmur dirges round his grave.
                              SIR W. SCOTT

97   SONG

OH, how hard it is to find
    the one just suited to our mind;
    and if that one should be
false, unkind, or found too late,
what can we do but sigh at fate,
    and sing 'Woe's me—Woe's me!'
Love's a boundless burning waste,
where Bliss's stream we seldom taste,
    and still more seldom flee
Suspense's thorns, Suspicion's stings;
yet somehow Love a something brings
    that's sweet—ev'n when we sigh 'Woe's me!'
                              T. CAMPBELL

98   PROSPERITY

WHEN mirth is full and free,
    some sudden gloom shall be;
when haughty power mounts high,
    the watcher's axe is nigh;
all growth has bound: when greatest found,
    it hastes to die.
When the rich town, that long
has lain its huts among,
builds court and palace vast
    and vaunts,—it shall not last!
Bright tints that shine are but a sign
    of summer past.

And when thine eye surveys,
with fond adoring gaze,
and yearning heart, thy friend,—
Love to its grave doth tend.
All gifts below, save Truth, but grow
towards an end.

LYRA APOSTOLICA

99   THE LOTOS-EATERS

HOW sweet it were, hearing the downward stream,
with half-shut eyes ever to seem
falling asleep in a half-dream!
to dream and dream, like yonder amber light,
which will not leave the myrrh-bush on the height;
to hear each other's whispered speech;
eating the Lotos day by day,
to watch the crisping ripples on the beach,
and tender curving lines of creamy spray;
to lend our hearts and spirits wholly
to the influence of mild-minded melancholy:
to muse and brood and live again in memory,
with the old faces of our infancy
heaped over with a mound of grass,
two handfuls of white dust, shut in an urn of brass

A. TENNYSON

100   THE VANITY OF FAME

WHERE is each boasted favourite of Fame,
whose wide expanded name
fill'd the loud echoes of the world around,
while shore to shore returned the lengthened sound?
The warriors where, who, in triumphal pride,
with weeping Freedom to the chariot tied,
to glory's Capitolian temple rode?
In undistinguished dust together trod,
victors and vanquished mingle in the grave;
worms prey upon the mouldering god,
nor know a Cæsar from his slave;
in empty air their mighty deeds exhale,
a school-boy's wonder, or an evening tale.

101   In vain with various arts they strive
            to keep their little names alive:
        bid to the skies th' ambitious tower ascend;
        the cirque its vast majestic length extend;
        bid arcs of triumph swell their graceful round;
        or mausoleums load th' encumbered ground;
        or sculpture speak in animated stone
        of vanquish'd monarchs tumbled from the throne;
            the rolling tide of years,
        rushing with strong and steady current, bears
        the pompous piles with all their fame away
            to black Oblivion's sea;
        deep in whose dread abyss the glory lies
        of empires, ages, never more to rise!

102   WHERE'S now imperial Rome,
        who erst to subject-kings denounced their doom
        and shook the sceptre o'er a trembling world?
        from her proud height by force barbarian hurl'd!
        Now, on some broken capital reclined,
            the sage of classic mind
        her awful relics views with pitying eye,
        and o'er departed grandeur heaves a sigh;
        or fancies, wandering in his moonlight walk,
            the prostrate fanes and mouldering domes among,
        he sees the mighty ghosts of heroes stalk
            in melancholy majesty along;
        or pensive hover o'er the ruins round,
        their pallid brows with faded laurel bound;
        while Cato's shade seems scornful to survey
        a race of slaves, and sternly strides away.

103   Where old Euphrates winds his storied flood,
        the curious traveller explores in vain
            the barren shores and solitary plain
        where erst majestic Babel's turret stood!
        all vanish'd from the view her proud abodes,
        her walls and brazen gates and palaces of gods!
        a shapeless heap o'erspreads the dreary space,
        of mingled piles an undistinguish'd mass:

there the wild tenants of the desert dwell:
the serpent's hiss is heard, the dragon's yell!
and doleful howlings o'er the waste affright,
and drive afar the wanderers of the night.

104   *ST JOHN THE EVANGELIST*

B ELOVED of God, to thee was given
    unscathed to see
the blaze of present Deity;
to see the veil in sunder riven,
and search the inmost court of Heaven.

Borne as on eagle-wings away
    through ether far,
thy soul outstrips the utmost star,
nor Heaven's own lightning's fiery ray
thy spirit from its God can stay.

'Tis thine Heaven's deepest notes to tell
    to seers divining;
thou op'st the light in darkness shining:
thou searchest life's o'er-flowing well,
and heaven-born light's primæval cell.

105   *SONNET TO THE MOON*

W ITH how sad steps, O Moon, thou climb'st the
    skies,
how silently, and with how wan a face!
what! may it be, and even in heavenly place,
that busy Archer his sharp arrows tries?
Sure, if that long with love acquainted eyes
can judge of love, thou feel'st a lover's case;
I read it in thy looks, thy languish'd grace
to me that feel the like thy state descries.
Then even of fellowship, O Moon, tell me,
is constant love deem'd there but want of wit?
are beauties there as proud as here they be?
do they above love to be lov'd, and yet
    those lovers scorn whom that love doth possess?
do they call virtue there ungratefulness?

                                   SIR P. SIDNEY

106   *TRUE BEAUTY*

MEN call you fayre, and you doe credit it,
    for that your selfe ye daily such doe see:
but the trew fayre, that is the gentle wit
and virtuous mind, is much more praysd of me:
for all the rest, how ever fayre it be,
shall turne to nought and loose that glorious hew;
but onely that is permanent, and free
from frayle corruption that doth flesh ensew.
That is true beautie: that doth argue you
to be divine, and borne of heavenly seed;
derived from that fayre Spirit, from whom al true
and perfect beauty did at first proceed:
   He onely fayre, and what he fayre hath made,
   all other fayre, lyke flowers, untymely fade.
                                        E. SPENSER

107   *SONNET*

LYKE as the culver on the bared bough
    sits mourning for the absence of her mate,
and in her songs sends many a wishfull vow
for his return that seemes to linger late:
so I alone, now left disconsolate,
mourn to myselfe the absence of my love;
and, wandering here and there all desolate,
seek with my plaints to match that mournful dove:
ne joy of ought that under heaven doth hove
can comfort me, but her owne joyous sight:
whose sweet aspect both God and man can move,
in her unspotted pleasauns to delight.
   Dark is my day whyles her fayre light I mis,
   And dead my life that wants such lively blis.
                                        E. SPENSER

108   *SONNET*

SWEET warriour! when shall I have peace with
       you?
High time it is this warre now ended were,
which I no longer can endure to sue,
nor your incessant battry more to beare:

so weake my powres, so sore my wounds appeare,
that wonder is how I should live a jot,
seeing my hart through launched everywhere
with thousand arrowes, which your eies have shot,
yet shoot ye sharpely still, and spare me not,
but glory thinke to make these cruel stoures.
Ye cruell one! what glory can be got,
in slaying him that would live gladly yours?
    Make peace therefore, and graunt me timely grace
that al my wound wil heale in little space.
E. SPENSER

109   *NON POSSVNT HÆC MONVMENTA MORI*

NOT marble, not the gilded monuments
   of princes, shall outlive this powerful rhyme;
but you shall shine more bright in these contents
than unswept stone, besmear'd with sluttish time.
When wasteful war shall statues overturn,
and broils root out the work of masonry,
nor Mars his sword nor war's quick fire shall burn
the living record of your memory.
'Gainst death and all oblivious enmity
shall you pace forth; your praise shall still find room
even in the eyes of all posterity
that wear this world out to the ending doom.
    So, till the judgement that yourself arise,
you live in this, and dwell in lovers' eyes.
W. SHAKESPEARE

110   *TIME AND LOVE*

WHEN I have seen by Time's fell hand defaced
   the rich-proud cost of outworn buried age;
when sometime lofty towers I see downrazed,
and brass eternal slave to mortal rage;
when I have seen the hungry ocean gain
advantage on the kingdom of the shore,
and the firm soil win of the watery main,
increasing store with loss and loss with store;
when I have seen such interchange of state,
or state itself confounded to decay;
ruin hath taught me thus to ruminate—
that Time will come and take my Love away:
    —This thought is as a death, which cannot choose
but weep to have that which it fears to lose.
W. SHAKESPEARE

111   *REMEMBRANCE*

WHEN to the sessions of sweet silent thought
     I summon up remembrance of things past,
I sigh the lack of many a thing I sought,
and with old woes new wail my dear time's waste;
then can I drown an eye, unused to flow,
for precious friends hid in death's dateless night,
and weep afresh love's long-since-cancell'd woe,
and moan the expense of many a vanish'd sight.
Then can I grieve at grievances foregone,
and heavily from woe to woe tell o'er
the sad account of fore-bemoanèd moan,
which I new pay as if not paid before:
    But if the while I think on thee, dear friend,
    all losses are restored, and sorrows end.
                                W. SHAKESPEARE.

112   *ON HIS OWN BLINDNESS*

WHEN I consider how my light is spent
     ere half my days, in this dark world and wide,
and that one talent, which is death to hide,
lodged with me useless, though my soul more bent
to serve therewith my Maker, and present
    my true account, lest He, returning, chide;
    Doth God exact day-labour, light denied?'
I fondly ask. But Patience, to prevent
that murmur, soon replies: 'God doth not need
either man's work, or his own gifts; who best
bear His mild yoke, they serve Him best. His state
is kingly. Thousands at His bidding speed
and post o'er land and ocean without rest;
they also serve who only stand and wait.'
                                J. MILTON.

113   *TO MR LAWRENCE*

LAWRENCE, of virtuous father virtuous son,
     now that the fields are dank, and ways all mire,
where shall we sometimes meet and by the fire
help waste a sullen day, what may be won
from the hard season gaining? Time will run
on smoother, till Favonius re-inspire
the frozen earth, and clothe in fresh attire
the lily and rose, that neither sowed nor spun.

What neat repast shall feast us, light and choice,
   of Attic taste with wine, whence we may rise
   to hear the lute well touched, or artful voice
warble immortal notes and Tuscan air?
   He, who of those delights can judge, and spare
   to interpose them oft, is not unwise.
J. MILTON

114   *TO THE NIGHTINGALE*

O NIGHTINGALE, that on yon bloomy spray
   warblest at eve, when all the woods are still;
   thou with fresh hopes the lover's heart dost fill,
while the jolly Hours lead on propitious May.
Thy liquid notes that close the eye of Day,
   first heard before the shallow cuckoo's bill,
   portend success in love. Oh! if Jove's will
have linked that amorous power to thy soft lay,
   now timely sing, ere the rude bird of hate
     foretell my hopeless doom, in some grove nigh
as thou from year to year hast sung too late
   for my relief, yet hadst no reason why:
whether the Muse or Love call thee his mate,
   both them I serve, and of their train am I.
J. MILTON

115   *THE POET'S HOUSE WHEN THE ASSAULT WAS
      INTENDED TO THE CITY OF LONDON*

CAPTAIN or Colonel, or Knight in arms,
   whose chance on these defenceless doors may seize,
if deed of honour did thee ever please,
   guard them, and him within protect from harms.
He can requite thee; for he knows the charms
   that call fame on such gentle acts as these,
   and he can spread thy name o'er lands and seas,
whatever clime the sun's bright circle warms.
Lift not thy spear against the Muses' bower:
   the great Emathian conqueror bid spare
   the house of Pindarus, when temple and tower
went to the ground: and the repeated air
   of sad Electra's poet had the pow'r
   to save the Athenian walls from ruin bare.
J. MILTON

116   *ON THE LATE MASSACRE IN PIEMONT*

AVENGE, O Lord, thy slaughter'd saints, whose bones
   lie scattered on the Alpine mountains cold;
   even them who kept thy truth so pure of old,
   when all our fathers worshipt stocks and stones,
forget not: in thy book record their groans
   who were thy sheep, and in their ancient fold
   slain by the bloody Piemontese, that rolled
   mother with infant down the rocks; their moans
the vales redoubled to the hills, and they
   to heaven. Their martyred blood and ashes sow
o'er all the Italian fields, where still doth sway
the triple tyrant; that from these may grow
   a hundredfold, who, having learned thy way,
   early may fly the Babylonian woe.

                                J. MILTON

117   *ON THE DEATH OF SIR PHILIP SIDNEY*

GIVE pardon, blessed soul, to my bold cries,
   if they, importunate, interrupt the song
which now, with joyful notes, thou sing'st among
the angel-choristers of heavenly skies.
Give pardon eke, sweet soul, to my slow eyes,
   that since I saw thee now it is so long,
   and yet the tears that unto thee belong,
to thee as yet they did not sacrifice.
   I did not know that thou wert dead before,
I did not feel the grief I did sustain;
   the greater stroke astonisheth the more;
astonishment takes from us sense of pain;
   I stood amazed when others' tears begun,
   and now begin to weep when they have done.

                               H. CONSTABLE

118   *SONNET*

AS when it happeneth that some lovely town
   unto a barbarous besieger falls,
who both by sword and flame himself installs,
and shameless it in tears and blood doth drown;

her beauty spoiled, her citizens made thralls,
his spite yet cannot so her all throw down,
but that some statue, arch, fane of renown,
yet lurks unmaimed within her weeping walls:
so after all the spoil, disgrace and wreck,
that time, the world and death could bring combined,
amidst that mass of ruins they did make,
safe and all scarless yet remains my mind:
   from this so high transcendent rapture springs,
   that I, all else defaced, not envy kings.
                           W. DRUMMOND

119   *PLEASURES OF RETIREMENT*

THRICE happy he, who by some shady grove,
   far from the clamorous world doth live his own,
though solitary, who is not alone,
but doth converse with that eternal love.
O how more sweet is birds' harmonious moan,
or the hoarse sobbings of the widowed dove,
than those smooth whisperings near a prince's throne,
which good make doubtful, do the evil approve!
O how more sweet is zephyr's wholesome breath,
and sighs embalmed, which new-born flow'rs unfold,
than that applause vain honour doth bequeath!
how sweet are streams to poison drunk in gold!
   the world is full of horrors, falehoods, slights:
   woods' harmless shades have only true delights.
                           W. DRUMMOND

120   *SONNET*

LOOK as the flow'r which lingeringly doth fade;
   the morning's darling late, the summer's Queen,
spoil'd of that juice which kept it fresh and green,
as high as it did raise, bows low the head;
(right so the pleasures of my life being dead,
or in their contraries but only seen)
with swifter speed declines than erst it spread,
and, blasted, scarce now shows what it hath been:
therefore, as doth the pilgrim, whom the night
hastes darkly to imprison on his way,

think on thy home, my soul! and think aright,
of what's yet left thee of life's wasting day;
the sun posts westward, passed is thy morn,
and twice it is not given thee to be born.
W. DRUMMOND

121 DOTH then the world go thus, doth all thus move?
is this the justice which on Earth we find?
is this that firm decree which all doth bind?
are these your influences Powers above?
Those souls which vice's moody mists most blind,
blind Fortune, blindly, most their friend doth prove:
and they who thee, poor idol Virtue! love,
ply like a feather tossed by storm and wind.
Ah! if a providence doth sway this all,
why should best minds groan under most distress?
or why should pride humility make thrall,
and injuries the innocent oppress?
Heavens! hinder, stop this fate; or grant a time
when good may have, as well as bad, their prime!
W. DRUMMOND

122   *THE ROSE*

LOOK, Delia, how we esteem the half-blown Rose,
the image of thy blush and summer's honour!
whilst yet her tender bud doth undisclose
that full of beauty Time bestows upon her.
No sooner spreads her glory in the air,
but straight her wide-blown pomp comes to decline;
she then is scorn'd that late adorn'd the fair;
so fade the roses of those cheeks of thine!
No April can revive thy wither'd flowers,
whose springing grace adorns thy glory now;
swift speedy time, feather'd with flying hours,
dissolves the beauty of the fairest brow.
Then do not thou such treasure waste in vain;
but love now, whilst thou mayst be loved again.
S. DANIEL

123   *TO SLEEP*

CARE-charmer sleep, son of the sable Night,
brother to Death, in silent darkness born,
relieve my languish, and restore the light,
with dark forgetting of my care, return.

And let the day be time enough to mourn
the shipwreck of my ill-adventured youth;
let waking eyes suffice to wail their scorn,
without the torment of the night's untruth.
Cease, dreams, the images of day-desires,
to model forth the passions of the morrow;
never let rising sun approve you liars,
to add more grief to aggravate my sorrow:
   still let me sleep, embracing clouds in vain,
   and never wake to feel the day's disdain.
S. DANIEL.

124   SWEET CONTENT

ART thou poor, yet hast thou golden slumbers?
   Oh, sweet content!
Art thou rich, yet in thy mind perplexed?
   Oh, punishment!
dost thou laugh to see, how fools are vexed,
to add to golden numbers golden numbers?
   Oh, sweet content!
canst drink the waters of the crisped spring?
   Oh, sweet content!
swimm'st thou in wealth, yet sink'st in thine own tears?
   Oh, punishment!
then he, that patiently want's burden bears,
no burden bears, but is a king, a king!
   Oh, sweet content!
DEKKER AND HAUGHTON

125   TO SLEEP

FOND words have oft been spoken to thee, Sleep!
   and thou hast had thȳ store of tenderest names;
the very sweetest fancy culls or frames,
when thankfulness of heart is strong and deep!
dear Bosom-child we call thee, that dost steep
in rich reward all suffering; Balm that tames
all anguish; Saint, that evil thoughts and aims
takest away, and into souls dost creep,
like to a breeze from heaven. Shall I alone,
I surely not a man ungently made,
call thee worst Tyrant by which Flesh is crost?
perverse, self-willed to own and to disown,
mere slave of them who never for thee prayed,
still last to come where thou art wanted most!
W. WORDSWORTH

126   *LONDON MDCCCII*

MILTON! thou shouldst be living at this hour:
England hath need of thee: she is a fen
of stagnant waters: altar, sword, and pen,
fireside, the heroic wealth of hall and bower,
have forfeited their ancient English dower
of inward happiness. We are selfish men:
O! raise us up, return to us again;
and give us manners, virtue, freedom, power.
Thy soul was like a Star, and dwelt apart:
thou hadst a voice whose sound was like the sea,
pure as the naked heavens, majestic, free;
so didst thou travel on life's common way
in cheerful godliness; and yet thy heart
the lowliest duties on herself did lay.

W. WORDSWORTH

127   *SEPTEMBER 1815*

WHILE not a leaf seems faded; while the fields,
with ripening harvest prodigally fair,
in brightest sunshine bask; this nipping air,
sent from some distant clime where Winter wields
his icy scimitar, a foretaste yields
of bitter change, and bids the flowers beware;
and whispers to the silent birds, 'Prepare
against the threatening foe your trustiest shields.'
For me, who under kindlier laws belong
to Nature's tuneful quire, this rustling dry
through leaves yet green, and yon crystalline sky,
announce a season potent to renew,
mid frost and snow, the instinctive joys of song,
and nobler cares than listless summer knew.

W. WORDSWORTH

128   *ON THE DEPARTURE OF SIR WALTER SCOTT
FROM ABBOTSFORD FOR NAPLES*

A TROUBLE, not of clouds, or weeping rain,
nor of the setting sun's pathetic light
engendered, hangs o'er Eildon's triple height:
Spirits of Power, assembled there, complain
for kindred Power departing from their sight:
while Tweed, best pleased in chanting a blithe strain,
saddens his voice again, and yet again.

Lift up your hearts, ye Mourners! for the might
of the whole world's good wishes with him goes;
blessings and prayers in nobler retinue
than sceptred king or laurelled conqueror knows,
follow this wondrous Potentate. Be true,
ye winds of Ocean, and the midland sea,
wafting your charge to fair Parthenope.
W. WORDSWORTH

129 *ON THE EXTINCTION OF THE VENETIAN REPUBLIC*

ONCE did She hold the gorgeous east in fee;
and was the safeguard of the west: the worth
of Venice did not fall below her birth,
Venice the eldest child of liberty.
She was a maiden city, bright and free;
no guile seduced, no force could violate;
and when she took unto herself a Mate,
she must espouse the everlasting Sea.
And what if she had seen those glories fade,
those titles vanish, and that strength decay;
yet shall some tribute of regret be paid,
when her long life hath reached its final day:
men are we, and must grieve when even the shade
of that which once was great is pass'd away.
W. WORDSWORTH

130 *SONNET*

NOT Love, not War, nor the tumultuous swell
of civil conflict, nor the wrecks of change,
nor Duty, struggling with afflictions strange—
not these *alone* inspire the tuneful shell;
but where untroubled peace and concord dwell,
there also is the Muse not loth to range,
watching the twilight smoke of cot or grange
sky-ward ascending from a woody dell.
Meek aspirations please her, lone endeavour,
and sage content, and placid melancholy;
she loves to gaze upon a crystal river—
diaphanous because it travels slowly;
soft is the music that would charm for ever;
the flower of sweetest smell is shy and lowly.
W. WORDSWORTH

131   ARION

NOT song, nor beauty, nor the wondrous power
  of the clear sky, nor stream, nor mountain-glen,
nor the wide ocean, turn the hearts of men
to love, nor give the world-embracing dower
of inward gentleness: up from the bed
blest by chaste beauty, men have risen to blood,
and life hath perished in the flow'ry wood,
and the poor traveller beneath starlight bled.
Thus that musician, in his wealth of song
pouring his numbers, even with the sound
swimming around them would the heartless throng
have thrust into his death; but with a bound
  spurning the cursed ship, he sought the wave,
  and Nature's children did her poet save.

132   SONNET TO THE RIVER OTTER

DEAR native brook! wild streamlet of the West!
  how many various-fated years have past,
what happy, and what mournful hours, since last
I skimm'd the smooth thin stone along thy breast,
numbering its light leaps! yet so deep imprest
sink the sweet scenes of childhood, that mine eyes
  I never shut amid the sunny ray,
but straight with all their tints thy waters rise,
  thy crossing plank, thy marge with willows grey,
and bedded sand that, veined with various dyes,
gleamed through thy bright transparence! On my way,
  visions of childhood! oft have ye beguiled
lone manhood's cares, yet waking fondest sighs:
  ah! that once more I were a careless child!
                                S. T. COLERIDGE

133   TO APRIL

EMBLEM of life, see changeful April sail
  in varying vest along the shadowy skies,
now bidding summer's softest zephyrs rise,
anon recalling winter's stormy gale,
and pouring from the cloud her sudden hail;
then, smiling through the tear that dims her eyes,
while Iris with her braid the welkin dyes,

promise of sunshine, not so prone to fail.
So to us, sojourners in life's low vale,
the smiles of Fortune flatter to deceive,
while still the Fates the web of misery weave:
so Hope exultant spreads her airy sail,
and from the present gloom the soul conveys
to distant summers and far happier days.
H. K. WHITE

134   *TO CAPEL LOFFT ESQ.*

LOFFT, unto thee one tributary song
   the simple Muse, admiring, fain would bring;
she longs to lisp thee to the listening throng,
and with thy name to bid the woodlands ring.
Fain would she blazon all thy virtues forth,
thy warm philanthropy, thy justice mild,
would say how thou didst foster kindred worth,
and to thy bosom snatched Misfortune's child:
firm she would paint thee, with becoming zeal,
upright and learned as the Pylian sire,
would say how sweetly thou couldst sweep the lyre,
and show thy labours for the public weal,
ten thousand virtues tell with joys supreme,
but ah! she shrinks abashed before the arduous theme.
H. K. WHITE

135   *TO CONSUMPTION*

SWEET to the gay of heart is Summer's smile,
   sweet the wild music of the laughing Spring;
but ah! my soul far other scenes beguile,
where gloomy storms their sullen shadows fling.
Is it for me to strike the Idalian string,
raise the soft music of the warbling wire,
while in my ears the howls of furies ring
and melancholy wastes the vital fire?
Away with thoughts like these!—To some lone cave
where howls the shrill blast and where sweeps the wave,
direct my steps; there, in the lonely drear,
I'll sit remote from worldly noise and muse,
till through my soul shall Peace her balm infuse,
and whisper sounds of comfort in my ear.
H. K. WHITE

136   THE PAINS OF MEMORY

WHAT time my heart unfolded its fresh leaves
    in spring-time gay, and scattered flowers around,
a whisper warned of earth's unhealthy ground,
and all that there faith's light and pureness grieves;
    sun's ray and canker-worm,
    and sudden-whelming storm:—
but, ah! my self-will smiled, nor recked the gracious sound.

So now defilement dims life's morning springs;
    I cannot hear an early-cherished strain,
    but first a joy, and then it brings a pain—
fear and self-hate, and vain remorseful stings:
    tears lull my grief to rest,
    not without hope, this breast
may one day lose its load, and youth yet bloom again.
                        LYRA APOSTOLICA

137   HOPE

NOW sober Cynthia spreads her lucid beam,
    with quivering ray the silent glen pervades,
tints the brown wood that crowns yon silvery stream,
and darts fine lustres on the full cascades:
through drear autumnal scenes her rays diffuse
that gentle charm which soothes the pensive sigh:
now Spring no more presents her blushing hues,
and Summer's gaudy pageants fading fly!
'tis thus, sweet Hope! through sorrow's blasting day
thy meek-eyed light kind solace can impart,
give to departing joy a lingering ray
and cheer with promised good the drooping heart;
    with radiant hands life's sable clouds remove,
    and ere the future dawns its blessings prove.

138   TO DEATH

WHY art thou slow, thou rest of trouble, Death,
    to stop a wretch's breath,
that calls on thee and offers her sad heart
    a prey unto thy dart?

I am nor young nor fair; be, therefore, bold:
   sorrow hath made me old,
deformed and wrinkled; all that I can crave
   is quiet in my grave.
Such as live happy hold long life a jewel;
   but to me thou art cruel,
if thou end not my tedious misery;
   and I soon cease to be.
Strike, and strike home, then: pity unto me,
   in one short hour's delay, is tyranny.

         P. MASSINGER.

139 AD SEIPSUM DE ADVENTU HYEMIS

SUMMER'S last lingering rose is flown,
   the leaf has withered from the tree;
I hear the coming winter moan
   through the sad forest sullenly.

The north wind's rage soft Zephyr flies;
   and all the songsters of the grove,
borne on his wing, 'mid brighter skies
   trill their sweet lays of joy and love.

Then quit we too the rural plain;
   till spring, with coronal so gay,
woo young Favonius back again,
   and chide his coy, his long delay.

Farewell ye flowers, ye streams, and thou
   my home, than princely hall more dear,
seat of my soul's delight, adieu!
   I go—but leave my spirit here.

         F. WRANGHAM

140   TO VIOLETS

WELCOME, maids of Honour,
   you do bring
   in the spring;
and wait upon her.

She has Virgins many,
   fresh and fair;
   yet you are
more sweet than any.

Ye are the maiden posies,
    and so grac'd
    to be plac'd
'fore damask roses.

Yet though thus respected,
    by and by
    ye do lie,
poor girls, neglected.
R. HERRICK

141   THE RULE OF LOVE

AND said I that my limbs were old;
   and said I that my blood was cold,
and that my kindly fire was fled,
and my poor withered heart was dead,
   and that I might not sing of love?—
how could I to the dearest theme,
that ever warmed a minstrel's dream,
   so foul, so false a recreant prove?
how could I name love's very name,
nor wake my heart to notes of flame!
in peace Love tunes the shepherd's reed;
in war he mounts the warrior's steed;
in halls, in gay attire is seen;
in hamlets, dances on the green.
SIR W. SCOTT

142   OF THE SEA

FOR lo the Sea that fleets about the land,
   and like a girdle clips her solid waist,
music and measure both doth understand;
for his great crystal eye is always cast
up to the moon, and on her fixed fast:
and as she danceth in her pallid sphere,
so danceth he about the centre here.

Sometimes his proud green waves in order set,
one after other, flow unto the shore,
which when they have with many kisses wet,
they ebb away in order as before;
and to make known his courtly love the more,
he oft doth lay aside his three-forked mace,
and with his arms the timorous Earth embrace.
SIR J. DAVIES

143 HARK! whence that rushing sound?
'tis like the wondrous strain
that round a lonely ruin swells,
which, wandering on the echoing shore,
   the enthusiast hears at evening:
'tis softer than the west wind's sigh;
'tis wilder than the unmeasured notes
of that strange lyre whose strings
   the genii of the breezes sweep:
those lines of rainbow light
are like the moonbeams when they fall
through some cathedral window, but the teints
   are such as may not find
   comparison on earth.
P. B. SHELLEY

144 *A NIGHT-PIECE ON DEATH*

NOR can the parted body know,
   nor wants the soul, these forms of woe;
as men who long in prison dwell
with lamps that glimmer round the cell,
whene'er their suffering years are run,
spring forth to greet the glittering sun:
such joy, though far transcending sense,
have pious souls at parting hence.
On earth, and in the body placed,
a few and evil years they waste:
but, when their chains are cast aside,
see the glad scene unfolding wide,
clap the glad wing and tower away,
and mingle with the blaze of day.
T. PARNELL

145 *TO ENGLAND*

NOT yet enslaved, not wholly vile,
   O Albion! O my mother isle!
thy valleys, fair as Eden's bowers,
glitter green with sunny showers;
thy grassy uplands' gentle swells
   echo to the bleat of flocks;
(those grassy hills, those glittering dells,
   proudly ramparted with rocks)

and Ocean mid his uproar wild
speaks safety to his island-child,
   hence for many a fearless age
   has social Quiet loved thy shore,
nor ever proud invader's rage
or sacked thy towers or stained thy fields with gore.
S. T. COLERIDGE

146   SONG TO ECHO

SWEET Echo, sweetest nymph, that livest unseen
   within thy airy shell,
by slow Meander's margent green,
and in the violet-embroidered vale
where the love-lorn nightingale
nightly to thee her sad song mourneth well;
canst thou not tell me of a gentle pair
   that likest thy Narcissus are?
     Oh! if thou have
   hid them in some flowery cave,
     tell me but where,
sweet queen of parley, daughter of the sphere,
so mayest thou be translated to the skies,
and give resounding grace to all Heaven's harmonies.
J. MILTON

147   INGRATITUDE

NOT faster yonder rowers' might
   flings from their oars the spray,
not faster yonder rippling bright,
that tracks the shallop's course in light,
   melts in the lake away,
than men from memory erase
the benefits of former days.

Then if in life's uncertain main
   mishap shall mar thy sail;
if faithful, wise and brave in vain,
woe, want and exile thou sustain
   beneath the fickle gale;
waste not a sigh on fortune changed,
on thankless courts or friends estranged.
SIR W. SCOTT

148   *TO CONTEMPLATION*

I VIEW thee on the calmy shore
    when Ocean stills his waves to rest;
or when slow-moving on the surges hoar
meet with deep hollow roar
    and whiten o'er his breast;
or lo! the moon with softer radiance gleams,
and lovelier heave the billows in her beams.

When the low gales of evening moan along,
    I love with thee to feel the calm cool breeze,
and roam the pathless forest wilds among,
    listening the mellow murmur of the trees
full-foliaged, as they lift their arms on high
and wave their shadowy heads in wildest melody.
                             R. SOUTHEY

149   *ON THE WINTER SOLSTICE* 1740

O THOU my lyre, awake, arise,
    and hail the sun's returning force;
even now he climbs the northern skies,
and health and hope attend his course.
Then louder howl the aerial waste,
be earth with keener cold embraced,
yet gentle hours advance their wing;
and Fancy, mocking Winter's might,
with flowers and dews and streaming light
already decks the new-born spring.
O fountain of the golden day,
could mortal vows promote thy speed,
how soon before thy vernal ray
should each unkindly damp recede!
how soon each hovering tempest fly,
whose stores for mischief arm the sky!
                             M. AKENSIDE

150   *DAVID'S SONG TO MICHAL*

AWAKE, awake, my Lyre!
    and tell thy silent master's humble tale
in sounds that may prevail;
sounds that gentle thoughts inspire.

        Though so exalted she,
        and I so lowly be,
tell her, such different notes make all thy harmony.
        Hark! how the strings awake:
and, though the moving hand approach not near,
        themselves with awful fear
a kind of numerous trembling make.
        Now all thy forces try;
        now all thy charms apply;
revenge upon her ear the conquests of her eye.

151   Weak Lyre! thy virtue sure
is useless here, since thou art only found
        to cure, but not to wound,
and she to wound, but not to cure.
        Too weak too wilt thou prove
        my passion to remove;
physic to other ills, thou'rt nourishment to love.
        Sleep, sleep again, my Lyre!
for thou canst never tell my humble tale
        in sounds that will prevail,
nor gentle thoughts in her inspire;
        all thy vain mirth lay by,
        bid thy strings silent lie,
sleep, sleep again, my Lyre, and let thy master die.
                            A. COWLEY

152   *REDEEM THE PAST*

'TIS vanished all—in hurried flight—
   ere yet I felt Time's trophies white
were sprinkled on my brow,—or thought, that since
   the light
   beamed on me, what long years had flown;
time's snows are on my forehead thrown,
and many a winter now and many a spring are gone.
   But what doth this, all this, avail?
for soon, too soon, oblivion pale
will blot alike the good and evil of my tale.
   'Twill then be said—whoe'er thou be,
that world is lost, which flattered thee,
and all thou hast pursued is fruitless vanity.
   Oh! while thy sinful soul can cast
sin's robes away—redeem the past,
if not in deeds, in words to praise thy Maker haste.

153   LIFE

How short is Life's uncertain space!
  how quickly is it run!
how swift the wild precarious chase,
anxious and difficult the race!
  and what the prize when won!

Youth stops at first its wilful ears
  to Wisdom's kindest voice;
till now arrived to riper years,
experienced age, worn out with cares,
  repents its earlier choice.

What though its prospects now appear
  so grateful to the mind;
yet groundless Hope, and teasing Fear,
by turns the busy moments share,
  and leave a sting behind.

                        J. MERRICK

154   HEAVEN

This world is all a fleeting show,
  for man's illusion given;
the smiles of Joy, the tears of Woe,
deceitful shine, deceitful flow—
  there's nothing true but Heaven!

And false the light on Glory's plume,
  as fading hues of even;
and Love and Hope, and Beauty's bloom
are blossoms gathered from the tomb—
  there's nothing bright but Heaven!

Poor wanderers of a stormy day,
  from wave to wave we're driven,
and Fancy's flash and Reason's ray
serve but to light the troubled way—
  there's nothing calm but Heaven!

                        T. MOORE

155   ON REVISITING THE SCENES OF HIS CHILDHOOD

With lorn delight the scene I view'd,
  past joys and sorrows were renew'd;
my infant hopes and fears
look'd lovely through the solitude
  of retrospective years.

And still, in Memory's twilight bowers,
the spirits of departed hours,
　with mellowing tints, pourtray
the blossoms of life's vernal flowers
　for ever fall'n away.

Till youth's delirious dream is o'er,
sanguine with hope, we look before,
　the future good to find;
in age, when error charms no more,
　for bliss we look behind.

J. MONTGOMERY

156 MORPHEUS

MORPHEUS, the humble god that dwells
　　in cottages and smoky cells,
hates gilded roofs and beds of down;
and though he fears no prince's frown,
flies from the circle of a crown.

Come, I say, thou powerful god,
and thy leaden charming rod
dipt in the Lethean lake,
o'er his wakeful temples shake,
lest he should sleep and never wake.

Nature, alas! why art thou so
obliged to thy greatest foe?
Sleep, that is thy best repast,
yet of death it bears a taste,
and both are the same thing at last.

SIR J. DENHAM

157 TO A CHILD EMBRACING HIS MOTHER

LOVE thy mother, little one!
　　kiss and clasp her neck again,—
hereafter she may have a son
will kiss and clasp her neck in vain.
　Love thy mother, little one!

Gaze upon her living eyes,
and mirror back her love for thee,—
hereafter thou may'st shudder sighs
to meet them when they cannot see.
　Gaze upon her living eyes!

Press her lips the while they glow
with love that they have often told,—
hereafter thou may'st press in woe,
and kiss them till thine own are cold.
  Press her lips the while they glow!
                              T. HOOD

158   THE RESTORATION OF HELLAS

THE world's great age begins anew,
    the golden years return,
the earth doth like a snake renew
    her winter weeds outworn:
a brighter Hellas rears its mountains
    from waves serener far;
a new Peneus rolls its fountains
    against the morning-star.
Where fairer Tempes bloom, there sleep
young Cyclads on a sunnier deep.
Another Athens shall arise,
    and to remoter time
bequeath, like sunset to the skies,
    the splendour of its prime;
and leave, if nought so bright may live,
all earth can take or heaven can give.
                              P. B. SHELLEY

159   SONG TO ECHO

SWEET Echo, sleeps thy vocal shell,
    where this high arch o'erhangs the dell;
while Tweed, with sun-reflecting streams,
chequers thy rocks with dancing beams!

Here may no clamours harsh intrude,
no brawling hound or clarion rude;
here no fell beast of midnight prowl,
and teach thy tortured cliffs to howl.

Be thine to pour these vales along
some artless shepherd's evening song;
while night's sweet bird from yon high spray
responsive listens to his lay.

And if, like me, some love-lorn maid
should sing her sorrows to thy shade,
O, soothe her breast, ye rocks around,
with softest sympathy of sound.
                              E. DARWIN

160   THE WISH

WELL, then, I now do plainly see
    this busy world and I shall ne'er agree;
the very honey of all earthly joy
does of all meats the soonest cloy:
and they (methinks) deserve my pity
who for it can endure the stings,
the crowd, and buz, and murmurings
of this great hive, the City.

Ah! yet, ere I descend to the grave,
may I a small house and large garden have!
and a few friends, and many books, both true,
both wise, and both delightful too!
and since Love ne'er will from me flee,
a Mistress moderately fair,
and good as guardian-angels are,
only beloved and loving me!

         A. COWLEY

161   LOVE OF SOLITUDE

I WOULD I were a careless child,
    still dwelling in my Highland cave,
or roaming through the dusky wild,
    or bounding o'er the dark blue wave;
the cumbrous pomp of Saxon pride
    accords not with the freeborn soul,
which loves the mountain's craggy side,
and seeks the rocks where billows roll.

Fortune! take back these cultured lands,
    take back this name of splendid sound!
I hate the touch of servile hands,
    I hate the slaves that cringe around.
Place me among the rocks I love,
    which sound to Ocean's wildest roar;
I ask but this—again to rove
    through scenes my youth hath known before.

162 Few are my years, and yet I feel
    the world was ne'er designed for me:
ah! why do dark'ning shades conceal
    the hour when man must cease to be?

Once I beheld a splendid dream,
 a visionary scene of bliss :
truth!—wherefore did thy hated beam
 awake me to a world like this?

I loved—but those I loved are gone;
 had friends—my early friends are fled:
how cheerless feels the heart alone
 when all its former hopes are dead!
Though gay companions o'er the bowl
 dispel awhile the sense of ill;
though pleasure stirs the maddening soul,
 the heart—the heart—is lonely still.

163 How dull! to hear the voice of those
 whom rank or chance, whom wealth or power,
have made, though neither friends nor foes,
 associates of the festive hour.
Give me again a faithful few,
 in years and feelings still the same,
and I will fly the midnight crew,
 where boisterous joy is but a name.

Fain would I fly the haunts of men—
 I seek to shun, not hate mankind;
my breast requires the sullen glen,
 whose gloom may suit a darkened mind.
Oh! that to me the wings were given
 which bear the turtle to her nest!
then would I cleave the vault of heaven,
 to flee away, and be at rest.
LORD BYRON

164 *THE POET'S TRANCE ENDED*

 THE solemn harmony
paused, and the spirit of that mighty singing
 to its abyss was suddenly withdrawn;
then as a wild swan, when sublimely winging
 its path athwart the thunder-smoke of dawn,
sinks headlong through the aerial golden light
 on the heavy sounding plain,
 when the bolt has pierced its brain;
as summer clouds dissolve unburthened of their rain;

        as a far taper fades with fading night;
        as a brief insect dies with dying day,
      my song, its pinions disarrayed of might,
            drooped; o'er it closed the echoes far away
      of the great voice which did its flight sustain,
      as waves which lately paved his watery way
      hiss round a drowner's head in their tempestuous play.
                                P. B. SHELLEY

165   DESPONDENCY

C AN Love again o'er this sad breast
    resume his long-forgotten reign?
again his downy plume invest
a heart, by sorrow chilled to stone?
again expand his infant wing
o'er the dark void of deep despair?
and bid the roseate blushes spring
e'en from the pallid cheek of care?
Can the quick pulse of fond alarm
in this cold bosom dare to beat?
the trembling joy, the anxious charm,
the bitter struggling with the sweet?
Ah! no, all cold and dark and void,
scarce beams one spark of genial fire;
the very power of Love destroyed,
O, Life! in mercy too expire.

166   THERMOPYLÆ

S HOUT for the mighty men,
    who died along this shore—
who died within this mountain glen!
for never nobler chieftain's head
was laid on Valour's crimson bed,
        nor ever prouder gore
sprang forth, than theirs who won the day
upon thy strand, Thermopylæ!

Shout for the mighty men,
        who on the Persian tents,
like lions from their midnight den
bounding on the slumbering deer,
rush'd—a storm of sword and spear;—
        like the roused elements,

let loose from an immortal hand,
to chasten or to crush a land!

G. CROLY

167   *THE BOWL*

WHEN the wearying cares of state
    oppress the monarch with their weight,
when from his pomp retired alone
he feels the duties of the throne,
feels that the multitude below
depend on him for weal or woe;
when his powerful will may bless
a realm with peace and happiness,
or with desolating breath
breathe ruin round and woe and death;
oh! give to him the flowing bowl,
bid it humanize his soul;
he shall not feel the empire's weight,
he shall not feel the cares of state,
the bowl shall each dark thought beguile,
and nations live and prosper from his smile.

R. SOUTHEY

168   *THE FOLLY OF MAKING TROUBLES*

WHEN we meet as when we part,
    why should sighs attend us,
making sad the gayest heart
    Heaven is pleased to send us?

Why, when all is bright to-day,
    should man choose to borrow
something from the darker ray
    destined for to-morrow?

If indeed to-morrow brings
    what is like to sear us,
why not seize by both its wings
    pleasure, while 'tis near us?

Why still float life's ocean o'er,
    missing joys designed us,
casting anxious eyes before,
    tearful ones behind us?

169   *SWEET EVENING HOUR*

SWEET evening hour! sweet evening hour!
that calms the air and shuts the flower,
that brings the wild bee to its nest,
the infant to its mother's breast.

Sweet hour! that bids the labourer cease,
that gives the weary team release,
and leads them home, and crowns them there
with rest and shelter, food and care.

O season of soft sounds and hues,
of twilight walks among the dews,
of feelings calm and converse sweet,
and thoughts too shadowy to repeat!

Yes, lovely hour! thou art the time
when feelings flow and wishes climb,
when timid souls begin to dare,
and God receives and answers prayer.

170   *SPRING*

SWEET daughter of a rough and stormy sire,
hoar Winter's blooming child, delightful Spring!
   whose unshorn locks with leaves
   and swelling buds are crowned;

from the green islands of eternal youth
(crowned with fresh blooms and ever-springing shade)
   turn, hither turn thy step,
   O thou, whose powerful voice,

more sweet than softest touch of Doric reed
or Lydian flute, can soothe the madding winds,
   and through the stormy deep
   breathe thy own tender calm.

Unlock thy copious stores; those tender showers
that drop their sweetness on the infant buds;
   and silent dews that swell
   the milky ear's green stem.

171 O nymph! approach, while yet the temperate sun,
with bashful forehead, through the cool moist air
   throws his young maiden beams,
   and with chaste kisses wooes

the earth's fair bosom; while the streaming veil
of lucid clouds with kind and frequent shade
    protects thy modest blooms
    from his severer blaze.

Sweet is thy reign, but short: the red dog-star
shall scorch thy tresses; and the mower's sithe
    thy greens, thy flowerets all,
    remorseless shall destroy.

Reluctant shall I bid thee then farewell;
for, O! not all that Autumn's lap contains,
    nor Summer's ruddiest fruits,
    can aught for thee atone.
                      A. L. BARBAULD

172   *FITZEUSTACE'S SONG*

WHERE shall the lover rest,
    whom the fates sever
from his true maiden's breast,
    parted for ever!
Where, through groves deep and high,
    sounds the far billow,
where early violets die
    under the willow.

There through the summer-day
    cool streams are laving;
there, while the tempests sway,
    scarce are boughs waving;
there thy rest shalt thou take,
    parted for ever,
never again to wake—
    never, O never!

173 Where shall the traitor rest,
    he, the deceiver,
who could win maiden's breast,
    ruin, and leave her!
In the lost battle,
    borne down by the flying,
where mingles war's rattle
    with groans of the dying.

Her wing shall the eagle flap
    o'er the false-hearted;
his warm blood the wolf shall lap
    ere life be parted:
shame and dishonour sit
    by his grave ever;
blessing shall hallow it
    never, O never!

                        SIR W. SCOTT

174. OCTOBER WINDS

OCTOBER winds, wi' biting breath,
    now nip the leaf that's yellow fading;
nae gowans glint upon the green,
    alas! they're co'er'd wi' winter's cleeding.
As through the woods I musing gang,
    nae birdies cheer me frae the bushes,
save little Robin's lanely sang,
    wild warbling where the burnie gushes.

The sun is jogging down the brae,
    dimly through the mist he's shining,
and cranreugh hoar creeps o'er the grass,
    as day resigns his throne to e'ening.
Oft let me walk at twilight grey,
    to view the face of dying nature,
till spring again with mantle green
    delights the heart o' ilka creature.

                        J. SCADLOCK

175. TO MEMORY

O MEMORY, celestial maid,
    who glean'st the flow'rets cropt by time,
and, suffering not a leaf to fade,
    preserv'st the blossoms of our prime:
bring, bring those moments to my mind,
when life was new, and all was kind;
and bring that garland to my sight,
    with which my favour'd crook was bound:
and bring that wreath of roses bright,
    which then my festive temples crown'd,

    and once more to my ear convey
the strains that wak'd a happier day;
and sketch with care the Muses' bower;
    nor yet omit a single flower,
of all that fling their sweetness round,
and seem to consecrate the ground!
W. SHENSTONE

176   THE LOSS

    YET ere I go,
       disdainful Beauty, thou shalt be
  so wretched, as to know
what joys thou fling'st away with me.

    A faith so bright,
as Time or Fortune could not rust;
  so firm, that lovers might
have read thy story in my dust,

    and crowned thy name
with laurel verdant as thy youth,
  whilst the shrill voice of Fame
spread wide thy beauty and my truth.

    This thou hast lost;
for all true lovers, when they find
  that my just aims were crost,
will speak thee lighter than the wind.
T. STANLEY

177   HORATIVS COCLES

    WHEN the oldest cask is opened,
        and the largest lamp is lit;
when the chestnuts glow in the embers,
  and the kid turns on the spit;
when young and old in circle
  around the firebrands close;
when the girls are weaving baskets,
  and the lads are shaping bows;

    when the goodman mends his armour,
  and trims his helmet's plume;
when the goodwife's shuttle merrily
  goes flashing through the loom;

with weeping and with laughter
　　still is the story told,
how well Horatius kept the bridge
　　in the brave days of old.
LORD MACAULAY

178　　　　　　　　*LUCY*

I TRAVELLED among unknown men
　　in lands beyond the sea;
nor, England! did I know till then
　　what love I bore to thee.

'Tis past, that melancholy dream!
　　nor will I quit thy shore
a second time; for still I seem
　　to love thee more and more.

Among thy mountains did I feel
　　the joy of my desire;
and she I cherished turned her wheel
　　beside an English fire.

Thy mornings showed, thy nights concealed
　　the bowers where Lucy played;
and thine too is the last green field
　　that Lucy's eyes surveyed.
W. WORDSWORTH

179　　　　　　*LOVE AND MUSIC*

WHAT woke the buried sound that lay
　　in Memnon's harp of yore?
what spirit on its viewless way
　　along the Nile's green shore?
Oh! not the night, and not the storm,
　　and not the lightning's fire;
but sunlight's torch, the kind, the warm—
　　this, this awoke the lyre.
What wins the heart's deep chords to pour
　　thus music forth on life—
like a sweet voice prevailing o'er
　　the truant sounds of strife?

Oh! not the conflict midst the throng,
  not e'en the trumpet's hour;
love is the gifted and the strong
  to wake that music's power!
F. HEMANS

180   *IL PENSEROSO*

AND when the sun begins to fling
  his flaring beams, me, Goddess, bring
to arched walks of twilight groves,
and shadows brown, that Sylvan loves,
of pine, or monumental oak,
where the rude axe with heaved stroke
was never heard the Nymphs to daunt,
or fright them from their hallowed haunt.
There in close covert by some brook,
where no profaner eye may look,
hide me from day's garish eye,
while the bee with honeyed thigh,
that at her flowery work doth sing,
and the waters murmuring,
with such consort as they keep,
entice the dewy-feathered Sleep.
J. MILTON

181   *TO DAFFODILS*

FAIR Daffodils, we weep to see
   you haste away so soon:
as yet the early-rising Sun
   has not attain'd his noon.
          Stay, stay,
   until the hasting day
          has run
   but to the even-song;
and, having pray'd together, we
   will go with you along.
We have short time to stay, as you,
   we have as short a Spring;
as quick a growth to meet decay
   as you, or any thing.

We die,
as your hours do, and dry
away
like to the Summer's rain;
or as the pearls of morning's dew,
ne'er to be found again.

R. HERRICK

182   *ON THE DEATH OF A SON*

TYRANT of man! Imperious Fate!
   I bow before thy dread decree,
nor hope in this uncertain state
   to find a seat secure from thee.

Life is a dark, tumultuous stream,
   with many a care and sorrow foul,
yet thoughtless mortals vainly deem
   that it can yield a limpid bowl.

Think not that stream will backward flow,
   or cease its destined course to keep;
as soon the blazing spark shall glow
   beneath the surface of the deep.

Believe not Fate at thy command
   will grant a meed she never gave;
as soon the airy tower shall stand,
   that's built upon a passing wave.

J. D. CARLYLE

183   *A LAMENT*

SWIFTER far than summer's flight,
   swifter far than youth's delight,
swifter far than happy night,
   art thou come and gone:

as the earth when leaves are dead,
as the night when sleep is sped,
as the heart when joy is fled,
   I am left lone, alone.

Lilies for a bridal bed,
roses for a matron's head,
violets for a maiden dead,
    pansies let my flowers be:

on the living grave I bear,
scatter them without a tear,
let no friend, however dear,
    waste one hope, one fear for me.

P. B. SHELLEY

184   *THE MOUNTAIN BOY*

WHAT liberty so glad and gay,
    as where the mountain boy,
reckless of regions far away,
    a prisoner lives in joy?

The dreary sounds of crowded earth,
    the cries of camp or town,
never untuned his lonely mirth,
    nor drew his visions down.

The snow-clad peaks of rosy light,
    that meet his morning view,
the thwarting cliffs that bound his sight,
    they bound his fancy too.

Two ways alone his roving eye
    for aye may onward go,
or in the azure deep on high
    or darksome mere below.

J. KEBLE

185   *ELEGY*

O SNATCH'D away in beauty's bloom!
    on thee shall press no ponderous tomb;
but on thy turf shall roses rear
their leaves, the earliest of the year,
and the wild cypress wave in tender gloom:

and oft by yon blue gushing stream
shall Sorrow lean her drooping head,
and feed deep thought with many a dream,
and lingering pause and lightly tread;
fond wretch! as if her step disturb'd the dead!

Away! we know that tears are vain,
that Death nor heeds nor hears distress:
will this unteach us to complain?
or make one mourner weep the less?
And thou, who tell'st me to forget,
thy looks are wan, thine eyes are wet.
LORD BYRON

186   *ON THE DEATH OF A YOUNG LADY*

THE peace of Heaven attend thy shade,
my early friend, my favourite maid!
when life was new, companions gay,
we hailed the morning of our day.

Ah, with what joy did I behold
the flower of beauty fair unfold!
and feared no storm to blast thy bloom,
or bring thee to an early tomb!

Untimely gone! for ever fled
the roses of the cheek so red;
the affection warm, the temper mild,
the sweetness that in sorrow smiled.

Alas! the cheek where beauty glowed,
the heart where goodness overflowed,
a clod amid the valley lies,
and 'dust to dust' the mourner cries.

187 O from thy kindred early torn,
and to thy grave untimely borne!
vanished for ever from my view,
thou sister of my soul, adieu!

Fair, with my first ideas twined,
thine image oft will meet my mind;
and, while remembrance brings thee near,
affection sad will drop a tear.

How oft does sorrow bend the head,
before we dwell among the dead!
scarce in the years of manly prime,
I've often wept the wrecks of time.

What tragic tears bedew the eye!
what deaths we suffer ere we die!
our broken friendships we deplore,
and loves of youth that are no more!

188 No after-friendship e'er can raise
the endearments of our early days;
and ne'er the heart such fondness prove,
as when it first began to love.

Affection dies, a vernal flower;
and love, the blossom of an hour;
the spring of fancy cares control,
and mar the beauty of the soul.

Versed in the commerce of deceit,
how soon the heart forgets to beat!
the blood runs cold at Interest's call;—
they look with equal eyes on all.

Then lovely Nature is expelled,
and Friendship is romantic held;
then Prudence comes with hundred eyes:
the veil is rent: the vision flies.

189 The dear illusions will not last;
the era of enchantment's past;
the wild romance of life is done;
the real history is begun.

The sallies of the soul are o'er,
the feast of fancy is no more;
and ill the banquet is supplied
by form, by gravity, by pride.

Ye gods! whatever ye withhold,
let my affections ne'er grow old;
ne'er may the human glow depart,
nor Nature yield to frigid Art!

Still may the generous bosom burn,
though doomed to bleed o'er beauty's urn;
and still the friendly face appear,
though moistened with a tender tear!

190 THE ALPS AT DAYBREAK

THE sun-beams streak the azure skies,
and line with light the mountain's brow:
with hounds and horns the hunters rise,
and chase the roebuck through the snow.

From rock to rock, with giant-bound,
high on their iron poles they pass;
mute, lest the air, convulsed by sound,
rend from above a frozen mass.

The goats wind slow their wonted way,
up craggy steeps and ridges rude;
marked by the wild wolf for his prey,
from desert cave or hanging wood.

And while the torrent thunders loud,
and as the echoing cliffs reply,
the huts peep o'er the morning-cloud,
perched, like an eagle's nest, on high.

S. ROGERS

191 MUTABILITY

WE are as clouds that veil the midnight moon:
　　how restlessly they speed and gleam and quiver,
streaking the darkness radiantly!—yet soon
　　night closes round, and they are lost for ever:

or like forgotten lyres, whose dissonant strings
　　give various response to each varying blast,
to whose frail frame no second motion brings
　　one mood or modulation like the last.

We rest—a dream has power to poison sleep;
　　we rise—one wandering thought pollutes the day;
we feel, conceive or reason, laugh or weep;
　　embrace fond woe, or cast our cares away:

it is the same! For, be it joy or sorrow,
　　the path of its departure still is free;
man's yesterday may ne'er be like his morrow;
　　nought may endure but Mutability.

P. B. SHELLEY

192   *THE YEAR*

IN childhood, when with eager eyes
 the season-measured year I viewed,
   all, garbed in fairy guise,
     pledged constancy of good.

Spring sang of heaven; the summer-flowers
 let me gaze on, and did not fade;
   even suns o'er autumn's bowers
     heard my strong wish, and stayed.

They came and went—the short-lived four,
 yet as their varying dance they wove,
   to my young heart each bore
     its own sure claim of love.

Far different now;—the whirling year
 vainly my dizzy eyes pursue;
   and its fair tints appear
     all blent in one dusk hue.

                      LYRA APOSTOLICA

193   *HYMN TO LIGHT*

FIRST-BORN of Chaos, who so fair did'st come
 from the old Negro's darksome womb!
   which when it saw the lovely child,
the melancholy mass put on kind looks and smiled.

Thou tide of glory, which no rest doth know,
   but ever ebb and ever flow!
   thou golden shower of a true Jove!
who does in thee descend, and Heaven to Earth
     make love!

Hail active Nature's watchful life and health!
   her joy, her ornament and wealth!
   hail to thy husband heat and thee!
thou the world's beauteous Bride, the lusty Bride-
     groom he!

Say from what golden quivers of the sky
   do all thy winged arrows fly?

swiftness and power by birth are thine:
from thy great Sire they came, thy Sire the Word
divine.

194 Swift as light thoughts their empty career run,
    thy race is finished, when begun:
    let a Post-angel start with thee,
and thou the goal of Earth shalt reach as soon as he.

Thou in the Moon's bright chariot, proud and gay,
    dost the bright wood of stars survey;
    and all the year doth with thee bring
a thousand flowery lights, thine own nocturnal spring.

Night and her ugly subjects thou dost fright,
    and sleep, the lazy owl of Night;
    asham'd and fearful to appear,
they screen their horrid shapes with the black Hemisphere.

With them there hastes, and wildly takes th' alarm,
    of painted dreams a busy swarm;
    at the first opening of thine eye
the various clusters break, the antic atoms fly.

The guilty serpents and obscener beasts
    creep conscious to their secret rests;
    Nature to thee does reverence pay,
ill omens and ill sights removes out of thy way.

195 At thy appearance, Grief itself is said
    to shake his wings and rouse his head;
    and cloudy Care has often took
a gentle beamy smile reflected from thy look.

At thy appearance, Fear itself grows bold:
    thy sunshine melts away his cold:
    encouraged at the sight of thee,
to the cheek colour comes and firmness to the knee.

Even Lust, the master of a hardened face,
    blushes if thou be'st in the place;
    to darkness' curtains he retires,
in sympathising night he rolls his smoky fires.

When, Goddess, thou lift'st up thy wak'ned head
    out of the morning's purple bed,

    thy quire of birds about thee play,
and all the joyful world salutes the rising day.

The ghosts and monster spirits, that did presume
    a body's privilege to assume,
    vanish again invisibly
and bodies gain again their visibility.

196 All the world's bravery, that delights our eyes,
    is but thy several liveries:
    thou the rich dye on them bestow'st,
thy nimble pencil paints this landscape as thou go'st.

A crimson garment in the rose thou wear'st;
    a crown of studded gold thou bear'st,
    the virgin lilies in their white
are clad but with the lawn of almost naked light.

The violet, spring's little infant, stands
    girt in thy purple swaddling-bands:
    on the fair tulip thou dost dote;
thou cloth'st it with a gay and party-coloured coat.

With flame condens'd thou dost the jewels fix,
    and solid colours in it mix:
    Flora herself envies to see
flowers fairer than her own, and durable as she.

Ah, Goddess! would thou could'st thy hand withhold
    and be less liberal to gold;
    didst thou less value to it give
of how much care, alas! might'st thou poor man relieve!

197 To me the Sun is more delightful far,
    and all fair days much fairer are;
    but few, ah wondrous few there be
who do not gold prefer, O Goddess! ev'n to thee.

Through the soft ways of heaven and air and sea,
    which open all their pores to thee,
    like a clear river thou dost glide,
and with thy living stream through the close channels
    slide.

But, where firm bodies thy free course oppose,
    gently thy source the land o'erflows;

takes there possession and does make,
of colours mingled, light, a thick and standing lake.

But the vast ocean of unbounded day
    in th' empyrean heaven does stay:
    thy rivers, lakes and springs below,
from thence took first their rise, thither at last must flow.

A. COWLEY

198   LOVE'S PHILOSOPHY

THE fountains mingle with the river
    and the rivers with the ocean,
the winds of heaven mix for ever
    with a sweet emotion;
nothing in the world is single,
    all things by a law divine
in one another's being mingle—
    why not I with thine!

See the mountains kiss high heaven
    and the waves clasp one another;
no sister flower would be forgiven
    if it disdain'd its brother:
and the sunlight clasps the earth,
    and the moonbeams kiss the sea—
what are all these kissings worth,
    if thou kiss not me?

P. B. SHELLEY

199   SONG FOR THE WANDERING JEW

THOUGH the torrents from their fountains
    roar down many a craggy steep,
yet they find among the mountains
    resting-places calm and deep.

Clouds that love through air to hasten,
    ere the storm its fury stills,
helmet-like themselves will fasten
    on the heads of towering hills.

If on windy days the Raven
    gambol like a dancing skiff,
not the less she loves her haven
    in the bosom of the cliff.

Day and night my toils redouble,
never nearer to the goal;
night and day, I feel the trouble
of the Wanderer in my soul.
W. WORDSWORTH

200   *CALM AFTER A STORM IN ASIA*

HOW calm, how beautiful comes on
the stilly hour, when storms are gone;
when warring winds have died away,
and clouds, beneath the glancing ray,
melt off, and leave the land and sea
sleeping in bright tranquillity,—
fresh, as if Day again were born,
again upon the lap of Morn!—
When the light blossoms, rudely torn
and scattered at the whirlwind's will,
hang floating in the pure air still,
filling it all with precious balm,
in gratitude for this sweet calm;—
and every drop the thunder-showers
have left upon the grass and flowers
sparkles, as 'twere that lightning gem,
whose liquid flame is born of them!
T. MOORE

201   *SONG OF THE PRIEST OF PAN*

SHEPHERDS, rise and shake off sleep!
see, the blushing morn doth peep
through the windows, whilst the sun
to the mountain-tops is run,
gilding all the vales below
with its rising flames, which grow
greater by his climbing still.
Up, ye lazy grooms, and fill
bag and bottle for the field!
Clasp your cloaks fast, lest they yield
to the bitter north-east wind.
Call the maidens up, and find
who lay longest, that she may
go without a friend all day;

  then reward your dogs, and pray
  Pan to keep you from decay:
  so, unfold, and then away!
J. FLETCHER

202   *DOMINUS DOMINANTIUM*

SUPREME Divinity! who yet
 could ever find
by the cold scrutiny of wit
 the treasury where Thou lock'st up the wind?
What majesty of princes can
 a tempest awe,
when the distracted ocean
 swells to sedition, and obeys no law?
How wretched doth the tyrant stand
 without a boast,
when his rich fleet even touching land
 he by some storm in his own port sees lost!
Vain pomp of life! what narrow bound
 ambition
is circled with! How false a ground
 hath human pride to build its triumphs on!
W. HABINGTON

203   *REQUIESCAT*

STREW on her roses, roses,
 but never a spray of yew:
in silence she reposes,
 ah! would that I did too.

Her mirth the world required,
 she bathed it in smiles and glee:
but her heart was tired, tired,
 and now they let her be.

Her life was turning, turning,
 in mazes of heat and sound:
but for peace her soul was yearning,
 and now peace laps her round:

Her cabined, ample Spirit,
 it fluttered and failed for breath:
to-night it doth inherit
 the vasty Hall of Death.
M. ARNOLD

204   *A MOTHER'S DIRGE OVER HER CHILD*

BRING me flowers all young and sweet,
that I may strew the winding sheet
where calm thou sleepest, baby fair,
with roseless cheek and auburn hair.

No more, my baby, shalt thou lie,
with drowsy smile and half-shut eye,
pillowed upon my fostering breast,
serenely sinking into rest!

The grave must be thy cradle now,
the wild flowers o'er thy breast shall grow,
while still my heart, all full of thee,
in widowed solitude shall be.

No taint of earth, no thought of sin,
e'er dwelt thy stainless breast within,
and God hath laid thee down to sleep,
like a pure pearl below the deep.

                            D. M. MOIR

205   *IN MEMORIAM*

CALM is the morn without a sound,
  calm as to suit a calmer grief,
  and only through the faded leaf
the chesnut pattering to the ground:

calm and deep peace on this high wold,
    and on these dews that drench the furze,
    and all the silvery gossamers
that twinkle into green and gold:

calm and still light on yon great plain
    that sweeps with all its autumn bowers,
    and crowded farms and lessening towers
to mingle with the bounding main:

calm and deep peace in this wide air,
    these leaves that redden in the fall;
    and in my heart if calm at all,
if any calm, a calm despair:

calm on the seas, and silver sleep,
  and waves that sway themselves in rest,
  and dead calm in that noble breast
which heaves but with the heaving deep.
A. TENNYSON

206   THE LAST CONQUEROR

VICTORIOUS men of earth, no more
    proclaim how wide your empires are;
though you bind in every shore,
  and your triumphs reach as far
    as night or day,
yet you, proud monarchs, must obey,
and mingle with forgotten ashes, when
death calls ye to the crowd of common men.

Devouring Famine, Plague, and War,
  each able to undo mankind,
death's servile emissaries are;
  nor to these alone confined,
    he hath at will
  more quaint and subtle ways to kill;
a smile or kiss, as he will use the art,
shall have the cunning skill to break a heart.
J. SHIRLEY

207   SONNET

TRUST not, sweet soul, those curlèd waves of gold
    with gentle tides that on your temples flow,
nor temples spread with flakes of virgin snow,
nor snow of cheeks with Tyrian grain enrolled.
Trust not those shining lights which wrought my woe
when first I did their azure rays behold,
nor voice whose sounds more strange effects do show
than of the Thracian harper have been told;
look to this dying lily, fading rose,
dark hyacinth, of late whose blushing beams
made all the neighbouring herbs and grass rejoice,
and think how little is twixt's life's extremes:
—the cruel tyrant that did kill those flowers
  shall once, ay me! not spare that spring of yours.
W. DRUMMOND

208   *A FAREWELL*

F LOW down, cold rivulet, to the sea,
 thy tribute wave deliver;
no more by thee my steps shall be,
 for ever and for ever.

Flow, softly flow, by lawn and lea,
 A rivulet then a river;
no where by thee my steps shall be,
 for ever and for ever.

But here will sigh thine alder tree,
 and here thine aspen shiver;
and here by thee will hum the bee,
 for ever and for ever.

A thousand suns will stream on thee,
 A thousand moons will quiver;
but not by thee my steps shall be,
 for ever and for ever.
       A. TENNYSON

209 *LITANY OF THE HOLY SPIRIT*

I N the hour of my distress,
 when temptations sore oppress,
and when I my sins confess,
  sweet Spirit, comfort me!

When I lie within my bed,
sick in heart and sick in head,
and with doubts discomfited,
  sweet Spirit, comfort me!

When the house doth sigh and weep,
and the world is drowned in sleep,
yet mine eyes their vigils keep,
  sweet Spirit, comfort me!

When the Judgment is revealed,
and that open which was sealed,
when to Thee I have appealed,
  sweet Spirit, comfort me!
       R. HERRICK

210   *JOHN ANDERSON*

   JOHN Anderson my jo, John,
      when we were first acquent
your locks were like the raven,
   your bonnie brow was brent;
but now your brow is bald, John,
   your locks are like the snow;
but blessings on your frosty pow,
   John Anderson my jo.

John Anderson my jo, John,
   we clamb the hill thegither,
and monie a cantie day, John,
   we've had wi' ane anither;
now we maun totter down, John,
   but hand in hand we'll go,
and sleep thegither at the foot,
   John Anderson my jo.

                              R. BURNS

211   *TO THE DAISY*

   THEE Winter in the garland wears
      that thinly decks his few grey hairs;
Spring parts the clouds with softest airs,
   that she may sun thee;
whole Summer-fields are thine by right;
and Autumn, melancholy Wight!
doth in thy crimson head delight
   when rains are on thee.

Be violets in their secret mews
the flowers the wanton Zephyrs choose;
proud be the rose, with rains and dews
   her head impearling;
thou liv'st with less ambitious aim,
yet·hast not gone without thy fame;
thou art indeed by many a claim
   the Poet's darling.

212   If to a rock from rains he fly,
   or, some bright day of April sky,
   imprisoned by hot sunshine lie
      near the green holly,

and wearily at length should fare;
he needs but look about, and there
thou art!—a friend at hand, to scare
    his melancholy.

Child of the year! that round dost run
thy pleasant course,—when day's begun
as ready to salute the sun
    as lark or leveret,
thy long-lost praise thou shalt regain;
nor be less dear to future men
than in old time;—thou not in vain
    art Nature's favourite.
W. WORDSWORTH

213   PROOF TO NO PURPOSE

YOU see this gentle stream that glides,
   shov'd on by quick succeeding tides:
try if this sober stream you can
follow to the wilder ocean:
and see, if there it keeps unspent
in that congesting element:
next, from that world of waters, then
by pores and caverns back again
induc'd that inadulterate same
stream to the spring from whence it came:
this with a wonder when ye do,
as easy, and else easier too,
then may ye recollect the grains
of my particular remains;
after a thousand lustres hurl'd,
by ruffling winds, about the world.
R. HERRICK

214   TO THE CORAL INSECT

TOIL on! toil on! ye ephemeral train,
   who build in the tossing and treacherous main;
toil on,—for the wisdom of man ye mock,
with your sand-based structures and domes of rock;
your columns the fathomless fountains lave,
and your arches spring up through the crested wave;
you're a puny race, thus to boldly rear
a fabric so vast in a realm so drear.

But why do ye plant 'neath the billows dark
the wrecking reef, for the gallant bark?
there are snares enough on the tented field;
'mid the blossomed sweets that the valleys yield;
there are serpents to coil ere the flowers are up;
there's a poison-drop in man's purest cup;
there are foes that watch for his cradle breath,
and why need ye sow the floods with death?

L. H. SIGOURNEY

215   *AN EPITAPH*

THIS little vault, this narrow room,
   of love and beauty is the tomb:
the dawning beam, that 'gan to clear
our clouded sky, lies darkened here;
for ever set to us by death,
sent to enflame the world beneath.
'Twas but a bud, yet did contain
more sweetness than shall spring again,
a budding star that might have grown
into a sun, when it had blown.
This hopeful beauty did create
new life in love's declining state;
but now his empire ends, and we
from fire and wounding darts are free;
his brand, his bow, let no man fear;
the flames, the arrows all lie here.

T. CAREW

216   *EXTREME OF LOVE OR HATE*

GIVE me more love or more disdain;
   the torrid or the frozen zone
bring equal ease unto my pain,
   the temperate affords me none;
either extreme of love or hate
is sweeter than a calm estate.

Give me a storm;—if it be love,
   like Danaë in that golden shower,
I swim in pleasure; if it prove
   disdain—that torrent will devour
my vulture hopes, and he's possessed
of heaven, that's but from hell released;
then crown my joys or cure my pain;
give me more love or more disdain.

T. CAREW

217   THE WATERFALL

MARK how, a thousand streams in one,
    one in a thousand, on they fare,
  now flashing to the sun,
    now still as beast in lair.

How round the rock, now mounting o'er,
  in lawless dance they win their way,
    still seeming more and more
      to swell as we survey.

They win their way, and find their rest
  together in their ocean home,
    from East and weary West,
      from North and South they come.

They rush and roar, they whirl and leap,
  not wilder drives the wintry storm:
    yet a strong law they keep,
      strange powers their course inform.

                      J. KEBLE.

218   YOUNG LOVE

COME, little infant, love me now,
    while thine unsuspected years
clear thine aged father's brow
    from cold jealousy and fears.

Pretty surely 'twere to see
    by young Love old Time beguiled,
while our sportings are as free
    as the nurse's with the child

Now then love me: time may take
    thee before thy time away;
of this need we'll virtue make,
    and learn love before we may.

So we win of doubtful fate,
    and, if good to us she meant,
we that good shall antedate,
    or, if ill, that ill prevent.

                      A. MARVELL.

219   THE MEANS TO ATTAIN HAPPY LIFE

MARTIAL, the things that do attain
   the happy life, be these I find:
the riches left, not got with pain;
   the fruitful ground, the quiet mind:

the equal friend, no grudge, no strife;
   no charge of rule, nor governance;
without disease, the healthful life;
   the household of continuance:

the mean diet, no delicate fare;
   true wisdom joined with simpleness;
the night discharged of all care;
   where wine the wit may not oppress:

the faithful wife, without debate;
   such sleeps as may beguile the night;
contented with thine own estate,
   ne wish for death, ne fear his might.

                            EARL OF SURREY

220   THE RETURN OF SPRING

GLOOMY winter's now awa',
   soft the westlin' breezes blaw:
'mang the birks o' Stanley-shaw
   the mavis sings fu' cheerie O.
towering o'er the Newton woods,
laverocks fan the snaw-white clouds;
siller saughs, wi' downie buds,
   adorn the banks sae brierie O.

Round the sylvan fairy nooks,
feathery breckans fringe the rocks,
'neath the brae the burnie jouks,
   and ilka thing is cheerie O.
Trees may bud, and birds may sing,
flowers may bloom, and verdure spring,
joy to me they canna bring,
   unless wi' thee, my dearie O.

                            R. TANNAHILL

221   *PAST AND FUTURE*

BROOD not on things gone by,
  on friendships lost, and high designs o'erthrown,
and old opinions swept away like leaves
  before the autumn blast.
brood not on things gone by!
thy house is left unto thee desolate,
thou canst not be again what once thou wert,
  away, my soul, away!
no longer weakly cower
o'er the white ashes of extinguish'd hope,
nor hover ghostlike round the sepulchre
  of thy departed joys:
another star hath risen,
another voice is calling thee aboard,
thy bark is launch'd, the wind is in thy sail;
  away, my soul, away!
                                W. S. WALKER

222   *ON HEARING A LADY SINGING*

NO nightingale did ever chant
  so sweetly to reposing bands
of travellers in some shady haunt
  among Arabian sands:
no sweeter voice was ever heard
in Spring-time from a cuckoo bird,
breaking the silence of the seas
among the farthest Hebrides.

Will no one tell me what she sings?
perhaps the plaintive numbers flow
for old, unhappy, far-off things,
  and battles long ago:
or is it some more humble lay,
familiar matter of to-day?
some natural sorrow, loss, or pain
that has been, and may be again?

223   *ON TIME*

TIME'S an hand's-breadth; 'tis a tale;
  'tis a vessel under sail;
'tis an eagle in its way,
  darting down upon its prey;

'tis an arrow in its flight,
mocking the pursuing sight;
'tis a short-lived fading flower;
'tis a rainbow on a shower;
'tis a momentary ray,
smiling in a winter's day;
'tis a torrent's rapid stream;
'tis a shadow; 'tis a dream;
'tis the closing watch of night,
dying at the rising light;
'tis a bubble; 'tis a sigh;
be prepared, O man, to die.
F. QUARLES

224 *HERRICK*

MY dearest love, since thou wilt go,
    and leave me here behind thee;
for love or pity, let me know
    the place where I may find thee.

AMARYLLIS

In country meadows, pearled with dew,
    and set about with lilies:
there, filling maunds with cowslips, you
    may find your Amaryllis.

HERRICK

What have the meads to do with thee,
    or with thy youthful hours?
live thou at court, where thou may'st be
    the queen of men, not flowers.
Let country wenches make 'em fine
    with posies, since 'tis fitter
for thee with richest gems to shine,
    and like the stars to glitter.
R. HERRICK

225 *THE PURSUIT OF THE IDEAL*

IT is not Beauty I demand,
    a crystal brow, the moon's despair,
nor the snow's daughter, a white hand,
    nor mermaid's yellow pride of hair:

give me, instead of Beauty's bust,
    a tender heart, a loyal mind
which with temptation I would trust,
    yet never linked with error find,—

one in whose gentle bosom I
　　　could pour my secret heart of woes,
　　like the care-burthen'd honey-fly
　　　that hides his murmurs in the rose,—

　　my earthly comforter! whose love
　　　so indefeasible might be,
　　that, when my spirit wonn'd above,
　　　hers could not stay, for sympathy.

226　　　　　CLAIM TO LOVE

ALAS! alas! thou turn'st in vain
　　thy beauteous face away,
which, like young sorcerers, rais'd a pain
　above its power to lay.

Love moves not, as thou turn'st thy look,
　but here doth firmly rest;
he long ago thy eyes forsook,
　to revel in my breast.

Thy power on him why hop'st thou more
　than his on me should be?
the claim thou lay'st to him is poor,
　to that he owns from me.

his substance in my heart excels
　his shadow in thy sight;
fire, where it burns, more truly dwells,
　than where it scatters light.
　　　　　　　　　　T. STANLEY

227　　　　　ELYSIUM

BEYOND the Acherontian pool
　and gloomy realms of Pluto's rule
　　the happy soul hath come:
and hark, what music on the breeze?
'Twas like the tune of summer-bees
　　a myriad-floating hum.

From spirits like himself it flowed
a welcome to his blest abode,
　　that melody of sound:
and lo, the sky all azure clear,
and liquid-soft the atmosphere:
　　it is Elysian ground.

To mortals, who on earth fulfil
the great Olympian Father's will,
   are given these happy glades;
where they, from all corruption free,
in unrestricted liberty
   may dwell, etherial shades.

228 There is no bound of time or place;
each spirit moves in endless space
   advancing as he wills:
the summer lightnings gleam not so,
as life with ever-varying flow
   the tender bosom thrills.

And memory is unmixed with pain,
though consciousness they still retain
   of joys they left behind;
whate'er on earth they held most dear,
to pure enjoyment hallowed here
   in golden dream they find.

The pilgrim oft by whispering trees
hath stretcht his weary limbs at ease,
   and laid his burden down;
the reaping man hath dropt his scythe,
around him gather'd harvests blithe
   the field with plenty crown.

229 The warrior-chief in soft repose
bethinks him of his vanquisht foes,
   and martial sounds begin
to rattle in his slumbering ear,
the rolling drum, the soldier's cheer,
   and dreadful battle-din.

The lover, whom untimely fate
hath sever'd from a worthy mate,
   expects the destined hour,
when she shall come, his bliss to share,
in beauty clad, divinely fair,
   with love's immortal dower.

Meanwhile in many a vision kind
he sees her imaged to his mind;

and for her brow he weaves
a mystic bridal coronal,
such as no poet's tongue can tell
nor human heart conceive.
Translated from SCHILLER

230   THE OAK

COME take a woodland walk with me,
and mark the rugged old Oak Tree,
how steadily his arm he flings
where from the bank the fresh rill springs,
and points the waters' silent way
down the wild marge of reed and spray.
Two furlongs on they glide unseen,
known only by the livelier green.

There stands he, in each time and tide,
the new-born streamlet's guard and guide.
To him spring shower and summer sun,
brown autumn, winter's sleet, are one:
but firmest in the bleakest hour
he holds his root in faith and power,
the splinter'd bark, his girdle stern,
his robe, grey moss and mountain fern.

J. KEBLE

231   A HYMN TO THE LARES

IT was, and still my care is,
to worship ye, the Lares,
with crowns of greenest parsley,
and garlick chives not scarcely:
for favours here to warm me,
and not by fire to harm me:
for gladding so my hearth here
with inoffensive mirth here;
that while the wassaile bowle here
with north-down ale doth trowl here,
no syllable doth fall here,
to mar the mirth at all here.
For which, whene'er I am able,
to keep a country-table,
great be my fare or small cheer,
I'le eat and drink up all here.

R. HERRICK

232   TO THE LADY MARGARET, COUNTESS OF
            CUMBERLAND

HE that of such a height hath built his mind,
    and rear'd the dwelling of his thoughts so strong,
as neither fear nor hope can shake the frame
of his resolved powers ; nor all the wind
of vanity or malice pierce to wrong
his settled peace, or to disturb the same:
what a fair seat hath he, from whence he may
the boundless wastes and wilds of man survey!
And with how free an eye doth he look down
upon these lower regions of turmoil,
where all the storms of passions mainly beat
on flesh and blood : where honour, power, renown,
are only gay afflictions, golden toil ;
where greatness stands upon as feeble feet,
as frailty doth ; and only great doth seem
to little minds, who do it so esteem.

233   He is not moved with all the thunder-cracks
of tyrants' threats, or with the surly brow
of power, that proudly sits on others' crimes ;
charged with more crying sins than those he checks.
The storms of sad confusion, that may grow
up in the present for the coming times,
appal not him ; that hath no side at all,
but of himself, and knows the worst can fall.
And whilst distraught Ambition compasses
and is encompassed ; whilst as craft deceives,
and is deceived : whilst man doth ransack man,
and builds on blood, and rises by distress ;
and th' inheritance of desolation leaves
to great-expecting hopes : he looks thereon,
as from the shore of peace, with unwet eye,
and bears no venture in impiety.

                                    S. DANIEL.

234   THE GRAVE

THERE is a calm for those who weep;
    a rest for weary pilgrims found,
they softly lie and sweetly sleep
            low in the ground.

The storm that wrecks the winter sky
no more disturbs their deep repose,
than summer-evening's latest sigh
    that shuts the rose.

There is a calm for those who weep;
a rest for weary pilgrims found;
and, while the mouldering ashes sleep
    low in the ground,

the soul, of origin divine,
God's glorious image, freed from clay,
in heaven's eternal sphere shall shine,
    a Star of Day.
                  J. MONTGOMERY

235   PROOF AGAINST FORTUNE

FORTUNE, that with malicious joy
   does man her slave oppress,
proud of her office to destroy,
   is seldom pleased to bless:
still various and inconstant still,
but with an inclination to be ill,
   promotes, degrades, delights in strife,
   and makes a lottery of life.
I can enjoy her while she's kind;
but when she dances in the wind,
   and shakes the wings and will not stay,
   I puff the prostitute away;
the little or the much she gave is quietly resigned:
content with poverty my soul I arm,
and virtue, though in rags, will keep me warm.

236   What is't to me,
who never sail in her unfaithful sea,
   if storms arise, and clouds grow black;
   if the mast split and threaten wreck?
Then let the greedy merchant fear
   for his ill-gotten gain;
   and pray to gods that will not hear,
while the debating winds and billows bear
   his wealth into the main.
For me, secure from Fortune's blows,
secure of what I cannot lose,

in my small pinnace I can sail,
contemning all the blustering roar;
  and running with a merry gale,
with friendly stars my safety seek
within some little winding creek;
  and see the storm, ashore

J. DRYDEN

237   ON RETURNING A BLANK BOOK

TAKE back the virgin page,
  white and unwritten still;
some hand, more calm and sage,
  the leaf must fill:
thoughts come, as pure as light,
  pure as e'en you require:
but oh! each word I write
  love turns to fire.

Yet let me keep the book;
  oft shall my heart renew,
when on its leaves I look,
  dear thoughts of you:
like you 'tis fair and bright;
  like you, too bright and fair,
to let wild passion write
  one wrong wish there.

238
Haply when from those eyes
  far, far away I roam,
should calmer thoughts arise
  towards you and home;
fancy may trace some line,
  worthy those eyes to meet;
thoughts that not burn, but shine,
  pure, calm and sweet.

And, as o'er ocean far
  seamen their records keep,
led by some hidden star
  through the cold deep;
so may the words I write
  tell through what storms I stray;
you still the unseen light,
  guiding my way.

T. MOORE

239   *THE PROGRESS OF POESY FROM GREECE TO
ITALY AND FROM ITALY TO ENGLAND*

WOODS, that wave o'er Delphi's steep,
    isles, that crown th' Ægean deep,
fields, that cool Ilissus laves,
or where Mæander's amber waves
in lingering lab'rinths creep;
how do your tuneful echoes languish,
mute, but to the voice of anguish!
Where each old poetic mountain
   inspiration breathed around;
every shade and hallow'd fountain
   murmur'd deep a solemn sound;
till the sad Nine, in Greece's evil hour,
   left their Parnassus for the Latian plains.
Alike they scorn the pomp of tyrant Power,
   and coward Vice, that revels in her chains.
When Latium had her lofty spirit lost,
they sought, O Albion! next thy sea-encircled coast.
                                   T. GRAY

240   *TO A STAR*

O FAIR and goodly star, upon the brow of night,
   that from thy silver car shootest thy friendly light,
thy path is calm and bright
through the clear azure of the starry way;
and from thy heavenly height
thou see'st how empires rise and pass away,
thou view'st the birth of human hopes—
   their blossom and decay.

Oh! that my spirit could cast off its mould of clay,
and with the wise and good fly from this toil away;
   that with thy bright array
we might look down upon the world of woe,
   even as the god of day
looks on the listless ocean's flow,
and eyes the fighting waves
that part and foam below.

241   *THE SOUL OF BEAUTY*

THE shape alone let others prize,
    the features of the fair;
I look for spirit in her eyes,
    and meaning in her air.

A damask cheek, an ivory arm,
    shall ne'er my wishes win;
give me an animated form
    that speaks a mind within;

a face where awful honour shines,
    where sense and sweetness move,
and angel innocence refines
    the tenderness of love.

These are the soul of beauty's frame;
    without whose vital aid
unfinished all her features seem,
    and all her roses dead.
                          M. AKENSIDE

242   *HEAVEN IN PROSPECT*

THEY are all gone into the world of light!
    And I alone sit ling'ring here!
Their very memory is fair and bright,
    and my sad thoughts doth clear.

It glows and glitters in my cloudy breast,
    like stars upon some gloomy grove,
or those faint beams in which this hill is drest
    after the sun's remove.

I see them walking in an air of glory,
    whose light doth trample on my days;
my days, which are at best but dull and hoary,
    meer glimmering and decays.

He that hath found some fledg'd bird's nest may know
    at first sight if the bird be flown:
but what fair dell or grove he sings in now,
    that is to him unknown.

243 And yet, as Angels in some brighter dreams
    call to the soul when man doth sleep,
so some strange thoughts transcend our wonted themes,
    and into glory peep.

If a star were confin'd into a tomb,
    her captive flames must needs burn there;
but when the hand that lockt her up gives room,
    she'll shine through all the sphere.

O Father of eternal life, and all
    created glories under thee,
resume thy spirit from this world of thrall
    into true liberty!

Either disperse these mists, which blot and fill
    my perspective still as they pass;
or else remove me hence unto that hill
    where I shall need no glass.
H. VAUGHAN

244   INSENSIBILITY TO GOD'S MERCIES

HUES of the rich unfolding morn,
that, ere the glorious sun be born,
by some soft touch invisible
around his path are taught to swell;—

thou rustling breeze so fresh and gay,
that dancest forth at opening day,
and brushing by with joyous wing,
wakenest each little leaf to sing;—

ye fragrant clouds of dewy steam,
by which deep grove and tangled stream
pay, for soft rains in season given,
their tribute to the genial Heaven:—

why waste your treasures of delight
upon our thankless, joyless sight;
who day by day to sin awake,
seldom of Heaven and you partake?
J. KEBLE

245   THE SEAMEN'S SONG

O'ER the rolling waves we go,
where the stormy winds do blow,
to quell with fire and sword the foe,
    that dares give us vexation.

Sailing to each foreign shore,
despising hardships we endure,
wealth we often do bring o'er
  that does enrich the nation.

Noble-hearted seamen are
those that do no labour spare,
nor no danger shun or fear,
  to do their country pleasure.

In loyalty they do abound,
nothing base in them is found,
but they bravely stand their ground
  in calm and stormy weather.

246   THE LIVING AUTHOR'S EPITAPH

FROM life's superfluous cares enlarg'd,
  his debt of human toil discharg'd,
here Cowley lies, beneath this shed,
to every worldly interest dead:
with decent poverty content;
his hours of ease not idly spent;
to fortune's goods a foe profess'd,
and hating wealth, by all caress'd.
'Tis sure, he's dead; for lo! how small
a spot of earth is now his all!
O! wish that earth may lightly lay,
and every care be far away!
bring flowers, the short-liv'd roses bring,
to life deceas'd fit offering!
and sweets around the poet strow,
whilst yet with life his ashes glow.
                                J. ADDISON

247   HYMN OF PAN

LIQUID Peneus was flowing,
    and all dark Tempe lay
in Pelion's shadow, outgrowing
  the light of the dying day,
    speeded with my sweet pipings.

I sang of the dancing stars,
I sang of the dædal Earth,
and of Heaven—and the giant wars,
and Love, and Death, and Birth,—
   and then I changed my pipings,—
singing how down the vale of Menalus
I pursued a maiden and clasped a reed:
gods and men, we are all deluded thus!
it breaks in our bosom and then we bleed:
all wept, as I think both ye now would,
if envy or age had not frozen your blood,
   at the sorrow of my sweet pipings.
                              P. B. SHELLEY

248   *JUNO'S OFFER TO PARIS*

LET ambition fire thy mind,
   thou wert born o'er men to reign;
not to follow flocks design'd,
   scorn thy crook and leave the plain.

Crowns I'll throw beneath thy feet;
   thou on necks of kings shalt tread;
joys in circles joys shall meet,
   which way e'er thy fancy's led.

Let not toils of empire fright,
   toils of empire pleasures are;
thou shalt only know delight,
   all the joy but not the care.

Shepherd, if thou'lt yield the prize,
   for the blessings I bestow,
joyful I'll ascend the skies,
   happy thou shalt reign below.
                              W. CONGREVE

249   *THE WINTER OF LIFE*

BUT lately seen in gladsome green
   the woods rejoice the day,
through gentle showers the laughing flowers
   in double pride were gay:
but now our joys are fled,
   on winter blasts awa'!
yet maiden May, in rich array,
   again shall bring them a'.

But my white pow, nae kindly thowe
   shall melt the snaws of age;
my trunk of eild, but buss or bield,
   sinks in time's wintry rage.
Oh, age has weary days
   and nights o' sleepless pain!
Thou golden time o' youthful prime,
   why com'st thou not again!
R. BURNS

250   HUSH, SWEET LUTE

HUSH, sweet Lute, thy songs remind me
   of past joys, now turn'd to pain;
of ties that long have ceas'd to bind me,
   but whose burning marks remain.
In each tone, some echo falleth
   on my ears of joys gone by:
every note some dream recalleth
   of bright hopes but born to die.

Yet, sweet Lute, though pain it bring me,
   once more let thy numbers thrill;
though death were in the strain they sing me,
   I must woo its anguish still.
Since no time can e'er recover
   love's sweet light when once 'tis set,—
better to weep such pleasures over,
   than smile o'er any left us yet.
T. MOORE

251   INDIFFERENCE TO FAME

AH! who can tell how hard it is to climb
   the steep where Fame's proud temple shines afar;
ah! who can tell how many a soul sublime
has felt the influence of malignant star,
and wag'd with fortune an eternal war;
checked by the scoff of Pride, by Envy's frown,
and Poverty's unconquerable bar,
in life's low vale remote has pined alone,
then dropt into the grave, unpitied and unknown!
And yet the languor of inglorious days
not equally oppressive is to all:
him, who ne'er listen'd to the voice of praise,
the silence of neglect can ne'er appal.

There are, who, deaf to mad Ambition's call,
would shrink to hear th' obstreperous trump of Fame;
supremely blest, if to their portion fall
health, competence and peace.
                                          J. BEATTIE

252 THERE be none of Beauty's daughters
    with a magic like thee;
and like music on the waters
    is thy sweet voice to me:
when, as if its sound were causing
the charmed ocean's pausing,
the waves lie still and gleaming,
and the lulled winds seem dreaming:

and the midnight moon is weaving
    her bright chain o'er the deep,
whose breast is gently heaving
    as an infant's asleep:
so the spirit bows before thee
to listen and adore thee,
with a full but soft emotion,
like the swell of Summer's ocean.
                                          LORD BYRON

253   *THE POET'S RECOLLECTIONS OF CHILDHOOD*

THUS, while I ape the measure wild
    of tales that charmed me yet a child,
rude though they be, still with the chime
return the thoughts of early time;
and feelings, roused in life's first day,
glow in the line, and prompt the lay.
Then rise those crags, that mountain tower,
which charmed my fancy's wakening hour:
though no broad river swept along,
to claim, perchance, heroic song;
though sighed no groves in summer gale,
to prompt of love a softer tale;
though scarce a puny streamlet's speed
claimed homage from a shepherd's reed;
yet was poetic impulse given
by the green hill and clear blue heaven.
                                          SIR W. SCOTT

254   *AUTUMN WOODS*

ERE, in the northern gale,
  the summer tresses of the trees are gone,
the woods of Autumn, all around our vale,
  have put their glory on.

The mountains that infold,
in their wide sweep, the coloured landscape round,
seem groups of giant kings, in purple and gold,
  that guard the enchanted ground.

I roam the woods that crown
the upland, where the mingled splendours glow,
where the gay company of trees look down
  on the green fields below.

My steps are not alone
in these bright walks; the sweet south-west, at play,
flies, rustling, where the painted leaves are strewn
  along the winding way.
                                        W. C. BRYANT

255   *THE POWER OF MUSIC*

THE Gift to king Amphion
  that walled a city with its melody
was for belief no dream:—thy skill, Arion!
could humanise the creatures of the sea,
where men were monsters. A last grace he craves,
leave for one chant;—the dulcet sound
steals from the deck o'er willing waves,
and listening dolphins gather round.
Self-cast, as with a desperate course,
'mid that strange audience, he bestrides
a proud One docile as a managed horse;
and singing, while the accordant hand
sweeps his harp, the Master rides;
so shall he touch at length a friendly strand,
and he, with his preserver, shine star-bright
in memory, through silent night.
                                        W. WORDSWORTH

256   *THE SPIRIT IN COMUS TO SABRINA*

VIRGIN, daughter of Locrine,
   sprung of old Anchises' line,
may thy brimmed waves for this
their full tribute never miss,
from a thousand petty rills,
that tumble down the snowy hills:
summer-drouth or singed air
never scorch thy tresses fair,
nor wet October's torrent-flood
thy molten crystal fill with mud:
may thy billows roll ashore
the beryl, and the golden ore;
may thy lofty head be crowned
with many a tower and terrace round;
and here and there thy banks upon
with groves of myrrh and cinnamon.
J. MILTON

257   *A WISH*

I WISH I was by that dim Lake,
  where sinful souls their farewell take
of this vain world, and half-way lie
in death's cold shadow, ere they die.
There, there, far from thee,
deceitful world, my home should be;
where, come what might of gloom and pain,
false hope should ne'er deceive again.

The lifeless sky, the mournful sound
of unseen waters falling round;
the dry leaves, quivering o'er my head,
like man, unquiet, ev'n when dead!
these, aye, these shall wean
my soul from life's deluding scene,
and turn each thought, o'ercharged with gloom,
like willows downwards tow'rds the tomb.
T. MOORE

258   *INVOCATION*

RARELY, rarely, comest thou,
    Spirit of Delight!
wherefore hast thou left me now
    many a day and night?
many a weary night and day
'tis since thou art fled away.

How shall ever one like me
    win thee back again?
with the joyous and the free
    thou wilt scoff at pain.
Spirit false! thou hast forgot
all but those who need thee not.

As a lizard with the shade
    of a trembling leaf,
thou with sorrow art dismayed;
    even the sighs of grief
reproach thee, that thou art not near,
and reproach thou wilt not hear.

259 I love all that thou lovest,
    Spirit of Delight!
the fresh Earth in new leaves drest
    and the starry night;
autumn evening, and the morn
when the golden mists are born.

I love snow and all the forms
    of the radiant frost;
I love waves, and winds, and storms,
    everything almost
which is Nature's, and may be
untainted by man's misery.

I love Love—though he has wings,
    and like light can flee,
but above all other things,
    Spirit, I love thee—
thou art love and life! O come!
make once more my heart thy home!

P. B. SHELLEY

260   ECHOES

How sweet the answer Echo makes
to Music at night
when, roused by lute or horn, she wakes,
and far away o'er lawns and lakes
goes answering light!

yet Love hath echoes truer far
and far more sweet
than e'er, beneath the moonlight's star,
of horn or lute or soft guitar
the songs repeat.

'Tis when the sigh,—in youth sincere
and only then,
the sigh that's breathed for one to hear—
is by that one, that only Dear,
breathed back again.

T. MOORE

261   THE WINTER'S EVENING

The sun is sinking in the fiery west;
the clouds are rushing on their wild, wet wings;
the lightning, like an eagle from its nest,
   in dazzling circles round the mountain springs;
   the groaning forest in the whirlwind swings,
strewing the marble cliffs with branches hoar;
   with cries of startled wolves the valley rings:
and when the sullen sounds of earth are o'er,
ocean lifts up his voice, and thunders on the shore.
Now close the portal!—'Tis the hour of hours!
   though ancient Winter lords it o'er the sky,
and the snow thickens on our leafless bowers;
   for now the few we love on earth are nigh.
   Ianthe! shall the livelong eve pass by
without one song from that red lip of thine?
   come, fill the bowls, and heap the faggots high!
to birds and flowers let Summer's morning shine,
to nobler man alone the Winter eve's divine.

G. CROLY

262   TO LUCASTA, ON GOING BEYOND THE SEAS

IF to be absent were to be
    away from thee;
or that when I am gone
    you or I were alone;
      then, my Lucasta, might I crave
pity from blustering wind, or swallowing wave.

Though seas and land betwixt us both,
    our faith and troth,
like separated souls,
    all time and space controls:
      above the highest sphere we meet
unseen, unknown, and greet as Angels greet.

So then we do anticipate
    our after-fate,
and are alive i' the skies,
    if thus our lips and eyes
      can speak like spirits unconfined
in Heaven, their earthy bodies left behind.

                      R. LOVELACE

263   MODERN GREECE

WHEN riseth Lacedæmon's hardihood,
    when Thebes Epaminondas rears again,
when Athens' children are with hearts endued,
when Grecian mothers shall give birth to men,
then may'st thou be restored; but not till then.
A thousand years scarce serve to form a state;
an hour may lay it in the dust, and when
can man its shatter'd splendour renovate,
recall its virtues back, and vanquish Time and Fate?

Yet are thy skies as blue, thy crags as wild;
sweet are thy groves, and verdant are thy fields,
thine olive ripe as when Minerva smiled,
and still his honied wealth Hymettus yields;
there the blithe bee his fragrant fortress builds,
the freeborn wanderer of thy mountain-air;
Apollo still thy long, long summer gilds,
still in his beam Mendeli's marbles glare;
Art, Glory, Freedom fail, but Nature still is fair.

                      LORD BYRON

264   THE DEATH OF ASTROPHEL

BUT that immortall spirit, which was deckt
with all the dowries of celestiall grace,
by soveraine choyce from th' hevenly quires select,
and lineally derived from Angels race,
   O! what is now of it become aread?
   Ay me! can so divine a thing be dead?

Ah! no: it is not dead, ne can it die,
but lives for aie in blissfull Paradise,
where like a new-borne babe it soft doth lie,
in bed of lillies wrapt in tender wise;
   and compast all about with roses sweet,
   and daintie violets from head to feet.

There thousand birds, all of celestiall brood,
to him do sweetly caroll day and night;
and with straunge notes, of him well understood,
lull him asleep in Angelick delight;
   whilest in sweet dreame to him presented bee
   immortall beauties, which no eye may see.
E. SPENSER

265   HOPE

I PRAISED the Earth, in beauty seen
with garlands gay of various green;
I praised the sea, whose ample field
shone glorious as a silver shield;
and earth and ocean seem'd to say,
"Our beauties are but for a day."

I praised the sun, whose chariot roll'd
on wheels of amber and of gold;
I praised the moon, whose softer eye
gleam'd sweetly through the summer sky;
and moon and sun in answer said,
"Our days of light are numbered."

O God! O good beyond compare!
if thus Thy meaner works are fair,
if thus Thy bounties gild the span
of ruin'd earth and sinful man,
how glorious must the mansion be,
where Thy redeem'd shall dwell with Thee!
R. HEBER

266 TO MY LORD OF LEICESTER

NOT that thy trees at Penshurst groan
   oppressed with their timely load;
and seem to make their silent moan,
   that their great Lord is now abroad:
they, to delight his taste or eye,
would spend themselves in fruit, and die.

Not that thy harmless deer repine,
   and think themselves unjustly slain
by any other hand than thine,
   whose arrows they would gladly stain:
no, nor thy friends, which hold too dear
that peace with France, which keeps thee there.

All these are less than that great cause
   which now exacts your presence here;
wherein there meet the divers laws
   of public and domestic care:
for one bright Nymph our youth contends,
and on your prudent choice depends.

                                     E. WALLER

267 HYMN TO DIANA

QUEEN and Huntress, chaste and fair,
   now the sun is laid to sleep,
seated in thy silver chair,
   state in wonted manner keep;
      Hesperus entreats thy light,
      goddess excellently bright.

Earth, let not thy envious shade
   dare itself to interpose;
Cynthia's shining orb was made
   heaven to clear when day did close:
      bless us then with wishèd sight,
      goddess excellently bright.

Lay thy bow of pearl apart
   and thy crystal-shining quiver:
give unto the flying hart
   space to breathe, how short soever:
      thou that makest a day of night,
      goddess excellently bright!

                                     B. JONSON

268 THALABA

OR when the winter torrent rolls
    down the deep-channel'd rain course, foamingly,
dark with its mountain spoils,
with bare feet pressing the wet sand,
    there wanders Thalaba,
the rushing flow, the flowing roar,
    filling his yielded faculties,
a vague, a dizzy, a tumultuous joy.

Or lingers it a vernal brook,
    gleaming o'er yellow sands?
beneath the lofty bank reclined,
with idle eye he views its little waves
    quietly listening to the quiet flow;
while in the breathings of the stirring gale
    the tall canes bend above,
floating like streamers on the wind
    their lank uplifted leaves.

                R. SOUTHEY

269 IONA

HERE, as to shame the temples decked
    by skill of earthly architect,
Nature herself, it seemed, would raise
a minster to her Maker's praise:
not for a meaner use ascend
her columns, or her arches bend;
nor of a theme less solemn tells
that mighty surge that ebbs and swells,
and still between each awful pause,
from the high vault an answer draws,
in varied tone prolonged and high,
that mocks the organ's melody.
Nor doth its entrance front in vain
to old Iona's holy fane,
that Nature's voice might seem to say,
'Well hast thou done, frail child of clay!
thy humble powers that stately shrine
tasked high and hard—but witness mine.'

                SIR W. SCOTT

270   TO BLOSSOMS

FAIR pledges of a fruitful tree,
   why do ye fall so fast?
Your date is not so past,
but you may stay yet here awhile
   to blush and gently smile,
      and go at last.

What, were ye born to be
   an hour or half's delight,
   and so to bid good night?
'Twas pity Nature brought ye forth,
   merely to show your worth,
      and lose you quite.

But you are lovely leaves, where we
   may read how soon things have
   their end, though ne'er so brave;
and after they have shown their pride,
   like you, awhile, they glide
      into the grave.

                        R. HERRICK

271   SONG FOR THE SPINNING-WHEEL

SWIFTLY turn the murmuring wheel!
   night has brought the welcome hour,
when the weary fingers feel
help, as if from faery power;
dewy night o'ershades the ground;
turn the swift wheel round and round!

Now beneath the starry sky
couch the widely-scattered sheep;—
ply the pleasant labour, ply!
for the spindle, while they sleep,
runs with motion smooth and fine,
gathering up a trustier line.

Short-lived likings may be bred
by a glance from fickle eyes;
but true love is like the thread
which the kindly wool supplies,
when the flocks are all at rest
sleeping on the mountain's breast.

                        W. WORDSWORTH

272   *MORNING SOUNDS*

BUT who the melodies of morn can tell?
    the wild brook babbling down the mountain-side;
the lowing herd; the sheepfold's simple bell;
the pipe of early shepherd dim descried
in the low valley; echoing far and wide
the clamorous horn along the cliffs above;
the hollow murmur of the ocean-tide;
the hum of bees, the linnet's lay of love,
and the full choir that wakes the universal grove.
The cottage-curs at early pilgrim bark;
crown'd with her pail the tripping milk-maid sings;
the whistling ploughman stalks afield; and hark!
down the rough slope the ponderous waggon rings;
through rustling corn the hare astonished springs;
slow tolls the village-clock the drowsy hour;
the partridge bursts away on whirring wings;
deep mourns the turtle in sequester'd bower,
and shrill lark carols clear from her aerial tower.
                                    J. BEATTIE

273   *ORPHEUS*

BUT when through all the infernal bounds,
    which flaming Phlegethon surrounds,
    Love, strong as Death, the Poet led
    to the pale nations of the dead,
    what sounds were heard,
    what scenes appeared,
        o'er all the dreary coasts!
            dreadful gleams,
            dismal screams,
            fires that glow,
            shrieks of woe,
            sullen moans,
            hollow groans,
    and cries of tortured ghosts!
But hark! he strikes the golden lyre;
and see! the tortured ghosts respire,
        see, shady forms advance!
    thy stone, O Sisyphus, stands still,
    Ixion rests upon his wheel,
            and the pale spectres dance;
the Furies sink upon their iron beds,
and snakes uncurled hang listening round their heads.
                                    A. POPE

274 THE HOPELESS LOVER

TELL me not how fair she is;
   I have no mind to hear
the story of that distant bliss
   I never shall come near:
by sad experience I have found
that her perfection is my wound.

And tell me not how fond I am
   to tempt my daring fate
from whence no triumph ever came,
   but to repent too late:
there is some hope ere long I may
in silence dote myself away.

I ask no pity, Love, from thee,
   nor will thy justice blame,
so that thou wilt not envy me
   the glory of my flame:
which crowns my heart whene'er it dies,
in that it falls her sacrifice.

H. KING

275 THE RESTORATION OF HELLAS

AS an eagle, fed with morning,
   scorns the embattled tempest's warning,
when she seeks her aerie hanging
   in the mountain-cedar's hair,
and her brood expect the clanging
   of her wings through the wild air,
sick with famine;—Freedom so
to what of Greece remaineth now
returns; her hoary ruins glow
like orient mountains lost in day;
   beneath the safety of her wings
her renovated nurselings play,
   and in the naked lightnings
of truth they purge their dazzled eyes.
Let Freedom leave, where'er she flies,
a Desert, or a Paradise;
let the beautiful and the brave,
share her glory, or a grave.

P. B. SHELLEY

276 THE TREASURES OF THE DEEP

WHAT hidest thou in thy treasure-caves and cells,
  thou hollow-sounding and mysterious main?
pale glistening pearls, and rainbow-coloured shells,
bright things which gleam unrecked of and in vain.
Keep, keep thy riches, melancholy sea!
  We ask not such from thee.

Yet more! the billows and the depths have more!
high hearts and brave are gathered to thy breast!
they hear not now the booming waters roar,
the battle-thunders will not break their rest:
keep thy red gold and gems, thou stormy grave—
  give back the true and brave!

Give back the lost and lovely! those for whom
the place was kept at board and hearth so long;
the prayer went up through midnight's breathless
  gloom,
and the vain yearning woke midst festal song!
Hold fast thy buried isles, thy towers o'erthrown,
  —But all is not thine own!
         F. HEMANS

277 *OUR SORROWES STILL PURSUE—*

TO MY HONOURED FRIEND, SIR E. P. KNIGHT

GOE find some whispering shade neare Arne or Poe,
  and gently 'mong their violets throw
your weary'd limbs, and see if all those faire
  enchantments can charme griefe or care.
Our sorrowes still pursue us, and when you
  the ruined capitoll shall view
and statues, a disordered heape; you can
  not cure yet the disease of man,
and banish youre owne thoughts. Goe travaile where
  another Sun and starres appeare,
and land not toucht by any covetous fleet,
  and yet even there youre selfe youle meete.

Stay here then, and while curious exiles find
new toyes for a fantastique mind;
enjoy at home what's reall: here the Spring
by her aeriall quires doth sing
as sweetly to you as if you were laid
vnder the learned Thessalian shade.

W. HABINGTON

278 *HYMN TO CONTENTMENT*

"LOVELY, lasting peace of mind!
sweet delight of human kind!
heavenly-born and bred on high,
to crown the favourites of the sky
with more of happiness below
than victors in a triumph know;
lovely, lasting peace appear!
this world itself, if thou art here,
is once again with Eden blest,
and man contains it in his breast."
'Twas thus, as under shade I stood,
I sung my wishes to the wood:
it seemed as all the quiet place
confessed the presence of the Grace;
when thus she spoke:—"Go rule thy will:
bid thy wild passions all be still;
know God, and bring thy heart to know
the joys which from religion flow:
then every grace shall prove its guest,
and I'll be there to crown the rest."

T. PARNELL

279 *PHILLIS*

PHILLIS is my only joy,
faithless as the winds or seas:
sometimes coming, sometimes coy,
yet she never fails to please;
    if with a frown
    I am cast down,
    Phillis smiling
    and beguiling
makes me happier than before.

Though, alas! too late I find,
nothing can her fancy fix;
yet the moment she is kind,
I forgive her all her tricks;
   which though I see,
   I can't get free;
   she deceiving,
   I believing;
what need lovers wish for more?
SIR C. SEDLEY

280   FAITHFUL LOVE

ASK me no more, my truth to prove,
what I would suffer for my love;
with thee I would in exile go
to regions of eternal snow;
o'er floods by solid ice confined:
thro' forest bare with northern wind;
while all around my eyes I cast
where all is wild and all is waste.
If there the timorous stag you chase,
or rouse to fight a fiercer race,
undaunted I thy arms would bear
and give thy hand the hunter's spear:
beneath the mountain's hollow brow,
or in its rocky cells below,
thy rural feast I would provide;
nor envy palaces their pride;
the softest moss should dress thy bed,
with savage spoils about thee spread:
while faithful love the watch should keep,
to banish danger from thy sleep.
E. TOLLET

281   THE DESCRIPTION OF CASTARA

LIKE the violet which alone
prospers in some happy shade;
my Castara lives unknown,
to no looser eye betrayed;
   for she's to herself untrue
   who delights i' the public view.
Such is her beauty, as no arts
have enriched with borrowed grace;
her high birth no pride imparts,
for she blushes in her place.

Folly boasts a glorious blood,
  she is noblest being good.

She sails by that rock, the court,
where oft honour splits her mast;
and retiredness thinks the port
where her fame may anchor cast;
  virtue safely cannot sit
  where vice is enthroned for wit.
                            W. HABINGTON

282   THE EDUCATION OF NATURE

SHE shall be sportive as the fawn
  that wild with glee across the lawn
    or up the mountain springs;
and her's shall be the breathing balm,
and her's the silence and the calm
    of mute insensate things.

The floating clouds their state shall lend
to her; for her the willow bend:
    nor shall she fail to see
e'en in the motions of the storm
grace that shall mould the maiden's form
    by silent sympathy.

The stars of midnight shall be dear
to her; and she shall lean her ear
    in many a secret place
where rivulets dance their wayward round,
and beauty born of murmuring sound
    shall pass into her face.
                            W. WORDSWORTH

283   NE NIMIVM ADOLESCENTIÆ FIDAT

LET not thy youth and false delights
    cheat thee of life; those heady flights
but waste thy time, which posts away
like wings unseen and swift as they.
Beauty is but meer paint, whose dye
with time's breath will dissolve and flye,
'tis wax, 'tis water, 'tis a glass,
it melts, breaks and away doth pass.

'tis like a rose, which in the dawn
the air with gentle breath doth fawn
and whisper too, but in the hours
of night is sullied with smart showers.
Life spent is wish'd for but in vain,
nor can past years come back again:
happy the Man who in this vale
redeems his time, shutting out all
thoughts of the world, whose longing eyes
are ever pilgrims in the skies,
that views his bright home, and desires
to shine amongst those glorious fires.
H. VAUGHAN

284   *ADVERSA ÆQUO ANIMO FERENDA ESSE*

IF weeping eyes could wash away
  those evils they mourn for night and day,
then glad I to cure my fears
with my best jewels would buy tears.
But, as dew feeds the growing corn,
so crosses that are grown forlorn
increase with grief, tears make tears way,
and cares kept up keep cares in pay.
That wretch whom Fortune finds to fear
and melting still into a tear,
she strikes more boldly; but a face
silent and dry doth her amaze.
Then leave thy tears, and tedious tale
of what thou dost misfortunes call:
what thou by weeping think'st to ease,
doth by thy passion but increase,
hard things to soft will never yield,
'tis the dry eye that wins the field;
a noble patience quells the spite
of Fortune, and disarms her quite.
H. VAUGHAN

285   *THE WARRIOR TO HIS DEAD BRIDE*

IF in the fight my arm was strong
  and forced my foes to yield,

if conquering and unhurt I came
    back from the battle-field—
it is because thy prayers have been
    my safeguard and my shield.

Thy heart, my own, still beats in Heaven
    with the same love divine
that made thee stoop to such a soul,
    so hard, so stern, as mine—
my eyes have learnt to weep, beloved,
    since last they looked on thine.

I hear thee murmur words of peace
    through the dim midnight air,
and a calm falls from the angel stars,
    and soothes my great despair—
the Heavens themselves look brighter, love,
    since thy sweet soul is there.

A. A. PROCTER

286 TO THE JEWS TO MOURN FOR THEIR DESTRUCTION

CONSIDER ye and call for the mourning women
        that they may come;
and send for cunning women, that they may come:
and let them make haste,
and take up a wailing for us,
that our eyes may run down with tears,
and our eyelids gush out with waters.
For a voice of wailing is heard out of Zion,
' How are we spoiled, we are greatly confounded,
because we have forsaken the land,
because our dwellings have cast us out!'
Yet hear the word of the Lord, O ye women,
and let your ear receive the word of his mouth,
and teach your daughters wailing,
and every one her neighbour lamentation.
For death is come up into our windows,
to cut off the children from without
and the young men from the streets:
the carcases of men shall fall as dung
upon the open field,
and as the handful after the harvestman,
and none shall gather them.

JEREMIAH

287   *DIRGE AT SEA*

SLEEP!—we give thee to the wave,
red with life-blood from the brave:
thou shalt find a noble grave:
    fare thee well!

Sleep! thy billowy field is won,
proudly may the funeral gun,
midst the hush at set of sun,
    boom thy knell!

Lonely, lonely is thy bed,
never there may flower be shed,
marble reared, or brother's head
    bowed to weep.

Yet thy record on the sea,
borne through battle high and free,
long the red-cross flag shall be;
    sleep! oh, sleep!
                     F. HEMANS

288   *BRIGHTLY HAST THOU FLED*

BRIGHTLY, brightly hast thou fled,
ere one grief had bowed thy head!
    brightly didst thou part!
with thy young thoughts pure from spot,
with thy fond love wasted not,
    with thy bounding heart.

Ne'er by sorrow to be wet,
calmly smiles thy pale cheek yet,
    ere with dust o'erspread:
lilies ne'er by tempest blown,
white rose which no stain hath known,
    be about thee shed!

So we give thee to the earth,
and the primrose shall have birth
    o'er thy gentle head;
thou that, like a dewdrop borne
on a sudden breeze of morn,
    brightly thus hast fled!

289   *DIRGE OF A CHILD*

NO bitter tears for thee be shed,
 blossom of being! seen and gone!
with flowers alone we strew thy bed,
  O blest departed One!
whose all of life, a rosy ray,
blushed into dawn and passed away.

We rear no marble o'er thy tomb;
no sculptured image there shall mourn:
ah! fitter far the vernal bloom
  such dwelling to adorn.
Fragrance and flowers and dews must be
the only emblems meet for thee.

Thy grave shall be a blessed shrine,
adorned with Nature's brightest wreath;
each glowing season shall combine
  its incense there to breathe;
and oft, upon the midnight air,
shall viewless harps be murmuring there.
        F. HEMANS

290   *TO WOMAN*

O THOU by heaven ordained to be
 arbitress of man's destiny!
from thy sweet lip one tender sigh,
one glance from thine approving eye,
can raise or bend him at thy will,
to virtue's noblest flights or worst extremes of ill!

Be angel-minded! and despise
thy sex's little vanities;
and let not passion's lawless tide
thy better purpose sweep aside;
for woe awaits the evil hour
that tends to man's annoy thy heaven-entrusted power.

Woman! 'tis thine to cleanse his heart
from every gross, unholy part;
thine, in domestic solitude,
to win him to be wise and good;
his pattern guide and friend to be,
to give him back the heaven he forfeited for thee.

291   MEMORIALS OF DEATH

THE leaves around me falling
    are preaching of decay;
the hollow winds are calling,
    "come, pilgrim, come away!"
the day, in night declining,
    says, I too must decline;
the year its life resigning,
    its lot foreshadows mine.

The light my path surrounding,
    the loves to which I cling,
the hopes within me bounding,
    the joys that round me wing;
all melt, like stars of even,
    before the morning's ray,
pass upward into Heaven,
    and chide at my delay.

                                H. F. LYTE

292   SONG

IF wine and music have the power
    to ease the sickness of the soul;
let Phœbus every string explore,
and Bacchus fill the sprightly bowl:
let them their friendly aid employ
to make my Cloe's absence light;
and seek for pleasure, to destroy
the sorrow of this lifelong night.

But she to-morrow will return,
Venus, be thou to-morrow great;
thy myrtles strew, thy odours burn;
and meet thy favourite nymph in state.
Kind goddess, to no other powers
let us to-morrow's blessings own:
thy darling loves shall guide the hours,
and all the day be thine alone.

293   CHRISTMAS DAY

Though rude winds usher thee, sweet day,
   though clouds thy face deform,
though nature's grace is swept away
before thy sleety storm;
ev'n in thy sombrest wintry vest,
of blessed days thou art most blest.

Nor frigid air nor gloomy morn
shall check our jubilee;
bright is the day when Christ was born,
no sun need shine but He;
let roughest storms their coldest blow,
with love of Him our hearts shall glow.

Oft, as this joyous morn doth come
to speak our Saviour's love,
oh, may it bear our spirits home,
where He now reigns above;
that day which brought Him from the skies,
and man restores to Paradise!
                                    S. RICKARDS

294   TO THE EVENING STAR

Star that bringest home the bee,
   and sett'st the weary labourer free!
if any star shed peace, 'tis Thou
   that send'st it from above,
appearing when Heaven's breath and brow
   are sweet as hers we love.

Come to the luxuriant skies,
   whilst the landscape's odours rise,
whilst far-off lowing herds are heard
   and songs when toil is done,
from cottages whose smoke unstirr'd
   curls yellow in the sun.

Star of love's soft interviews,
parted lovers on thee muse;
their remembrancer in Heaven
   of thrilling vows thou art,
too delicious to be riven
   by absence from the heart.
                                    T. CAMPBELL

295   TO MEMORY

HAIL, Memory, hail! in thy exhaustless mine
from age to age unnumber'd treasures shine!
thought and her shadowy brood thy call obey,
and Place and Time are subject to thy sway!
Thy pleasures most we feel, when most alone;
the only pleasures we can call our own.
Lighter than air, Hope's summer-visions die,
if but a fleeting cloud obscure the sky;
if but a beam of sober Reason play,
lo, Fancy's fairy frost-work melts away!
but can the wiles of Art, the grasp of Power,
snatch the rich relics of a well-spent hour?
these, when the trembling spirit wings her flight,
pour round her path a stream of living light;
and gild those pure and perfect realms of rest,
where Virtue triumphs, and her sons are blest!
                              S. ROGERS

296   LOVE OF LUCRE

WHAT man in his wits had not rather be poor,
than for lucre his freedom to give;
ever busy the means of his life to secure,
and so ever neglecting to live!

Environ'd from morning to night in a crowd,
not a moment unbent, or alone;
constrain'd to be abject, though never so proud,
and at every one's call but his own!

Still repining and longing for quiet each hour,
yet studiously flying it still;
with the means of enjoying his wish in his power,
but accurst with his wanting the will!

For a year must be past or a day must be come,
before he has leisure to rest:
he must add to his store this or that pretty sum,
and then will have time to be blest.

But his gains, more bewitching the more they increase,
only swell the desire of his eye:
such a wretch let mine enemy live, if he please,
but not even my enemy die.

297 WINTER

SWEET are the harmonics of Spring;
  sweet is the Summer's evening gale,
and sweet the autumnal winds that shake
  the many-colour'd grove.

And pleasant to the sober'd soul
the silence of the wintry scene,
when nature shrouds herself, entranced
  in deep tranquillity.

Not undelightful now to roam
the wild heath sparkling on the sight;
not undelightful now to pace
  the forest's ample rounds;

and see the spangled branches shine,
and mark the moss of many a hue
that varies the old tree's brown bark,
  or o'er the grey stone spreads;

and mark the clustered berries bright
amid the holly's gay green leaves;
the ivy round the leafless oak
  that clasps its foliage close.

R. SOUTHEY

298 THE NEW-BORN RILL

GO up and watch the new-born rill
  just trickling from its mossy bed,
streaking the heath-clad hill
  with a bright emerald thread.

Canst thou her bold career foretel,
what rocks she shall o'erleap or rend,
how far in Ocean's swell
  her freshening billows send?

Perchance that little brook shall flow
the bulwark of some mighty realm,
bear navies to and fro
  with monarchs at their helm.

Or canst thou guess, how far away
some sister nymph, beside her urn
reclining night and day,
  'mid reeds and mountain fern,

nurses her store, with thine to blend
when many a moor and glen are past,
   then in the wide sea end
      their spotless lives at last?
                              J. KEBLE

299   TO MEMORY

OH! sacred Memory, tablet of the heart,
   thou breathing shadow of departed days,
still ever prompt to wake the slumb'ring smart,
   and backward lure the visionary gaze;
thou tellest but of scenes that melted by
   are vanished now, like wreaths of winter snow;
the tear of sorrow gems thy lucid eye,
   and yet, so beauteous is thy garb of woe,
we love thee still and clasp thy fond regret,
too tender to renounce, too pleasing to forget!

why should Mem'ry weep, that frowning truth
   so early chased the mockeries of delight,
the idle dreams that flushed the cheek of youth,
   and glittered baneful on the dazzled sight?
She hath not murdered Hope, though distant far,
   and trembling at her voice, with drooping plume,
gay Fancy flies; nor quenched that better star,
   whose radiant orb can cheer the wintry gloom,
where sacred Virtue rears her hallowed nest,
there Peace shall linger still, companion of the breast.

300   THE ISER—DRINKING SONG OF MUNICH

SWEET Iser! were thy sunny realm,
   and flowery gardens mine,
thy waters I would shade with elm
      to prop the tender vine;
my golden flagons I would fill
   with rosy draughts from every hill;
      and, under every myrtle bower,
      my gay companions should prolong
      the laugh, the revel and the song,
         to many an idle hour.

Like rivers crimsoned with the beam
   of yonder planets bright,
our balmy cups should ever stream
      profusion of delight;

no care should touch the mellow heart,
and sad or sober none depart;
　for wine can triumph over woe;
and Love and Bacchus, brother powers,
could build in Iser's sunny bowers
　　a paradise below.

T. CAMPBELL

301　　　　　*THE LONGEST DAY*

LET us quit the leafy harbour,
　and the terrent murmuring by;
for the sun is in his harbour,
weary of the open sky.

Summer ebbs;—each day that follows
is a reflux from on high,
tending to the darksome hollows
where the frosts of winter lie.

He who governs the creation,
in his providence, assigned
such a gradual declination
to the life of human kind.

Yet we mark it not;—fruits redden,
fresh flowers blow, as flowers have blown,
and the heart is loth to deaden
hopes that she so long hath known.

Be thou wiser, youthful Maiden!
and when thy decline shall come,
let not flowers, or boughs fruit-laden,
hide the knowledge of thy doom.

W. WORDSWORTH

302　　　　　*TO FANCY*

O Queen of numbers, once again
　animate some chosen swain,
who, filled with unexhausted fire,
may boldly smite the sounding lyre;
who with some new unequalled song
may rise above the rhyming throng;
o'er all our listening passions reign,
o'erwhelm our souls with joy and pain,
with terror shake, and pity move,
rouse with revenge, or melt with love;

O deign to attend his evening walk,
with him in groves and grottoes talk;
teach him to scorn with frigid art
feebly to touch the unraptured heart;
like lightning, let his mighty verse
the bosom's inmost foldings pierce;
with native beauties win applause
beyond cold critics' studied laws;
O let each Muse's fame increase,
O bid Britannia rival Greece!

J. WARTON

303   THE INCARNATION

FOR Thou wert born of woman! Thou didst come,
O Holiest! to this world of sin and gloom,
not in Thy dread omnipotent array;
       and not by thunders strewed
       was Thy tempestuous road;
nor indignation burnt before Thee on Thy way.
    But Thee, a soft and naked child,
       thy mother undefiled,
       in the rude manger laid to rest
       from off her virgin breast.

The heavens were not commanded to prepare
a gorgeous canopy of golden air;
nor stooped their lamps th' enthroned fires on high:
       a single silent star
       came wandering from afar,
gliding unchecked and calm along the liquid sky;
       the Eastern Sages leading on
       as at a kingly throne
       to lay their gold and odours sweet
       before Thy infant feet.

304 The Earth and Ocean were not hushed to hear
bright harmony from every starry sphere;
nor at Thy presence brake the voice of song
       from all the cherub choirs,
       and seraphs' burning lyres,
pour'd thro' the host of heaven the charmed clouds
    along.

One angel troop the strain began,
   of all the race of man
by single shepherds heard alone
   that soft Hosanna's tone.

And when Thou didst depart, no car of flame
to bear Thee hence in lambent radiance came;
nor visible Angels mourned with drooping plumes:
   nor didst Thou mount on high
      from fatal Calvary
with all Thine own redeemed outbursting from their
      tombs:
         for Thou didst bear away from earth
            but one of human birth,
         the dying felon by Thy side, to be
            in Paradise with Thee.

H. H. MILMAN

305   *IN MEMORIAM*

THE time admits not flowers or leaves
   to deck the banquet. Fiercely flies
the blast of North and East, and ice
makes daggers at the sharpen'd eaves,

   and bristles all the brakes and thorns
      to yon hard crescent, as she hangs
      above the wood which grides and clangs
   its leafless ribs and iron horns

together, in the drifts that pass
   to darken on the rolling brine
   that breaks the coast. But fetch the wine,
arrange the board and brim the glass;

bring in great logs and let them lie,
   to make a solid core of heat;
   be cheerful-minded, talk and treat
of all things, ev'n as he were by;

we keep the day. With festal cheer,
   with books and music surely we
   will drink to him whate'er he be,
and sing the songs he loved to hear.

A. TENNYSON

306   *IN MEMORIAM*

R ISEST thou thus, dim dawn, again,
    so loud with voices of the birds,
so thick with lowings of the herds,
day, when I lost the flower of men;

who tremblest thro' thy darkling red
    on yon swoll'n brook that bubbles fast
by meadows breathing of the past,
and woodlands holy to the dead;

who murmurest in the foliaged caves
    a song that slights the coming care,
and Autumn laying here and there
a fiery finger on the leaves;

who wakenest with thy balmy breath
    to myriads on the genial earth
memories of bridal, or of birth,
and unto myriads more, of death.

O, wheresoever those may be,
    betwixt the slumber of the poles,
to-day they count as kindred souls;
they know me not, but mourn with me.

A. TENNYSON

307   *IN MEMORIAM*

F AIR ship, that from the Italian shore
    sailest the placid ocean-plains
with my lost Arthur's loved remains,
spread thy full wings, and waft him o'er.

So draw him home to those that mourn
    in vain; a favourable speed
ruffle thy mirror'd mast, and lead
thro' prosperous floods his holy urn.

All night no ruder air perplex
    thy sliding keel, till Phosphor, bright
as our pure love, thro' early light
shall glimmer on the dewy decks.

Sphere all your lights around, above;
    sleep, gentle heavens, before the prow;
sleep, gentle winds, as he sleeps now,
my friend, the brother of my love;

my Arthur, whom I shall not see
till all my widowed race be run:
dear as the mother to the son,
more than my brothers are to me.
A. TENNYSON

308   THE CHARACTER OF A HAPPY LIFE

HOW happy is he born and taught,
that serveth not another's will;
whose armour is his honest thought
and simple truth his utmost skill!

Whose passions not his masters are,
whose soul is still prepared for death,
not tied unto the world with care
of public fame or private breath;

Who envies none that chance doth raise
or vice; who never understood
how deepest wounds are given by praise;
nor rules of state, but rules of good:

Who hath his life from rumours freed;
whose conscience is his strong retreat;
whose state can neither flatterers feed,
nor ruin make oppressors great;

—This man is freed from servile bands
of hope to rise, or fear to fall;
lord of himself, though not of lands;
and having nothing, yet hath all.
SIR H. WOTTON

309   PEACE

MY soul, there is a country
    afar beyond the stars,
where stands a winged sentry
    all skilful in the wars:
There above noise and danger
    sweet peace sits crown'd with smiles,
and one born in a manger
    commands the beauteous files.
He is thy gracious friend,
    and (O my Soul awake!)
did in pure love descend,
    to die here for thy sake.

If thou canst get but thither,
   there grows the flower of peace;
the rose that cannot wither,
   thy fortress and thy ease.
Leave then thy foolish ranges;
   for none can thee secure,
but One, who never changes,
   thy God, thy Life, thy Cure.

H. VAUGHAN

310   *LOVE'S IMMORTALITY*

THEY sin who tell us Love can die.
   With life all other passions fly,
all others are but vanity:
in heaven ambition cannot dwell,
nor avarice in the vaults of hell:
earthly these passions, as of earth,
they perish where they have their birth.
But Love is indestructible;
its holy flame for ever burneth,
from heaven it came, to heaven returneth;
too oft on earth a troubled guest,
at times deceived, at times opprest,
it here is tried and purified,
and hath in heaven its perfect rest:
it soweth here with toil and care,
but the harvest-time of Love is there.
Oh! when a mother meets on high
the babe she lost in infancy,
hath she not then, for pains and fears,
the day of woe, the anxious night,
for all her sorrow, all her tears,
an over-payment of delight!

R. SOUTHEY

311   *KEPLER'S PRAYER*

O THOU, who by the light of Nature dost enkindle in us a desire after the light of grace, that by this Thou mayest translate us into the light of glory: I give Thee thanks, O Lord and Creator, that Thou hast gladdened me by Thy Creation, when I was enraptured by the work of Thy hands. Behold, I have completed a work of my calling with as much of intellectual strength as Thou hast granted me. I have declared the praise of Thy works to the men who will read the evidences of it, so far as my finite spirit could comprehend them in their infinity. My mind endeavoured to its utmost to reach the truth by philosophy; but if anything unworthy of Thee has been taught by me, a worm born and nourished in sin, do Thou teach me that I may correct it. Have I been seduced into presumption by the admirable beauty of Thy works, or have I sought my own glory amongst men in the construction of a work designed for Thine honour? O then graciously and mercifully forgive me; and finally grant me this favour, that this work may never be injurious; but may conduce to Thy glory and the good of souls.

J. KEPLER

312   *STILL LIKE HIS NATIVE STREAM*

IN glowing youth he stood beside
his native stream, and saw it glide
shewing each gem beneath its tide,
calm as though nought could break its rest,
reflecting heaven on its breast,
and seeming, in its flow, to be
like candour, peace and piety.

When life began its brilliant dream,
his heart was like his native stream:
the wave-shrined gems could scarcely seem
less hidden than each wish it knew;
its life flowed on as calmly too:
and heaven shielded it from sin,
to see itself reflected in.

He stood beside that stream again,
when years had fled in strife and pain;
he looked for its calm course in vain,—
for storms profaned its peaceful flow,
and clouds o'erhung its crystal brow:
and turning then, he sighed to deem
his heart still like his native stream.

B. W. PROCTER

313   *TO PHYLLIS*

PHYLLIS! why should we delay
pleasures shorter than the day?

Could we (which we never can)
stretch our lives beyond their span;
beauty like a shadow flies,
and our youth before us dies.
Or would youth and beauty stay,
Love hath wings, and will away.
Love hath swifter wings than Time:
change in love to heaven does climb;
gods, that never change their state,
vary oft their love and hate.
   Phyllis! to this truth we owe
all the love betwixt us two:
let not you and I enquire,
what has been our past desire:
on what shepherds you have smil'd,
or what nymphs I have beguil'd:
leave it to the planets too,
what we shall hereafter do:
for the joys we now may prove,
take advice of present love.
E. WALLER

314   *A TIME FOR EVERY THING*

WHEN the crab's fierce constellation
   burns with the beams of the bright sun,
then he that will go out to sow
shall never reap where he did plough;
but instead of corn may rather
the old world's diet, acorns gather.
Who the violet doth love,
must seek her in the flowery grove;
but never when the North's cold wind
the russet fields with frost doth bind.
If in the spring-time (to no end)
the tender vine for grapes we bend,
we shall find none, for only still
Autumn doth the wine-press fill.
Thus for all things, in the world's prime,
the wise God seal'd their proper time,
nor will permit those seasons, he
ordained by turns, should mingled be.
Then, whose wild actions out of season
cross to nature and her reason

would by new ways old orders rend,
shall never find a happy end.
H. VAUGHAN

315 SONG

Ask me no more where Jove bestows,
when June is past, the fading rose:
for in your beauties orient deep
these flowers, as in their causes, sleep.

Ask me no more, whither do stray
the golden atoms of the day;
for, in pure love, heaven did prepare
those powders to enrich your hair.

Ask me no more, whither doth haste
the nightingale, when May is past;
for in your sweet dividing throat
she winters and keeps warm her note.

Ask me no more, where those stars light
that downwards fall in dead of night;
for in your eyes they sit, and there
fixed become, as in their sphere.

Ask me no more, if east or west
the phœnix builds her spicy nest;
for unto you at last she flies
and in your fragrant bosom dies.
T. CAREW

316 THE SHORTNESS OF LIFE AND UNCERTAINTY OF RICHES

Why dost thou heap up wealth, which thou must quit,
   or, what is worse, be left by it?
Why dost thou load thyself, when thou'rt to fly,
   O man ordained to die?
Why dost thou build up stately rooms on high,
   thou who art under ground to lie?
Thou sow'st and plantest, but no fruit must see,
   for Death alas! is reaping thee.

Thou dost thyself wise and industrious deem:
   A mighty husband thou would'st seem;
fond man! like a bought slave, thou all the while
   dost but for others sweat and toil.

Ev'n aged men, as if they truly were
    children again, for age prepare;
provisions for long travel they design
    in the last point of their short line.

Wisely the ant against poor winter hoards
    the stock which summer's wealth affords;
in grasshoppers, which must in autumn die,
    how vain were such an industry!

317 Of power and honour the deceitful light
    might half excuse our cheated sight,
if it of life the whole small time would stay,
    and be our sunshine all the day.

Like lightning that begot but in a cloud,
    tho' shining bright and speaking loud)
whilst it begins, concludes its violent race,
    and where it gilds, it wounds the place.

O scene of Fortune, which dost fair appear
    only to men that stand not near!
proud poverty, that tinsel bravery wears!
    and, like a rainbow, painted tears!

Be prudent and the shore in prospect keep,
    in a weak boat trust not the deep,
placed beneath envy, above envying rise,
    pity great men, great things despise.

The wise example of the heavenly lark
    thy fellow-poet, Cowley, mark,
above the clouds let thy proud music sound,
    thy humble nest build on the ground.
A. COWLEY

318   *TO A DYING INFANT*

SLEEP, little baby, sleep!
    not in thy cradle bed,
not on thy mother's breast
henceforth shall be thy rest,
    but quiet with the dead.

Flee, little tender nursling,
    flee to thy place of rest!
there the first flowers shall blow,
the first pure flake of snow
    shall fall upon thy breast.

I've seen thee in thy beauty,
   a thing all health and glee!.
but never then wert thou
   so beautiful, as now,
      baby! thou seem'st to me.

Mount up, immortal essence!
   young spirit! haste, depart—
and is this Death!—Dread thing!
if such thy visiting,
   how beautiful thou art!

                            C. BOWLES

319   THE QUIET LIFE

HAPPY the man, whose wish and care
   a few paternal acres bound;
content to breathe his native air
   in his own ground.

Whose herds with milk, whose fields with bread,
whose flocks supply him with attire;
whose trees in summer yield him shade,
   in winter, fire.

Blest, who can unconcern'dly find
hours, days, and years, slide soft away,
in health of body, peace of mind,
   quiet by day,

sound sleep by night: study and ease
together mix'd; sweet recreation,
and innocence, which most doth please
   with meditation.

Thus let me live, unseen, unknown;
thus unlamented let me die;
steal from the world, and not a stone
   tell where I lie.

                            A. POPE

320   VERSES TO HIS WIFE

IF thou, my love, wert by my side,
   my children at my knee,
how gaily would our pinnace glide
   o'er Gunga's mimic sea!

I miss thee, at the dawning gray,
  when, on the deck reclined,
in careless ease my limbs I lay,
  and woo the cooler wind.

I miss thee when by Gunga's stream
  my twilight steps I guide;
but most beneath the lamp's pale beam
  I miss thee from my side.

I spread my books, my pencil try,
  the lingering noon to cheer,
but miss thy kind approving eye,
  thy meek attentive ear.

Yet when of morn and eve the star
  beholds me on my knee,
I feel, though thou art distant far,
  thy prayers ascend for me.

                    R. HEBER

321   THE GOOD ALONE ARE GREAT

WHEN winds the mountain oak assail,
  and lay its glories waste,
content may slumber in the vale,
  unconscious of the blast.
Thro' scenes of tumult while we roam,
the heart, alas! is ne'er at home,
it hopes in time to roam no more;
the mariner, not vainly brave,
combats the storm, and rides the wave,
to rest at last on shore.
Ye proud, ye selfish, ye severe,
how vain your mask of state!
the good alone have joy sincere,
that good alone are great:
great, when, amid the vale of peace,
they bid the plaint of sorrow cease,
and hear the voice of artless praise;
as when along the trophy'd plain
sublime they lead the victor train,
while shouting nations gaze.

                    J. BEATTIE

322   TO AN EARLY PRIMROSE

MILD offspring of a dark and sullen sire,
  whose modest form, so delicately fine,
    was nursed in whirling storms,
    and cradled in the winds;
thee when young spring first questioned winter's sway,
and dared the sturdy blusterer to the fight,
    thee on this bank he threw
    to mark the victory.

In this low vale, the promise of the year,
serene, thou openest to the nipping gale,
    unnoticed and alone,
    thy tender elegance.

So virtue blooms, brought forth amid the storms
of chill adversity; in some lone walk
    of life she rears her head,
    obscure and unobserved;

while every bleaching breeze that on her blows,
chastens her spotless purity of breast,
    and hardens her to bear
    serene the ills of life.

                      H. K. WHITE.

323   THE SONG OF DIANA

WITH horns and with hounds, I waken the day;
  and hie to the woodland-walks away:
I tuck up my robe, and am buskined soon,
and tie to my forehead a wexing moon.
I course the fleet stag, unkennel the fox,
  and chase the wild goats o'er summits of rocks,
with shouting and hooting we pierce through the sky,
and Echo turns hunter, and doubles the cry.

SONG OF MARS

Inspire the vocal brass, inspire;
the world is past its infant age:
    arms and honour,
    arms and honour,
set the martial soul on fire,
and kindle manly rage.

Mars has look'd the sky to red;
and Peace, the lazy good, is fled.
Plenty, peace, and pleasure fly:
  the sprightly green
in woodland-walks no more is seen;
the sprightly green has drunk the Tyrian dye.
J. DRYDEN

324   *TO APOLLO*

APOLLO!—king Apollo!
  in what enchanted region dost thou stay?—
is it in the azure air
or in the caverns hollow,
which Thetis at the set of day
in the sea waters far away
buildeth up, as blue and fair
as thy own bright kingdoms are?
O King of life and light!
O peerless Archer! O triumphant God!
  behold!—the golden rod
now pointeth to the promised hour,—twilight;
and she who loves thee so
is pale and full of woe.—
No wave nor throne have I,
no bower nor golden grove,
no palace built on high,
to tempt thee not to rove,
but truth, and such a love
as would not shame the sky,—
if these be nothing, Time
shall teach me how to die.
B. W. PROCTER

325   *THE LAND O' THE LEAL*

I'M wearing awa', Jean,
  like snaw when it is thaw, Jean,
I'm wearing awa'
  to the land o' the leal.
There's nae sorrow there, Jean,
there's neither cauld nor care, Jean,
the day is aye fair
  in the land o' the leal.

Ye were aye leal and true, Jean,
your task's ended noo, Jean,
and I'll welcome you
   to the land o' the leal.
Our bonnie bairn's there, Jean,
she was baith guid and fair, Jean;
O we grudged her right sair
   to the land o' the leal!
then dry that tearfu' e'e, Jean,
my soul langs to be free, Jean,
and angels wait on me
   to the land o' the leal.
now fare ye weel, my ain Jean,
this warld's care is vain, Jean;
we'll meet and aye be fain
   in the land o' the leal.

LADY NAIRN

326   *THE NIGHTINGALE*

HARK, how through many a melting note
   she now prolongs her lays;
how sweetly down the void they float!
the breeze their magic path attends:
the stars shine out; the forest bends:
   the wakeful heifers gaze.
Whoe'er thou art whom chance may bring
   to this sequestered spot,
if then the plaintive Siren sing,
O softly tread beneath her bower,
and think of heaven's disposing power,
   of man's uncertain lot.
O think, o'er all this mortal stage
   what mournful scenes arise;
what ruin waits on kingly rage;
how often virtue dwells with woe;
how many griefs from knowledge flow;
   how swiftly pleasure flies.
O sacred bird, let me at eve,
   thus wandering all alone,
thy tender counsel oft receive,
bear witness to thy pensive airs,
and pity Nature's common cares
   till I forget my own.

M. AKENSIDE

327 *LOUISA*

I MET Louisa in the shade,
and having seen that lovely maid
why should I fear to say
that nymph-like she is fleet and strong,
and down the rocks can leap along
    like rivulets in May?

And smiles has she to earth unknown;
smiles, that with motion of their own
    do spread and sink and rise;
that come and go with endless play,
and ever as they pass away
    are hidden in her eyes.

She loves her fire, her cottage-home ;
yet o'er the moorland will she roam
    in weather rough and bleak;
and, when against the wind she strains,
O might I kiss the mountain rains
    that sparkle on her cheek !

Take all that's mine beneath the moon,
if I with her but half a noon
    may sit beneath the walls
of some old cave or mossy nook,
when up she winds along the brook
    to hunt the waterfalls.
                    W. WORDSWORTH

328 *VIRTUE MAN'S SUREST STAY*

THE sturdy rock, for all his strength,
    by raging seas is rent in twain:
the marble stone is pierced at length
    with little drops of drizzling rain:
the ox doth yield unto the yoke;
the steel obeyeth the hammer stroke.

The stately stag, that seems so stout,
    by yelping hounds at bay is set:
the swiftest bird, that flies about,
    is caught at length in fowler's net:
the greatest fish in deepest brook
is soon deceived by subtle hook.

Yea, man himself, unto whose will
   all things are bounden to obey,
for all his wit and worthy skill,
   doth fade at length and fall away.
There is no thing but time doth waste;
the heavens, the earth, consume at last.

But virtue sits, triumphing still,
   upon the throne of glorious Fame:
though spiteful death man's body kill,
   yet hurts he not his virtuous name.
By life or death what so betides,
the state of virtue never slides.

329   LAPLAND LOVE-SONG

THOU rising sun, whose gladsome ray
   invites my fair to rural play,
dispel the mist, and clear the skies,
and bring my Orra to my eyes.

O! were I sure my dear to view,
I'd climb that pine-tree's topmost bough,
fast by the roots enraged I'd tear
the trees that hide my promised fair.

Oh! could I ride the clouds and skies,
or on the raven's pinions rise;
ye storks, ye swans, a moment stay,
and waft a lover on his way.

My bliss too long my bride denies,
apace the wasting summer flies:
nor yet the wintry blasts I fear,
not storms or night shall keep me here.

What may for strength with steel compare?
O love has fetters stronger far:
by bolts of steel are limbs confined,
but cruel love enchains the mind.

No longer then perplex thy breast;
when thoughts torment, the first are best:
'tis mad to go, 'tis death to stay:
away to Orra, haste away.

                               A. PHILIPS

330   *LOVE-SONG*

MY dear and only love, I pray
that little world of thee
be governed by no other sway
but purest monarchy.
And in the empire of thy heart,
where I should solely be,
let none beside pretend a part,
or dare to share with me.

As Alexander I will reign,
and I will reign alone;
my thoughts did evermore disdain
a rival on my throne.
He either fears his fate too much,
or his deserts are small,
who dares not put it to the touch
to gain or lose it all.

But if no faithless action stain
thy love and constant word,
I'll make thee famous by my pen
and glorious by my sword;
I'll serve thee in such noble ways
as ne'er was known before;
I'll deck and crown thy head with bays
and love thee evermore.

MARQUIS OF MONTROSE

331   *NEW SELF*

WHY sittest thou on that sea-girt rock
with downward look and sadly-dreaming eye:
playest thou beneath with Proteus' flock,
or with the far-bound sea-bird wouldst thou fly?

OLD SELF

I sit upon this sea-girt rock
with downward look and dreaming eye;
But neither do I sport with Proteus' flock,
nor with the far-bound sea-bird would I fly.

I list the splash so clear and chill
of yon old fisher's solitary oar:
   I watch the waves that rippling still
chase one another o'er the marble shore.

NEW SELF

   Yet from the splash of yonder oar
no dreamy sound of sadness comes to me:
   and yon fresh waves that beat the shore,
how merrily they splash, how merrily!

OLD SELF

   I mourn for the delicious days,
when those calm sounds fell on my childish ear,
   a stranger yet to the wild ways
of triumph and remorse, of hope and fear.

NEW SELF

Mournest thou, poor soul! and thou wouldst yet call back the things which shall not, cannot be?
Heaven must be won, not dreamed: thy task is set, peace was not made for earth, nor rest for thee.

LYRA APOSTOLICA

332 *ON THE DEATH OF COLONEL CHARLES ROSS IN THE ACTION AT FONTENOY*

BLEST youth, regardful of thy doom
aërial hands shall build thy tomb,
   with shadowy trophies crowned:
whilst Honour bathed in tears shall rove
to sigh thy name through every grove,
   and call his heroes round.

By rapid Schelde's descending wave
his country's vows shall bless the grave,
   where'er the youth is laid:
that sacred spot the village hind
with every sweetest turf shall bind,
   and Peace protect the shade.

The warlike dead of every age,
who fill the fair recording page,

shall leave their sainted rest;
and, half reclining on his spear,
each wondering chief by turns appear,
to hail the blooming guest.

But lo, where sunk in deep despair,
her garments torn, her bosom bare,
impatient Freedom lies!
her matted tresses madly spread,
to every sod, which wraps the dead,
she turns her joyless eyes.

W. COLLINS

333   THE PROGRESS OF POESY

AWAKE, Aeolian lyre, awake,
and give to rapture all thy trembling strings.
From Helicon's harmonious springs
    a thousand rills their mazy progress take:
the laughing flowers that round them blow
drink life and fragrance as they flow.
Now the rich stream of Music winds along
deep, majestic, smooth, and strong,
through verdant vales, and Ceres' golden reign;
now rolling down the steep amain
headlong, impetuous, see it pour:
the rocks and nodding groves re-bellow to the roar.

    O Sovereign of the willing soul,
parent of sweet and solemn-breathing airs,
enchanting shell! the sullen Cares
    and frantic Passions hear thy soft control.
On Thracia's hills the Lord of War
has curb'd the fury of his car
and dropt his thirsty lance at thy command.
Perching on the sceptred hand
of Jove, thy magic lulls the feather'd king
with ruffled plumes, and flagging wing:
quench'd in dark clouds of slumber lie
the terror of his beak, and lightnings of his eye.

334 Thee the voice, the dance, obey,
temper'd to thy warbled lay.
O'er Idalia's velvet-green
the rosy-crowned Loves are seen
on Cytherea's day,

with antic Sport, and blue-eyed Pleasures,
frisking light in frolic measures;
now pursuing, now retreating,
    now in circling troops they meet:
to brisk notes in cadence beating
    glance their many-twinkling feet.
Slow melting strains their Queen's approach declare:
    where'er she turns the Graces homage pay:
with arms sublime that float upon the air
    in gliding state she wins her easy way:
o'er her warm cheek and rising bosom move
the bloom of young Desire and purple light of Love.
                           T. GRAY

335   *UPON THE SHORTNESS OF MAN'S LIFE*

MARK that swift arrow how it cuts the air,
    how it outruns thy following eye,
    use all persuasions now, and try
if thou canst call it back or stay it there;
    that way it went, but thou shalt find
    no track is left behind.

Fool, 'tis thy life, and the fond Archer thou,
    of all the time thou'st shot away
    I'll bid thee fetch but yesterday,
and it shall be too hard a task to do.
    Besides repentance, what canst find
    that it hath left behind?

Our life is carried with too strong a tide,
    a doubtful cloud our substance bears,
    and is the horse of all our years;
each day doth on a winged whirlwind ride.
    We and our glass run out, and must
    both render up our dust.

But his past life who without grief can see,
    who never thinks his end too near,
    but says to fame, thou art mine heir,
that man extends life's natural brevity:
    this is, this is the only way
    to outlive Nestor in a day.

336   *THE CYPRESS-WREATH*

O LADY, twine no wreath for me,
　or twine it of the cypress-tree.
Too lively glow the lilies light,
the varnished holly's all too bright,
the may-flower and the eglantine
may shade a brow less sad than mine;
but, lady, weave no wreath for me,
or weave it of the cypress-tree.

Let dimpled Mirth his temples twine
with tendrils of the laughing vine;
the manly oak, the pensive yew,
to patriot and to sage be due;
the myrtle-bough bids lovers live,
but that Matilda will not give;
then, lady, twine no wreath for me,
or twine it of the cypress-tree.

Yes, twine for me the cypress-bough,
but O, Matilda, twine not now:
stay 'till a few brief months are past,
and I have looked and loved my last.
When villagers my shroud bestrew
with pansies, rosemary, and rue,
then, lady, weave a wreath for me,
and weave it of the cypress-tree.
　　　　　　　　　　　SIR W. SCOTT

337   *INSTABILITY OF AFFECTION*

ALAS, how light a cause may move
　dissension between hearts that love;
hearts that the world in vain had tried,
and sorrow but more closely tied;
that stood the storm, when waves were rough,
yet in a sunny hour fall off,
a something light as air—a look,
　a word unkind or wrongly taken—
O love, that tempests never shook,
　a breath, a touch like this hath shaken.
And ruder words will soon rush in
to spread the breach that words begin;

and eyes forget the gentle ray
they wore in courtship's smiling day;
and voices lose the tone that shed
a tenderness round all they said;
till fast declining, one by one,
the sweetnesses of love are gone,
and hearts so lately mingled seem
like broken clouds, or like the stream,
that smiling left the mountain's brow,
   as though its waters ne'er could sever,
yet, ere it reach the plain below,
   breaks into floods that part for ever.
T. MOORE

338   THE OMNIPRESENCE OF THE GREAT SPIRIT

THERE is a tongue in every leaf,
   a voice in every rill—
a voice that speaketh everywhere,
in flood and fire, through earth and air—
   a tongue that's never still.

'Tis the Great Spirit, wide diffused
   through every thing we see,
that with our spirits communeth
of things mysterious—life and death,
   time and eternity!

I see him in the blazing sun
   and in the thunder-cloud;
I hear him in the mighty roar
that rusheth through the forests hoar
   when winds are raging loud.

I feel him in the silent dews
   by grateful earth betrayed;
I feel him in the gentle showers,
the soft south-wind, the breath of flowers,
   the sunshine and the shade.

I see him, hear him, everywhere,
   in all things—darkness, light,
silence, and sound; but most of all,
when slumber's dusky curtains fall,
   I' the silent hour of night.
C. BOWLES

339   *AD DIVINAM SAPIENTIAM*

ALMIGHTY Spirit! thou that by
set turns and changes from thy high
and glorious throne dost here below
rule all, and all things dost foreknow;
can those blind plots we here discuss
please thee, as thy wise counsels us?
When thou thy blessings here dost strow,
and pour on Earth, we flock and flow
with joyous strife and eager care,
struggling which shall have the best share
in thy rich gifts, just as we see
children about nuts disagree.
Some that a crown have got and foiled
break it; another sees it spoiled
ere it is gotten: thus the world
is all to piece-meal cut, and hurled
by factious hands. It is a ball
which fate and force divide 'twixt all
the sons of men. But O good God!
while these for dust fight and a clod,
grant that poor I may smile and be
at rest and perfect peace with Thee.

H. VAUGHAN

340   *THE POET TO HIS FARM*

DEAR mansion, once my father's home,
    sweet farm, his pride and joy,
ye could not shield, ye could not save,
when he was carried to the grave,
    his little orphan boy!

A stranger came with iron hand,
    lord of that evil day:
and drove me forth with weeping eye,
to seek through toil and poverty
    my miserable way.

But now my gracious Prince restores
    his poet's home again:
he comes with his victorious reed,
to teach the river, mount and mead
    a proud yet grateful strain.

He comes in yonder latticed room
    to dream of manhood's days;
he comes, beneath his father's trees
    to mix with rustic melodies
        the great Farnese's praise.

Break forth, my father's blessed home,
        thou prize of minstrelsy!
He comes, the good old master's son:
up with thy tuneful benison,
        give praise and melody!

E. W. BARNARD

341   *THE CASTLE OF ARLINKOW*

HIGH on a rock, whose castled shade
    darkened the lake below,
in ancient strength majestic stood
    the towers of Arlinkow.

The fisher in the lake below
    durst never cast his net,
nor ever swallow in its waves
    her passing wing would wet.

The cattle from its ominous banks
    in wild alarm would run,
though parched with thirst and faint beneath
    the summer's scorching sun.

For sometimes when no passing breeze
    the long lank sedges waved,
all white with foam and heaving high
    its deafening billows raved;

and when the tempest from its base
    the rooted pine would shake,
the powerless storm unruffled swept
    across the calm dead lake.

And ever then when death drew near
    the house of Arlinkow,
its dark unfathomed depths did send
    strange music from below.

R. SOUTHEY

342   *HIS POETRY HIS PILLAR*

ONLY a little more
    I have to write,
    then I'll give o'er,
and bid the world good-night.

'Tis but a flying minute,
    that I must stay,
    or linger in it,
and then I must away.

O Time that cut'st down all,
    and scarce leav'st here
    memorial
of any men that were;

How many lie forgot
    in vaults beneath;
    and piece-meal rot
without a fame in death?

Behold this living stone
    I rear for me,
    ne'er to be thrown
down, envious Time, by thee.

Pillars let some set up,
    if so they please,
    here is my hope,
and my pyramides.

                      R. HERRICK

343   *PRAISE OF A COUNTRY LIFE*

ABUSED mortals! did you know
   where joy, hearts-ease, and comforts grow,
    you'd scorn proud towers,
    and seek them in these bowers
where winds sometimes our woods perhaps may shake,
but blustering care could never tempest make,
    nor murmurs e'er come nigh us,
    saving of fountains that glide by us.

Here's no fantastic masque or dance,
but of our kids that frisk and prance;

nor wars are seen,
unless upon the green
two harmless lambs are butting one the other;
which done, both bleating run, each to his mother;
and wounds are never found,
save what the ploughshare gives the ground.

Go! let the diving Negro seek
for gems hid in some forlorn creek:
we all pearls scorn,
save what the dewy morn
congeals upon each little spire of grass,
which careless shepherds beat down as they pass:
and gold ne'er here appears,
save what the yellow Ceres bears.

SIR W. RALEIGH

344   *ODE ON THE DEATH OF JAMES THOMSON*

IN yonder grove a Druid lies,
  where slowly winds the stealing wave!
The year's best sweets shall duteous rise
  to deck its poet's sylvan grave.

In yon deep bed of whispering reeds
  his airy harp shall now be laid,
that he, whose heart in sorrow bleeds,
  may love through life the soothing shade.

The maids and youth shall linger here,
  and while its sounds at distance swell,
shall sadly seem in Pity's ear
  to hear the woodland pilgrim's knell.

Remembrance oft shall haunt the shore
  when Thames in summer wreaths is drest,
and oft suspend the dashing oar,
  to bid his gentle spirit rest!

And oft as ease and health retire
  to breezy lawn, or forest deep,
the friend shall view yon whitening spire,
  and 'mid the varied landscape weep.

345 But thou who own'st that earthly bed,
  Ah! what will every dirge avail?
or tears, which Love and Pity shed,
  that mourn beneath the gliding sail!

Yet lives there one, whose heedless eye
    shall scorn thy pale shrine glimmering near?
with him, sweet bard, may Fancy die,
    and Joy desert the blooming year.

But thou, lorn stream, whose sullen tide
    no sedge-crowned sisters now attend;
now waft me from the green hill's side,
    whose cold turf hides the buried friend!

And see, the fairy valleys fade;
    dun night has veiled the solemn view!
yet once again, dear parted shade,
    meek Nature's Child, again adieu!

The genial meads, assigned to bless
    thy life, shall mourn thy early doom;
their hinds and shepherd girls shall dress
    with simple hands thy rural tomb.

Long, long, thy stone and pointed clay
    shall melt the musing Briton's eyes:
O! vales, and wild woods, shall he say,
    in yonder grove your Druid lies!

W. COLLINS

346 A DIRGE

REST on your battle-fields, ye brave!
    let the pines murmur o'er your grave,
your dirge be in the moaning wave—
        we call you back no more!

O there was mourniug when ye fell,
in your own vales a deep-toned knell,
an agony, a wild farewell—
        but that hath long been o'er.

Rest with your still and solemn fame;
the hills keep record of your name,
and never can a touch of shame
        darken the buried brow.

But we on changeful days are cast
when bright names from their place fall fast;
and ye that with your glory passed,
        we cannot mourn you now.

F. HEMANS

347   THE HAMLET

THE hinds how blest, who ne'er beguiled
to quit their hamlet's hawthorn wild,
nor haunt the crowd, nor tempt the main
for splendid care and guilty gain!
When morning's twilight-tinctur'd beam
strikes their low thatch with slanting gleam,
they rove abroad in ether blue,
to dip the scythe in fragrant dew;
the sheaf to bind, the beech to fell,
that nodding shades a craggy dell.

'Midst gloomy glades, in warbles clear,
wild nature's sweetest notes they hear:
on green untrodden banks they view
the hyacinth's neglected hue:
in their lone haunts, and woodland rounds,
they spy the squirrel's airy bounds;
and startle from her ashen spray,
across the glen, the screaming jay:
each native charm their steps explore
of Solitude's sequestered store.

348 For them the moon with cloudless ray
mounts to illume their homeward way;
their weary spirits to relieve,
the meadows incense breathe at eve.
No riot mars the simple fare,
that o'er a glimmering hearth they share;
but when the curfew's measured roar
duly, the darkening valleys o'er,
has echoed from the distant town,
they wish no beds of cygnet-down,
no trophied canopies, to close
their drooping eyes in quick repose.

Their humble porch with honied flowers,
the curling woodbine's shade imbowers:
from the small garden's thymy mound
their bees in busy swarm resound:
nor fell Disease, before his time,
hastes to consume life's golden prime:

but when their temples long have wore
the silver crown of tresses hoar;
as studious still calm peace to keep,
beneath a flowery turf they sleep.

T. WARTON

349 *THE TIMBER*

SURE thou didst flourish once! and many Springs,
 many bright mornings, much dew, many showers
past o'er thy head; many light hearts and wings,
 which now are dead, lodg'd in thy living bowers.

And still a new succession sings and flies;
 fresh groves grow up and their green branches shoot
towards the old and still enduring skies;
 while the low violet thrives at their root.

But thou beneath the sad and heavy line
 of death dost waste all senseless, cold and dark;
where not so much as dreams of light may shine,
 nor any thought of greenness, leaf or bark.

And yet, as if some deep hate and dissent,
 bred in thy growth betwixt high winds and thee,
were still alive, thou dost great storms resent,
 before they come, and know'st how near they be.

Else all at rest thou lyest, and the fierce breath
 of tempests can no more disturb thy ease;
but this thy strange resentment after death
 means only those who broke in life thy peace.

H. VAUGHAN

350 *BLESSED ARE THEY THAT MOURN*

OH, deem not they are blest alone
 whose lives a peaceful tenor keep;
the Power who pities man, has shown
 a blessing for the eyes that weep.

The light of smiles shall fill again
 the lids that overflow with tears;
and weary hours of woe and pain
 are promises of happier years.

There is a day of sunny rest
for every dark and troubled night;
and grief may bide an evening guest,
but joy shall come with early light.

And thou, who o'er thy friend's low bier
sheddest the bitter drops like rain,
hope that a brighter, happier sphere
will give him to thy arms again.

For God has marked each sorrowing day
and numbered every secret tear,
and heaven's long age of bliss shall pay
for all his children suffer here.

W. C. BRYANT

351   ANACREONTIC

BENEATH a thick and silent shade
   that seem'd for pure devotion made
in holy rapture stretch'd along
   (Urania lay to aid my song)
I tun'd my voice and touch'd the lyre
   while heav'nly themes the Muse inspire;
I sung the beauties of the grove
I sung th' Almighty power above,
   but striving more my notes to raise,
   and to my subject suit my lays,
a string o'erstrain'd, in pieces flew,
   and sudden from its place withdrew.
Under my hand the chord I found,
   but lost alas! the sprightly sound.
So pierc'd by Death's relentless dart
   we view the lifeless earthly part,
the soul invisible takes wing
as sound that leaves the breaking string.

352   VITA EST BENEFACTIS EXTENDENDA

THE snow, that crowns each mountain's brow,
   and whitens every spray,
fom each high rock and loaded bough
   will quickly melt away;

soon as the sun's reviving ray
  shall warm the northern gale;
and Zephyrs mild their wing display
  to wanton in the vale.
When Time upon thine aged brow
  shall shed the fatal shower;
the hoary frost, the chilling snow,
  will melt from thence no more.
Quick summer flies, and autumn's suns,
  and winter's cheerless gloom;
in changeful turn each season runs,
  and spring breathes new perfume.
Unchanged o'er us the tempest low'rs,
  till death's last hour arrives:
nor robe, nor garland deck'd with flowers,
  the bloom of life revives.
What youth on us but once bestows,
  age once shall snatch away:
but Fame can stop the fatal blows,
  and double life's short day.
Long shall he live, whose bright career
  deserv'd a patriot's sigh;
all else flies with the fleeting year,
  but Fame can never die.
                              W. HERBERT

353   *THE SAME*

IT would less vex distressed man
  if Fortune in the same pace ran
to ruin him, as he did rise;
but highest states fall in a trice.
No great success held ever long:
a restless fate afflicts the throng
of Kings and Commons, and less days
serve to destroy them, than to raise.
Good luck smiles once an age, but bad
makes kingdoms in a minute sad,
and every hour of life we drive,
hath o'er us a prerogative.
Then leave (by wild Impatience driven,
and rash resents,) to rail at heaven,

leave an unmanly, weak complaint
that Death and Fate have no restraint.
In the same hour, that gave thee breath,
thou hadst ordained thy hour of death,
but he lives most, who here will buy
with a few tears eternity.

H. VAUGHAN

354   *THE EXODUS OF THE ISRAELITES*

WHEN Israel was from bondage led,
   led by th' Almighty's hand
from out a foreign land,
the great sea beheld and fled.
As men pursu'd, when that fear past they find,
stop on some higher ground to look behind,
   so whilst through wondrous ways
   the sacred army went,
the waves afar stood up to gaze,
and their own rocks did represent,
solid as waters are above the firmament.
Old Jordan's waters to their spring
   start back with sudden fright;
   the spring amazed at sight,
asks what news from sea they bring.
The mountains shook, and to the mountain's side
the little hills leapt round themselves to hide;
   as young affrighted lambs,
   when they ought dreadful spy,
run trembling to their helpless dams,
the mighty sea and river by
were glad for their excuse to see the hills to fly.

A. COWLEY

355   *PANEGYRIC ON THE HIGH PRIEST SIMON,*
              SON OF ONIAS

HOW was he honoured in the midst of the people
   in his coming out of the sanctuary!
He was as the morning star in the midst of the cloud,
and as the moon at the full;
as the sun shining upon the temple of the most High,
and as the rainbow giving light in the bright clouds:
and as the flower of roses in the spring of the year,
as lilies by the rivers of waters,

and as the branches of the frankincense tree in summer:
as fire and incense in the censer,
and as a vessel of gold set with precious stones,
as a fair olive-tree, budding forth fruit,
and as a cypress which groweth up to the clouds.
When he put on the robe of honour,
and was clothed with the perfection of glory,
when he went up to the holy altar,
he made the garment of holiness honourable.
He himself stood by the hearth of the altar,
compassed with his brethren round about,
as a young cedar in Libanus;
and as palm trees compassed they him round about.
ECCLESIASTICUS

356 *MUTABILITY*

THE flower that smiles to-day
    to-morrow dies;
all that we wish to stay
    tempts and then flies:
what is this world's delight?
lightning that mocks the night,
brief even as bright.

Virtue, how frail it is!
    friendship too rare!
Love, how it sells poor bliss
    for proud despair!
but we, though soon they fall,
survive their joy and all
which ours we call.

Whilst skies are blue and bright,
    whilst flowers are gay,
whilst eyes that change ere night
    make glad the day;
whilst yet the calm hours creep,
dream thou—and from thy sleep
then wake to weep.
P. B. SHELLEY

357 *SUMMER'S DEPARTURE AND RETURN*

FAREWELL! on wings of sombre stain,
    that blacken in the last blue skies,
thou fliest; but thou wilt come again
on the gay wings of butterflies:

spring at thy approach will sprout
her new Corinthian beauties out,
leaf-woven homes, where twitter-words
will grow to songs—and eggs to birds;
ambitious buds shall swell to flowers,
and April smiles to sunny hours.
Bright days shall be, and gentle nights
full of soft breath and echo lights,
as if the god of sun-time kept
his eyes half-open while he slept,
roses shall be where roses were,
   not shadows but reality,
as if they never perished there,
   but slept in immortality:
Nature shall thrill with new delight,
   and Time's relumined river run
warm as young blood, and dazzling bright
   as if its source were in the sun.

T. HOOD

358   THE TRUE KING

'TIS not wealth that makes a king,
   nor the purple's colouring,
nor a brow that's bound with gold,
nor gates on mighty hinges rolled.
The king is he who, void of fear,
looks abroad with bosom clear,
who can tread ambition down,
nor be swayed by smile or frown,
nor for all the treasure cares
that mine conceals or harvest bears,
or that golden sands deliver
bosomed in a glassy river.
What shall move his placid might?
nor the headlong thunder-light,
nor the storm that rushes out
to snatch the shivering waves about,
nor all the shapes of slaughter's trade,
with forward lance or fiery blade.
Safe with wisdom for his crown,
he looks on all things calmly down;
he welcomes fate, when fate is near,
nor taints his dying breath with fear.

359 COMPLAINT ON ENGLAND'S MISERIES

All, happy Isle, how art thou chang'd and curst,
   since I was born and knew thee first!
when Peace, which had forsook the world around,
(frighted with noise and the shrill trumpet's sound),
   thee for a private place of rest
   and a secure retirement chose
   wherein to build her halcyon nest;
no wind durst stir abroad the air to discompose.

When all the riches of the globe beside
   flowed in to thee with every tide;
when all that nature did thy soil deny
the growth was of thy fruitful industry;
   when all the proud and dreadful sea,
   and all his tributary-streams,
   a constant tribute paid to thee;
when all the liquid world was one extended Thames.

Unhappy Isle! no ship of thine at sea
   was ever tossed and torn like thee:
thy naked hulk loose on the waves does beat,
the rocks and banks around her ruin threat:
   what did thy foolish pilots ail,
   to lay the compass quite aside?
   without a law or rule to sail,
and rather take the winds than heavens to be their guide?

                    A. COWLEY

360 ADVERSITY THE SCHOOL OF HEROISM

So, when the wisest poets seek
   in all their liveliest colours to set forth
   a picture of heroic worth,
(the pious Trojan or the prudent Greek)
they choose some comely Prince of heavenly birth,
   (no proud gigantic Son of earth
who strives t' usurp the gods' forbidden seat);
they feed him not with nectar, and the meat
   that cannot without joy be eat;
but in the cold of want and storms of adverse chance
they harden his young virtue by degrees;
the beauteous drop first into ice does freeze,
and into solid crystal next advance.

His murdered friends and kindred he does see,
  and from his flaming country flee:
much is he tossed at sea and much at land,
does long the force of angry gods withstand:
he does long troubles and long wars sustain,
  ere he his fatal birthright gain.
With no less time or labour can
  destiny build up such a man,
who's with sufficient virtue fill'd
  his ruin'd country to rebuild.

A. COWLEY

361   DEATH THE LEVELLER

THE glories of our blood and state
  are shadows, not substantial things:
there is no armour against fate;
Death lays his icy hands on kings:
    Sceptre and Crown
    must tumble down
and in the dust be equal made
with the poor crooked scythe and spade.
Some men with swords may reap the field,
  and plant fresh laurels where they kill;
but their strong nerves at last must yield;
  they tame but one another still:
    early or late
    they stoop to fate,
and must give up their murmuring breath
when they, pale captives, creep to death.
The garlands wither on your brow;
  then boast no more your mighty deeds;
upon Death's purple altar now
  see where the victor-victim bleeds:
    your heads must come
    to the cold tomb;
only the actions of the just
smell sweet, and blossom in the dust.

J. SHIRLEY

362   THE GREAT LEVELLER

WHY should man's aspiring mind
  burn in him with so proud a breath,
when all his haughty views can find
  in this world yields to death?

The fair, the brave, the vain, the wise,
　　the rich, the poor, the great and small
are each but worms' anatomies,
　　to strew his quiet hall.

Power may make many earthly gods,
　　where gold and bribery's guilt prevails;
but death's unwelcome honest odds
　　kicks o'er the unequal scales.
The flatter'd great may clamours raise
　　of power,—and their own weakness hide;
but death shall find unlooked-for ways
　　to end the farce of pride.

Death levels all things, in his march
　　nought can resist his mighty strength;
the palace proud,—triumphal arch,
　　shall mete their shadow's length:
the rich, the poor, one common bed
　　shall find in the unhonoured grave,
where weeds shall crown alike the head
　　of tyrant and of slave.
　　　　　　　　　　　A. MARVELL

363　　　*THE GREEK BOY*

GONE are the glorious Greeks of old,
　　glorious in mien and mind;
their bones are mingled with the mould,
　　their dust is on the wind;
the forms they hewed from living stone
survive the waste of years alone,
and scattered with their ashes, shew
what greatness perished long ago.

Yet fresh the myrtles there—the springs
　　gush brightly as of yore;
flowers blossom from the dust of kings,
　　as many an age before;
there nature moulds as nobly now,
as e'er of old, the human brow;
and copies still the martial form
that braved Plataea's battle storm.

Boy! thy first looks were taught to seek
    their heaven in Hellas' skies;
her airs have tinged thy dusky cheek,
    her sunshine lit thine eyes;
and Greece, decayed, dethroned, doth see
    her youth renewed in such as thee;
a shoot of that old vine that made
the nations silent in its shade.
W. C. BRYANT

364   CONTEMPLATION

O VOICE divine, whose heavenly strain
    no mortal measure may attain,
O powerful to appease the smart
that festers in a wounded heart,
whose mystic numbers can assuage
the bosom of tumultuous rage,
can strike the dagger from despair,
and shut the watchful eye of care.
Oft lured by thee, when wretches call,
Hope comes, that cheers and softens all;
expelled by thee, and dispossest
Envy forsakes the human breast.
Full oft with thee the Bard retires,
and lost to earth to heaven aspires:
how nobly lost! with thee to rove
through the long deepening solemn grove,
or underneath the moonlight pale
to silence trust some plaintive tale
of nature's ills and mankind's woes,
while kings and all the proud repose:
or where some holy aged oak
a stranger to the woodman's stroke,
from the high rock's aërial crown
in twisting arches bending down,
bathes in the smooth pellucid stream;
full oft he waits the mystic dream
of mankind's joys right understood,
and of the all prevailing good.
Go forth invoked, O voice divine!
and issue from thy sacred shrine.
W. HAMILTON

365 TO A MOUNTAIN DAISY ON TURNING ONE DOWN WITH THE PLOUGH

WEE, modest, crimson-tipped flow'r,
  thou's met me in an evil hour;
for I maun crush amang the stoure
        thy tender stem;
to spare thee now is past my pow'r,
        thou bonnie gem!

Cauld blew the bitter-biting north
upon thy early, humble birth;
yet cheerfully thou glinted forth
        amid the storm,
scarce reared above the parent earth
        thy tender form.

The flaunting flow'rs our gardens yield
high sheltering woods and wa's maun shield;
but thou, beneath the random bield
        o' clod or stane,
adorns the histie stibble-field,
        unseen, alane.

There, in thy scanty mantle clad,
thy snawy bosom sun-ward spread,
thou lifts thy unassuming head
        in humble guise;
but now the share uptears thy bed,
        and low thou lies!

366
Such is the fate of artless maid,
sweet flowret of the rural shade,
by love's simplicity betrayed,
        and guileless trust,
till she, like thee, all soiled, is laid
        low i' the dust.

Such is the fate of simple bard,
on life's rough ocean luckless starred!
unskilful he to note the card
        of prudent lore,
till billows rage, and gales blow hard,
        and whelm him o'er!

Such fate to suffering worth is given,
who long with wants and woes has striven,
by human pride or cunning driven
  to misery's brink,
till, wrenched of every stay but Heaven,
  he, ruined, sink!

Even thou, who mourn'st the daisy's fate,
that fate is thine—no distant date;
stern Ruin's ploughshare drives, elate,
  full on thy bloom,
till crushed beneath the furrow's weight
  shall be thy doom!
R. BURNS

367   ON DISAPPOINTMENT

WHAT is this passing scene?
  a peevish April day!
a little sun—a little rain,
and then night sweeps along the plain,
  and all things fade away.
   Man (soon discussed)
   yields up his trust,
And all his hopes and fears lie with him in the dust.

Oh, what is Beauty's pow'r?
  it flourishes and dies!
Will the cold earth its silence break,
to tell how soft, how smooth a cheek
  beneath its surface lies?
   Mute, mute is all
   o'er Beauty's fall;
her praise resounds no more when mantled in her pall.

The most beloved on earth
  not long survives to-day:
so music past is obsolete,
and yet 'twas sweet, 'twas passing sweet,
  but now 'tis gone away.
   Thus does the shade
   in memory fade
when in forsaken tomb the form belov'd is laid.
H. K. WHITE

368   SOLITUDE

IT is not that my lot is low,
that bids this silent tear to flow;
it is not grief that bids me moan;
it is that I am all alone.

In woods and glens I love to roam,
when the tired hedger hies him home;
or by the woodland pool to rest,
when pale the star looks on its breast.

Yet when the silent evening sighs
with hallowed airs and symphonies,
my spirit takes another tone,
and sighs that it is all alone.

The autumn leaf is sere and dead,
it floats upon the water's bed;
I would not be a leaf to die
without recording sorrow's sigh!

the woods and winds, with sullen wail,
tell all the same unvaried tale;
I've none to smile when I am free,
And when I sigh, to sigh with me.

Yet in my dreams a form I view,
that thinks on me and loves me too:
I start, and then, the vision flown,
I weep that I am all alone.
                                    H. K. WHITE

369   TO VENUS

COME, gentle Venus, and assuage
a warring world, a bleeding age;
for nature lives beneath thy ray,
the wintry tempests haste away;
a lucid calm invests the sea,
thy native deep is full of thee:
the flowering earth, where'er you fly,
is all o'er spring, all sun the sky.
A genial spirit warms the breeze;
unseen among the blooming trees,
the feather'd lovers tune their throat,
the desert growls a soften'd note,

glad o'er the meads the cattle bound;
and love and harmony go round.
    Come, thou delight of heaven and earth!
to whom all creatures owe their birth;
O come, sweet smiling, tender, come!
and yet prevent our final doom.
For long the furious god of war
has crushed us with his iron car,
has raged along our ruined plains,
has soiled them with his cruel stains,
has sunk our youth in endless sleep,
and made the widowed virgin weep.

J. THOMSON

370   TO THE SWALLOW

O SWALLOW, Swallow, flying, flying South,
  fly to her and fall upon her gilded eaves,
and tell her, tell her what I tell to thee.

    O tell her, Swallow, thou that knowest each,
that bright and fierce and fickle is the South,
and dark and true and tender is the North.

    O Swallow, Swallow, if I could follow, and light
upon her lattice, I would pipe and trill,
and cheep and twitter twenty million loves.

    O were I thou that she might take me in,
and lay me on her bosom, and her heart
would rock the snowy cradle till I died.

    Why lingereth she to clothe her heart with love,
delaying as the tender ash delays
to clothe herself, when all the woods are green?

    O tell her, Swallow, that thy brood is flown:
say to her, I do but wanton in the South,
but in the North long since my nest is made.

    O tell her, brief is life but love is long,
and brief the sun of summer in the North,
and brief the moon of beauty in the South.

    O Swallow, flying from the golden woods,
fly to her, and pipe and woo her, and make her mine,
and tell her, tell her, that I follow thee.

A. TENNYSON

HYMN ON THE NATIVITY

NO war, or battle's sound
  was heard the world around;
the idle spear and shield were high up hung;
  the hooked chariot stood
  unstained with hostile blood;
the trumpet spake not to the arméd throng;
  and kings sat still with awful eye,
as if they surely knew their sovran Lord was by.

  But peaceful was the night,
  wherein the Prince of light
his reign of peace upon the earth began:
  the winds, with wonder whist,
  smoothly the waters kissed
whispering new joys to the mild ocean,
  who now hath quite forgot to rave,
while birds of calm sit brooding on the charméd wave.

  The stars, with deep amaze,
  stand fixed in steadfast gaze,
bending one way their precious influence,
  and will not take their flight,
  for all the morning-light,
or Lucifer that often warned them thence;
  but in their glimmering orbs did glow,
until their Lord himself bespake, and bid them go.

  The shepherds on the lawn
  or ere the point of dawn
sat simply chatting in a rustic row;
  full little thought they than
  that the mighty Pan
was kindly come to live with them below;
  perhaps their loves, or else their sheep
was all that did their silly thoughts so busy keep.

  When such music sweet
  their hearts and ears did greet
as never was by mortal finger strook;
  divinely-warbled voice
  answering the stringéd noise,
as all their souls in blissful rapture took:
  the air, such pleasure loth to lose,
with thousand echoes still prolongs each heavenly close.

Nature that heard such sound
  beneath the hollow round
of Cynthia's seat the airy region thrilling,
  now was almost won
  to think her part was done,
and that her reign had here its last fulfilling;
  she knew such harmony alone
could hold all heaven and earth in happier union.

373
  The oracles are dumb;
    no voice or hideous hum
  runs through the arched roof in words deceiving:
    Apollo from his shrine
    can no more divine,
  with hollow shriek the steep of Delphos leaving:
    no nightly trance or breathed spell
  inspires the pale-eyed priest from the prophetic cell.

  The lonely mountains o'er
    and the resounding shore
  a voice of weeping heard and loud lament;
    from haunted spring and dale
    edged with poplar pale
  the parting Genius is with sighing sent;
    with flower-inwoven tresses torn
  the nymphs in twilight shade of tangled thickets mourn.

  In consecrated earth,
    and on the holy hearth,
  the Lars and Lemures moan with midnight plaint;
    in urns and altars round
    a drear and dying sound
  affrights the Flamens at their service quaint;
    and the chill marble seems to sweat,
  while each peculiar Power foregoes his wonted seat.

J. MILTON

374 *ODE TO PEACE*

COME, peace of mind, delightful guest!
  return and make thy downy nest
once more in this sad heart:
nor riches I nor power pursue,
nor hold forbidden joys in view;
  we therefore need not part.

Where wilt thou dwell, if not with me,
from avarice and ambition free,
 and pleasure's fatal wiles?
For whom, alas! dost thou prepare
the sweets that I was wont to share,
 the banquet of thy smiles?

The great, the gay, shall they partake
the Heaven that thou alone canst make?
 And wilt thou quit the stream
that murmurs through the dewy mead,
the grove and the sequestered shed,
 to be a guest with them?

For thee I panted, thee I prized;
for thee I gladly sacrificed
 whate'er I loved before;
and shall I see thee start away,
and helpless, hopeless, hear thee say—
 farewell! we meet no more?

W. COWPER

375   ODE TO PEACE

O THOU! who had'st thy turtles bear
swift from his grasp thy golden hair,
 and sought'st thy native skies;
when War, by vultures drawn from far,
to Britain bent his iron car,
 and bade his storms arise!

Tired of his rude tyrannic sway
our youth shall fix some festive day,
 his sullen shrines to burn:
but thou, who hear'st the turning spheres,
what sounds may charm thy partial ears,
 and gain thy blest return!

O Peace, thy injured robes upbind!
O rise, and leave not one behind
 of all thy beamy train:
the British Lion, goddess sweet,
lies stretched on earth to kiss thy feet,
 and own thy holier reign.

Let others court thy transient smile,
but come to grace thy western isle,

by warlike Honour led;
and, while around her ports rejoice,
while all her sons adore thy choice,
with him for ever wed!

W. COLLINS

376   TO SPRING

THE bright-haired sun with warmth benign
   bids tree and shrub and swelling vine
  their infant buds display:
again the streams refresh the plains
which Winter bound in icy chains,
  and sparkling bless his ray.

Life-giving Zephyrs breathe around,
and instant glows th' enamel'd ground
  with Nature's varied hues:
not so returns our youth decayed,
alas! nor air nor sun nor shade
  the spring of life renews.

The sun's too quick-revolving beam
will soon dissolve the human dream,
  and bring th' appointed hour:
too late we catch his parting ray,
and mourn the idly-wasted day,
  no longer in our power.

Then happiest he, whose lengthened sight
pursues by virtue's constant light
  a hope beyond the skies;
where frowning Winter ne'er shall come,
but rosy Spring for ever bloom
  and suns eternal rise.

MISS FERRER

377   HAPPY INSENSIBILITY

IN a drear-nighted December,
  too happy, happy Tree,
thy branches ne'er remember
their green felicity;
the north cannot undo them,
with a sleety whistle through them,
nor frozen thawings glue them
from budding at the prime.

In a drear-nighted December,
too happy, happy Brook,
thy bubblings ne'er remember
Apollo's summer-look;
but with a sweet forgetting
they stay their crystal fretting,
never, never petting
about the frozen time.

Ah! would 'twere so with many
a gentle girl and boy!
But were there ever any
writhed not at passéd joy?
to know the change and feel it,
when there is none to heal it,
nor numbéd sense to steal it—
was never said in rhyme.

          J. KEATS

378   *SPRING*

NOW each creature joys the other,
 passing happy days and hours;
one bird reports unto another,
 in the fall of silver showers;
whilst the earth, our common mother,
 hath her bosom decked with flowers.
Whilst the greatest torch of heaven
 with bright rays warms Flora's lap,
making nights and days both even,
 cheering plants with fresher sap:
my field of flowers quite bereaven
 wants refresh of better hap.
Echo, daughter of the air,
 (babbling guest of rocks and hills)
knows the name of my fierce fair,
 and sounds the accents of my ills.
Each thing pities my despair,
 whilst that she her lover kills:
whilst that she (O cruel maid!)
 doth me and my love despise;
my life's flourish is decayed,
 that depended on her eyes:
but her will must be obeyed;
 and well he ends for love who dies.

379   TO MAY

QUEEN of fresh flowers,
    whom vernal stars obey,
bring thy warm showers,
    bring thy genial ray.
In nature's greenest livery drest
descend on earth's expectant breast,
to earth and heaven a welcome guest,
    thou merry month of May!

Mark! how we meet thee
    at dawn of dewy day!
hark! how we greet thee
    with our roundelay!
while all the goodly things that be
in earth and air and ample sea
are waking up to welcome thee,
    thou merry month of May!

Flocks on the mountains,
    and birds upon their spray,
tree, turf, and fountains
    all hold holiday;
and Love, the life of living things,
Love waves his torch and claps his wings,
and loud and wide thy praises sings,
    thou merry month of May.
                              R. HEBER

380   NORTHERN SPRING

YESTREEN the mountain's rugged brow
    was mantled o'er with dreary snow;
the sun set red behind the hill,
and every breath of wind was still;
but ere he rose, the southern blast
a veil o'er heaven's blue arch had cast:
thick rolled the clouds, and genial rain
poured the wide deluge o'er the plain:
fair glens and verdant vales appear,
and warmth awakes the budding year.
O 'tis the touch of fairy hand
that wakes the spring of Northern land!
it warms not there by slow degrees,
with changeful pulse, the uncertain breeze;

but sudden on the wondering sight
bursts forth the beam of living light;
and instant verdure springs around,
and magic flowers bedeck the ground:
returned from regions far away
the red-winged throstle pours his lay;
the soaring snipe salutes the spring,
as the breeze whistles through his wing;
and, as he hails the melting snows,
the heath-cock claps his wings and crows.

W. HERBERT

381   *THE SPRING*

NOW that the winter's gone, the earth hath lost
    her snow-white robes; and now no more the frost
candies the grasse, or castes an ycie creame
upon the silver lake or chrystall streame ;
but the warme sunne thawes the benummed earth,
and makes it tender; gives a sacred birth
to the dead swallow; wakes in hollow tree
the drowzie cuckow and the humble bee.
Now doe a quire of chirping minstrels bring
in tryumph to the world the youthfull Spring :
the vallies, hills, and woods, in rich arraye,
welcome the comming of the long'd-for May.
Now all things smile: only my Love doth lowre;
nor hath the scalding noon-day sunne the power
to melt that marble yce, which still doth hold
her heart congealed, and makes her pittie cold.
The oxe which lately did for shelter flie
into the stall, doth now securely lie
in open fields ; and love no more is made
by the fire-side; but, in the cooler shade,
Amyntas now doth with his Cloris sleepe
under a sycamoure, and all things keepe
time with the season—only she doth carry
June in her eyes, in her heart January.

T. CAREW

382   *ODE ON THE PLEASURE ARISING FROM
        VICISSITUDE*

NOW the golden Morn aloft
    waves her dew-bespangled wing,
with vermeil check and whisper soft
    she woos the tardy Spring:

till April starts, and calls around
the sleeping fragrance from the ground,
and lightly o'er the living scene
scatters his freshest, tenderest green.

New-born flocks, in rustic dance,
   frisking ply their feeble feet;
forgetful of their wintry trance
   the birds his presence greet:
but chief, the skylark warbles high
his trembling thrilling ecstacy;
and, lessening from the dazzled sight,
melts into air and liquid light.

Yesterday the sullen year
   saw the snowy whirlwind fly;
mute was the music of the air,
   the herd stood drooping by:
their raptures now that wildly flow
no yesterday nor morrow know;
'tis Man alone that joy descries
with forward and reverted eyes.

383 Smiles on past Misfortune's brow
   soft Reflection's hand can trace,
and o'er the cheek of Sorrow throw
   a melancholy grace;
while Hope prolongs our happier hour,
or deepest shades, that dimly lour
and blacken round our weary way,
gilds with a gleam of distant day.

Still, where rosy Pleasure leads,
   see a kindred Grief pursue;
behind the steps that Misery treads
   approaching Comfort view:
the hues of bliss more brightly glow
chastised by sabler tints of woe,
and blended form, with artful strife,
the strength and harmony of life.

See the wretch that long has tost
   on the thorny bed of pain,
at length repair his vigour lost
   and breathe and walk again:

the meanest floweret of the vale,
the simplest note that swells the gale,
the common sun, the air, the skies,
to him are opening Paradise.

T. GRAY

384   TIME BREEDETH CHANGE

IN time we see the silver drops
   the craggy stones make soft;
the slowest snail in time we see
   doth creep and climb aloft.
With feeble puffs the tallest pine
   in tract of time doth fall;
the hardest heart in time doth yield
   to Venus' luring call.
Where chilling frost alate did nip,
   there flasheth now a fire;
where deep disdain bred noisome hate,
   there kindleth now desire.
Time causeth hope to have his hap;
   what care in time's not eased?
in time I loathed that now I love
   in both content and pleased.

R. GREENE

385   PEACE

SLEEP, Ambition! Rage, expire!
   Vengeance, fold thy wing of fire!
close thy dark and lurid eye,
bid thy torch, forsaken, die;
furl thy banner, waving proud,
dreadful as the thunder-cloud;
shall destruction blast the plain?
shall the falchion rage again?
shall the sword thy bands dissever?
never, sweet Affection! never!
   As the halcyon o'er the ocean
   lulls the billow's wild commotion,
   so we bid dissension cease.
Bloom, O amaranth of peace!
twine the spear with vernal roses;
now the reign of discord closes;
goddess of th' unconquer'd isles,
Freedom! triumph in our smiles.

Blooming youth, and wisdom hoary,
bards of fame, and sons of glory;
Albion! pillar of the main,
monarchs, nations, join the strain;
swell to heaven the exulting voice;
mortals, triumph! earth, rejoice.

386   *THE FALCON ON THE WARRIOR'S WRIST*

THE Falcon is a noble bird,
and when his heart of hearts is stirred,
he'll seek the eagle, though he run
into his chamber near the sun.
Ne'er was there brute or bird,
whom the woods or mountains heard,
that could force a fear or care
from him,—the Arab of the air!

To-day he sits upon a wrist
whose purple veins a queen has kissed,
and on him falls a sterner eye
than he can face where'er he fly,
though he scale the summit cold
of the Grimsel, vast and old,—
though he search yon sunless stream,
that threads the forest like a dream.

Ah! noble Soldier! noble Bird!
will your name be ever heard,—
ever seen in future story,
crowning it with deathless glory?
Peace, ho!—the master's eye is drawn
away unto the bursting dawn!
arise, thou bird of birds, arise,
and seek thy quarry in the skies!

B. W. PROCTER

387   *INDEPENDENCE*

WHOSE calm soul in a settled state
kicks under foot the frowns of Fate,
and in his fortunes bad or good
keeps the same temper in his blood,
not him the flaming clouds above,
nor Ætna's fiery tempests move,

no fretting seas from shore to shore
boiling with indignation o'er,
nor burning thunderbolt that can
a mountain shake, can stir this man.
Dull cowards, then, why should we start
to see these tyrants act their part?
nor hope nor fear what may befall,
and you disarm their malice all.
But who doth faintly fear or wish,
and sets no law to what is his,
hath lost the buckler, and, poor elf!
makes up a chain to bind himself.

H. VAUGHAN

388 *QVID SIT FVTVRVM CRAS FVGE QVÆRERE*

SEES not my friend, what a deep snow
candies our country's woody brow?
the yielding branch his load scarce bears
opprest with snow and frozen tears,
while the dumb rivers slowly float
all bound up in an icy coat.
Let us meet then! and while this world
in wild eccentrics now is hurled,
keep we, like nature, the same key,
and walk in our forefathers' way;
why any more cast we an eye
on what may come, not what is nigh?
why vex ourselves with fear or hope,
and cares beyond our horoscope?
Sorrows and sighs and searches spend
and draw our bottom to an end,
but discreet joys lengthen the lease
without which life were a disease,
and who this age a mourner goes
does with his tears but feed his foes.

H. VAUGHAN

389   *THE ECSTACY*

I LEAVE mortality's low sphere:
ye winds and clouds, come lift me high,
and on your airy pinions bear
swift through the regions of the sky.

What lofty mountains downward fly!
and lo, how wide a space of air
extends new prospects to my eye!
the gilded fanes, reflecting light,
and royal palaces, as bright,
    (the rich abodes
of heavenly and of earthly gods)
retire apace; whole cities too
decrease beneath my rising view.
And now far off the rolling globe appears;
its scatter'd nations I survey,
and all the mass of earth and sea;
O object well-deserving tears!
capricious state of things below,
that changeful from their birth no fix'd duration know!

390   Here new-built towns, aspiring high,
ascend with lofty turrets crown'd;
there others fall, and mouldering lie,
obscure, or only by their ruins found.
Here peace would all its joys dispense,
the vines and olives unmolested grow,
but lo! a purple pestilence
unpeoples cities, sweeps the plains,
whilst vainly through deserted fields
her unreap'd harvests Ceres yields,
and at the noon of day a midnight silence reigns.
There milder heat the healthful climate warms,
but slaves to arbitrary power,
and pleas'd each other to devour,
the mad possessors rush to arms,
I see, I see them from afar,
I view distinct the mingled war!
I see the charging squadrons prest
hand to hand, and breast to breast.
Destruction, like a vulture, hovers nigh;
lur'd with the hope of human blood,
she hangs upon the wing, uncertain where to fly,
but licks her drowthy jaws, and waits the promised food.

                            J. HUGHES

391 *THE PRAISE OF A RELIGIOUS LIFE*

IN the calm spring, when the earth bears,
and feeds on April's breath and tears,
his eyes accustomed to the skies
find here fresh objects and like spies
or busy bees search the soft flowers,
contemplate the green fields and bowers;
he sadly sighing says, 'O how
these flowers with hasty stretched heads grow,
and strive for heaven, but rooted here
lament the distance with a tear!
The honeysuckles clad in white,
the rose in red, point to the light,
and the lilies hollow and bleak
look, as if they would something speak,
they sigh at night to each soft gale,
and at the day-spring weep it all.
Shall I then only, wretched I!
opprest with earth, on earth still lie?'
Thus speaks he to the neighbouring trees,
and many sad soliloquies
to springs and fountains doth impart,
seeking God with a longing heart.

392 Then feasted, to the flowery groves
or pleasant rivers he removes,
where near some fair oak hung with mast
he shuns the south's infectious blast:
on shady banks sometimes he lies,
sometimes the open current tries,
where with his line and feathered fly
he sports and takes the scaly fry.
Meanwhile each hollow wood and hill
doth ring with lowings long and shrill,
and shady lakes with rivers deep
echo the bleating of the sheep:
the blackbird with the pleasant thrush
and nightingale in every bush
choice music give and shepherds play
unto their flocks some loving lay;
the thirsty reapers in thick throngs
return home from the field with songs,

and the carts laden with ripe corn
come groaning to the well-stored barn.

H. VAUGHAN

393   *NOX NOCTI INDICAT SCIENTIAM*

WHEN I survay the bright
    cœlestiall spheare,
so rich with jewels hung, that night
doth like an Æthiop bride appeare;

my soule her wings doth spread,
    and heaven-ward flies,
the Almighty's Mysteries to read
in the large volumes of the skies.

For the bright firmament
    shootes forth no flame
so silent, but is eloquent
in speaking the Creator's name.

No unregarded star
    contracts its light
into so small a character
remov'd far from our humane sight:

but if we stedfast looke,
    we shall discerne
in it as in some holy booke,
how man may heavenly knowledge learne.

394
It tells the conqueror,
    that farre-stretcht powre,
which his proud dangers traffique for,
is but the triumph of an houre:

that from the farthest North
    some nation may
yet undiscovered issue forth,
and ore his new-got conquest sway:

some nation yet shut in
    with hils of ice
may be let out to scourge his sinne
till they shall equall him in vice:

and then they likewise shall
    their ruine have;
for as your selves your empires fall,
and every kingdome hath a grave.

Thus those cœlestiall fires,
    though seeming mute,
the fallacie of our desires
and all the pride of life confute.

For they have watcht since first
    the world had birth;
and found sinne in itselfe accurst,
and nothing permanent on earth.
W. HABINGTON

395   THE CHRISTIAN SOLDIER

'SERVANT of God! well done;
    rest from thy loved employ;
the battle fought, the victory won,
enter thy Master's joy.'
—The voice at midnight came;
he started up to hear:
a mortal arrow pierced his frame,
he fell,—but felt no fear.

Tranquil amidst alarms,
it found him in the field,
a veteran slumbering on his arms,
beneath his red-cross shield:
his sword was in his hand,
still warm with recent fight,
ready that moment, at command,
through rock and steel to smite.

It was a two-edged blade,
of heavenly temper keen;
and double were the wounds it made,
where'er it smote between:
'twas death to sin;—'twas life
to all that mourn'd for sin;
it kindled and it silenced strife,
made war and peace within.

396 Oft, with its fiery force,
his arm had quelled the foe,
and laid, resistless in its course,
the alien-armies low.
Bent on such glorious toils,
the world to him was loss;
yet all his trophies, all his spoils,
he hung upon the cross.

At midnight came the cry,
'To meet thy God, prepare!'
He woke, and caught his Captain's eye;
then, strong in faith and prayer,
his spirit, with a bound,
burst its encumbering clay:
his tent at sunrise, on the ground,
a darkened ruin lay.

The pains of death are past,
labour and sorrow cease,
and, life's long warfare closed at last,
his soul is found in peace.
Soldier of Christ! well done;
praise be thy new employ:
and while eternal ages run,
rest in thy Saviour's joy.

J. MONTGOMERY

397 *ODE ON THE SPRING*

LO! where the rosy-bosom'd Hours
  fair Venus' train, appear,
disclose the long-expecting flowers
  and wake the purple year!
the Attic warbler pours her throat
responsive to the cuckoo's note,
the untaught harmony of Spring:
while, whispering pleasure as they fly,
cool Zephyrs through the clear blue sky
  their gather'd fragrance fling.

Where'er the oak's thick branches stretch
  a broader, browner shade,
where'er the rude and moss-grown beech
  o'er-canopies the glade,

beside some water's rushy brink
with me the Muse shall sit, and think
(at ease reclined in rustic state)
how vain the ardour of the Crowd,
how low, how little are the Proud,
 how indigent the Great!

398 Still is the toiling hand of Care;
 the panting herds repose:
yet hark, how thro' the peopled air
 the busy murmur glows!
the insect youth are on the wing,
eager to taste the honied spring
and float amid the liquid noon:
some lightly o'er the current skim,
some show their gaily-gilded trim
 quick-glancing to the sun.

To Contemplation's sober eye
 such is the race of Man:
and they that creep, and they that fly
 shall end where they began.
Alike the busy and the gay
but flutter thro' life's little day,
in Fortune's varying colours drest:
brush'd by the hand of rough Mischance
or chill'd by Age, their airy dance
 they leave, in dust to rest.

 T. GRAY

399 *TO MUSIC*

O MUSIC, sphere-descended maid,
 friend of Pleasure, Wisdom's aid!
why, goddess, why, to us denied,
lay'st thou thy ancient lyre aside?
as in that loved Athenian bower
you learn'd an all-commanding power,
thy mimic soul, O nymph endear'd!
can well recall what then it heard.
Where is thy native simple heart
devote to Virtue, Fancy, Art?
Arise, as in that elder time,
warm, energic, chaste, sublime!
thy wonders, in that god-like age,
fill thy recording Sister's page;—

'tis said, and I believe the tale,
thy humblest reed could more prevail
had more of strength, diviner rage,
than all which charms this laggard age,
e'en all at once together found
Cecilia's mingled world of sound:—
O bid our vain endeavours cease:
revive the just designs of Greece:
return in all thy simple state!
confirm the tales her sons relate!

W. COLLINS

400   *HYMNUS IN HERMEAN ATARNENSEM*

Ἀρετὰ πολύμοχθε γένει βροτείῳ
θήραμα κάλλιστον βίῳ,
σᾶς πέρι, παρθένε, μορφᾶς
καὶ θανεῖν ζαλωτὸς ἐν Ἑλλάδι πότμος
καὶ πόνους τλῆναι μαλεροὺς ἀκάμαντας·
τοῖον ἐπὶ φρένα βάλλεις
καρπόν τ' ἀθάνατον χρυσοῦ τε κρείσσω
καὶ γονέων μαλακαυγήτοιό θ' ὕπνου.
σεῦ δ' ἕνεχ' οὐκ Διὸς Ἡρακλέης
Λήδας τε κοῦροι πόλλ' ἀνέτλασαν
ἔργοις σὰν ἀγρεύοντες δύναμιν.
σοῖς δὲ πόθοις Ἀχιλεὺς
Αἴας τ' Ἀίδαο δόμους ἦλθον·
σᾶς δ' ἕνεκεν φιλίου μορφᾶς καὶ Ἀταρνέος
ἔντροφος ἀελίου χήρωσεν αὐγάς·
τοιγὰρ ἀοίδιμος ἔργοις,
ἀθάνατόν τέ μιν αὐξήσουσι Μοῦσαι
Μναμοσύνας θύγατρες, Διὸς ξενίου σέβας
αὔξουσαι φιλίας τε γέρας βεβαίου.

ARISTOTELES

401   *THE LEGEND OF CYRENE*

Ἁ μὲν οὔθ' ἱστῶν παλιμβάμους ἐφίλησεν ὁδούς,
οὔτε δείπνων οἰκοριᾶν μεθ' ἑταιρᾶν τέρψιας,
ἀλλ' ἀκόντεσσίν τε χαλκέοις
φασγάνῳ τε μαρναμένα κεράϊζεν ἀγρίους

θῆρας, ἣ πολλάν τε καὶ ἀσύχιον
βουσὶν εἰράναν παρέχοισα πατρῴαις, τὸν δὲ σύγκοιτον
γλυκὺν
παῦρον ἐπὶ γλεφάροις
ὕπνον ἀναλίσκοισα ῥέποντα πρὸς ἀῶ.
Κίχε νιν λέοντί ποτ' εὐρυφαρέτρας
ὀμβρίμῳ μούναν παλαίοισαν
ἄτερ ἐγχέων ἑκάεργος Ἀπόλλων·
αὐτίκα δ' ἐκ μεγάρων Χείρωνα προσέννεπε φωνᾷ·
Σεμνὸν ἄντρον, Φιλυρίδα, προλιπὼν θυμὸν γυναικὸς καὶ
μεγάλαν δύνασιν
θαύμασον, οἷον ἀταρβεῖ νεῖκος ἄγει κραδίᾳ, μόχθον
καθύπερθε νεᾶνις
ἦτορ ἔχοισα· φόβῳ δ' οὐ κεχείμανται φρένες.
τίς νιν ἀνθρώπων τέκεν; ποίας δ' ἀποσπασθεῖσα φύτλας
ὀρέων κευθμῶνας ἔχει σκιοέντων,
γεύεται δ' ἀλκᾶς ἀπειράντου.

PINDARVS

402   *HYMN TO THE SUN UNDER ECLIPSE*

Ἀκτὶς Ἀελίου, τί, πολύσκοπε, μήδομένα, μᾶτερ ὀμ-
μάτων·
ἄστρον ὑπέρτατον ἐν ἀμέρᾳ κλεπτόμενον,
ἔθηκας ἀμάχανον ἰσχὺν ποτανὰν ἀνδράσιν
καὶ σοφίας ὁδόν,
ἐπίσκοτον ἀτραπὸν ἐσσυμένα
ἐλαύνειν τι νεώτερον ἢ πάρος;
ἀλλά σε πρὸς Διὸς ἵππους ζαθέας ἱκετεύω
ἀπήμον' ἐς ὄλβον τράποις Θήβαις,
ὦ πότνια, πάγκοινον τέρας.
πολέμου δ' εἰ σᾶμα φέρεις τινός, ἢ καρποῦ φθίσιν,
ἢ νιφετοῦ σθένος ὑπέρφατον,
ἢ στάσιν οὐλομέναν, ἢ πόντου κενέωσιν ἀνὰ πέδον,
ἢ παγετὸν χθονός, ἢ νότιον θέρος ὕδατι ζακότῳ διερόν,
ἢ γαῖαν κατακλύσαισα θήσεις ἀνδρῶν νέον ἐξ ἀρχᾶς
γένος,
ὀλοφύρομαι οὐδὲν ὅτι πάντων μέτα πείσομαι.

PINDARVS

403 THE BIRTH AND INFANCY OF HERACLES

Ἀλλ' ἐπεὶ σπλάγχνων ὕπο μάτερος αὐτίκα θαητὰν ἐς
  αἴγλαν παῖς Διὸς
ὠδῖνα φεύγων διδύμῳ σὺν κασιγνήτῳ μόλεν,
οὐ λαθὼν χρυσόθρονον
Ἥραν κροκωτὸν σπάργανον ἐγκατέβα·
ἀλλὰ θεῶν βασιλέα
σπερχθεῖσα θυμῷ πέμπε δράκοντας ἄφαρ·
τοὶ μὲν οἰχθεισᾶν πυλᾶν
ἐς θαλάμου μυχὸν εὐρὺν ἔβαν, τέκνοισιν ὠκείας γνάθους
ἀμφελίξασθαι μεμαῶτες· ὁ δ' ὀρθὸν μὲν ἄντεινεν κάρα,
  πειρᾶτο δὲ πρῶτον μάχας,
δισσαῖσι δοιοὺς αὐχένων
μάρψαις ἀφύκτοις χερσὶν ἑαῖς ὄφιας·
ἀγχομένοις δὲ χρόνος
ψυχὰς ἀπέπνευσεν μελέων ἀφάτων.
ἐκ δ' ἄρ' ἄτλατον βέλος
πλᾶξε γυναῖκας, ὅσαι τύχον Ἀλκμήνας ἀρήγοισαι λέχει·
καὶ γὰρ αὐτά, ποσσὶν ἄπεπλος ὀρούσαισ' ἀπὸ
  στρώμνας, ὅμως ἄμυνεν ὕβριν κνωδάλων.

404 Τάχυ δὲ Καδμείων ἀγοὶ χαλκέοις ἔδραμον σὺν ὅπλοις
  ἁθρόοι·
ἐν χερὶ δ' Ἀμφιτρύων κολεοῦ γυμνὸν τινάσσων φάσγανον
ἵκετ', ὀξείαις ἀνίαισι τυπείς· τὸ γὰρ οἰκεῖον πιέζει πάνθ'
  ὁμῶς·
εὐθὺς δ' ἀπήμων κραδία κᾶδος ἀμφ' ἀλλότριον.
ἔστα δὲ θάμβει δυσφόρῳ
τερπνῷ τε μιχθείς· εἶδε γὰρ ἐκνόμιον
λῆμά τε καὶ δύναμιν
υἱοῦ· παλίγγλωσσον δὲ οἱ ἀθάνατοι
ἀγγέλων ῥῆσιν θέσαν.
γείτονα δ' ἐκκάλεσεν Διὸς ὑψίστου προφάταν ἔξοχον,
ὀρθόμαντιν Τειρεσίαν· ὁ δὲ οἱ φράζε καὶ παντὶ
  στρατῷ, ποίαις ὁμιλήσει τύχαις,
ὅσσους μὲν ἐν χέρσῳ κτανών,
ὅσσους δὲ πόντῳ θῆρας ἀϊδροδίκας·
καί τινα σὺν πλαγίῳ
ἀνδρῶν κόρῳ στείχοντα τὸν ἐχθρότατον

φῆσέ νιν δώσειν μόρῳ.
καὶ γὰρ ὅταν θεοὶ ἐν πεδίῳ Φλέγρας γιγάντεσσιν μάχαν
ἀντιάζωσιν, βελέων ὑπὸ ῥιπαῖσι κείνου φαιδίμαν γαίᾳ
πεφύρσεσθαι κόμαν
ἔνεπεν· αὐτὸν μὰν ἐν εἰράνᾳ καμάτων μεγάλων ἐν σχερῷ
ἁσυχίαν τὸν ἅπαντα χρόνον ποίναν λαχόντ' ἐξαίρετον
ὀλβίοις ἐν δώμασι, δεξάμενον θαλερὰν Ἥβαν ἄκοιτιν
καὶ γάμον
δαίσαντα, πὰρ Δὶ Κρονίδᾳ σεμνὸν αἰνήσειν δόμον.

PINDARVS

405 *THE HAPPINESS OF THE GOOD IN A FUTURE STATE—
A DESCRIPTION OF THE ELYSIAN FIELDS*

Ἴσον δὲ νύκτεσσιν αἰεί,
ἴσα δ' ἐν ἁμέραις ἀέλιον ἔχοντες ἀπονέστερον
ἐσλοὶ δεδόρκαντι βίον, οὐ χθόνα ταράσσοντες ἐν χερὸς
ἀκμᾷ
οὐδὲ πόντιον ὕδωρ
κεινὰν παρὰ δίαιταν· ἀλλὰ παρὰ μὲν τιμίοις
θεῶν, οἵτινες ἔχαιρον εὐορκίαις, ἄδακρυν νέμονται
αἰῶνα· τοὶ δ' ἀπροσόρατον ὀκχέοντι πόνον.
ὅσοι δ' ἐτόλμασαν ἐστρὶς
ἑκατέρωθι μείναντες ἀπὸ πάμπαν ἀδίκων ἔχειν
ψυχάν, ἔτειλαν Διὸς ὁδὸν παρὰ Κρόνου τύρσιν· ἔνθα
μακάρων
νᾶσος ὠκεανίδες
αὖραι περιπνέοισιν, ἄνθεμα δὲ χρυσοῦ φλέγει,
τὰ μὲν χερσόθεν ἀπ' ἀγλαῶν δενδρέων, ὕδωρ δ' ἄλλα
φέρβει,
ὅρμοισι τῶν χέρας ἀναπλέκοντι καὶ κεφαλὰς
βουλαῖς ἐν ὀρθαῖς Ῥαδαμάνθυος,
ὃν πατὴρ ἔχει Κρόνος ἑτοῖμον αὑτῷ πάρεδρον,
πόσις ὁ πάντων Ῥέας ὑπέρτατον ἐχοίσας θρόνον.

PINDARVS

406 *THE SORROWS OF HELLAS FOR THE DEATH OF HER
HEROES BEFORE TROY*

Τὰ μὲν κατ' οἴκους ἐφ' ἑστίας ἄχη
τάδ' ἐστί, καὶ τῶνδ' ὑπερβατώτερα.

τὸ πᾶν δ' ἀπ' αἴας Ἑλλάδος ξυνορμένοις
πένθεια τλησικάρδιος
δόμων ἑκάστου πρέπει.
πολλὰ γοῦν θιγγάνει πρὸς ἧπαρ·
οὓς μὲν γάρ τις ἔπεμψεν
οἶδεν, ἀντὶ δὲ φωτῶν
τεύχη καὶ σποδὸς εἰς ἑκάστου δόμους ἀφικνεῖται.
ὁ χρυσαμοιβὸς δ' Ἄρης σωμάτων,
καὶ ταλαντοῦχος ἐν μάχῃ δορός,
πυρωθὲν ἐξ Ἰλίου
φίλοισι πέμπει βαρὺ
ψῆγμα δυσδάκρυτον, ἀν-
τήνορος σποδοῦ γεμίζων λέβητας εὐθέτου.
στένουσι δ' εὖ λέγοντες ἄν-
δρα τὸν μὲν ὡς μάχης ἴδρις,
τὸν δ' ἐν φοναῖς καλῶς πεσόντ' ἀλ-
λοτρίας διαὶ γυναικός·
τὰ δὲ σῖγά τις βαΰζει·
φθονερὸν δ' ὑπ' ἄλγος ἕρπει
προδίκοις Ἀτρείδαις.

AESCHYLUS

407 THE SCOURGE OF WAR

Ὄφελε πρότερον αἰθέρα δῦναι μέγαν ἢ τὸν πολύκοι-
νον Ἅιδαν
κεῖνος ἀνήρ, ὃς στυγερῶν ἔδειξ' ὅπλων
Ἕλλασι κοινὸν Ἄρη.
ἰὼ πόνοι πρόπονοι·
κεῖνος γὰρ ἔπερσεν ἀνθρώπους.
ἐκεῖνος οὐ στεφάνων
οὔτε βαθειᾶν κυλίκων
νεῖμεν ἐμοὶ τέρψιν ὁμιλεῖν,
οὔτε γλυκὺν αὐλῶν ὄτοβον
δύσμορος οὔτ' ἐννυχίαν
τέρψιν ἰαύειν.
ἐρώτων δ' ἐρώτων ἀπέπαυσεν, ὤμοι.
κεῖμαι δ' ἀμέριμνος οὕτως,
ἀεὶ πυκιναῖς δρόσοις
τεγγόμενος κόμας,
λυγρᾶς μνήματα Τροίας.

SOPHOCLES

408   ODE TO ROME

Χαῖρέ μοι, Ῥώμα, θυγάτηρ Ἄρηος,
χρυσεόμιτρα, δαΐφρων ἄνασσα,
σεμνὸν ἃ ναίεις ἐπὶ γᾶς Ὄλυμπον
    αἰὲν ἄθραυστον.

σοὶ μόνᾳ πρέσβειρα δέδωκε Μοῖρα
κῦδος ἀρρήκτω βασιλῆον ἀρχᾶς,
ὄφρα κοιρανῆον ἔχοισα κάρτος
    ἁγεμονεύῃς.

σᾷ δ' ὑπὸ σδεύγλᾳ κρατερῶν λεπάδνων
στέρνα γαίας καὶ πολιᾶς θαλάσσας
σφίγγεται· σὺ δ' ἀσφαλέως κυβερνᾷς
    ἄστεα λαῶν.

πάντα δὲ σφάλλων ὁ μέγιστος αἰών,
καὶ μεταπλάσσων βίον ἄλλοτ' ἄλλως,
σοὶ μόνᾳ πλησίστιον οὖρον ἀρχᾶς
    οὐ μεταβάλλει.

ἦ γὰρ ἐκ πάντων σὺ μόνα κρατίστους
ἄνδρας αἰχμητὰς μεγάλως λοχεύεις,
εὔσταχυν, Δάματρος ὅπως, ἀνεῖσα
    καρπὸν ἀπ' ἀνδρῶν.

                                MELINNO

409 *THE POWER OF HARMONY TO CURB THE TURBULENT
         PASSIONS OF THE SOUL*

Χρυσέα φόρμιγξ, Ἀπόλλωνος καὶ ἰοπλοκάμων
σύνδικον Μοισᾶν κτέανον· τᾶς ἀκούει μὲν βάσις, ἀ-
    γλαΐας ἀρχά,
πείθονται δ' ἀοιδοὶ σάμασιν,
ἁγησιχόρων ὁπόταν προοιμίων ἀμβολὰς τεύχῃς ἐλελι-
    ζομένα.
καὶ τὸν αἰχματὰν κεραυνὸν σβεννύεις
ἀενάου πυρός· εὕδει δ' ἀνὰ σκάπτῳ Διὸς αἰετός,
    ὠκεῖαν πτέρυγ' ἀμφοτέρωθεν χαλάξαις,
ἀρχὸς οἰωνῶν, κελαινῶπιν δ' ἐπὶ οἱ νεφέλαν

ἀγκύλῳ κρατί, γλεφάρων ἁδὺ κλαΐστρον, κατέχευας· ὁ
    δὲ κνώσσων
ὑγρὸν νῶτον αἰωρεῖ, τεαῖς
ῥιπαῖσι κατασχόμενος. καὶ γὰρ βιατὰς Ἄρης, τρα-
    χεῖαν ἄνευθε λιπὼν
ἐγχέων ἀκμὰν, ἰαίνει καρδίαν
κώματι, κῆλα δὲ καὶ δαιμόνων θέλγει φρένας,
        ἀμφί τε Λατοΐδα σοφίᾳ βαθυκόλπων τε Μοισᾶν.
Ὅσσα δὲ μὴ πεφίλακε Ζεὺς ἀτύζονται βοὰν
Πιερίδων ἀΐοντα, γᾶν τε καὶ πόντον κατ' ἀμαιμάκετον,
ὅς τ' ἐν αἰνᾷ Ταρτάρῳ κεῖται, θεῶν πολέμιος,
Τυφὼς ἑκατοντακάρανος· τόν ποτε
Κιλίκιον θρέψεν πολυώνυμον ἄντρον· νῦν γε μὰν
ταί θ' ὑπὲρ Κύμας ἁλιέρκεες ὄχθαι
Σικελία τ' αὐτοῦ πιέζει στέρνα λαχνάεντα· κίων δ' οὐ-
    ρανία συνέχει,
νιφόεσσ' Αἴτνα, πάνετες χιόνος ὀξείας τιθήνα.
                                            PINDARVS

410 *PELOPS' INVOCATION OF NEPTUNE FOR HELP TO
WIN HIPPODAMIA FROM HER FATHER OENOMAUS*

Πρὸς εὐάνθεμον δ' ὅτε φυὰν
λάχναι νιν μέλαν γένειον ἔρεφον,
ἑτοῖμον ἀνεφρόντισεν γάμον
Πισάτα παρὰ πατρὸς εὔδοξον Ἱπποδάμειαν
σχεθέμεν· ἀγχὶ δ' ἐλθὼν πολιᾶς ἁλὸς οἶος ἐν ὄρφνᾳ
ἄπυεν βαρύκτυπον
Εὐτρίαιναν· ὁ δ' αὐτῷ
πὰρ ποδὶ σχεδὸν φάνη.
τῷ μὲν εἶπε· Φίλια δῶρα Κυπρίας ἄγ' εἴ τι, Ποσείδαον,
    ἐς χάριν
τέλλεται, πέδασον ἔγχος Οἰνομάου χάλκεον,
ἐμὲ δ' ἐπὶ ταχυτάτων πόρευσον ἁρμάτων
ἐς Ἆλιν, κράτει δὲ πέλασον.
ἐπεὶ τρεῖς τε καὶ δέκ' ἄνδρας ὀλέσαις
ἐρῶντας ἀναβάλλεται γάμον
θυγατρός. ὁ μέγας δὲ κίνδυνος ἄναλκιν οὐ φῶτα λαμ-
    βάνει.

into Latin Lyric Verse 195

θανεῖν δ' οἷσιν ἀνάγκα, τί κέ τις ἀνώνυμον
γῆρας ἐν σκότῳ καθήμενος ἕψοι μάταν,
ἁπάντων καλῶν ἄμμορος; ἀλλ' ἐμοὶ μὲν οὗτος ἄεθλος
ὑποκείσεται· τὺ δὲ πρᾶξιν φίλαν δίδοι.
Ὣς ἔννεπεν· οὐδ' ἀκράντοις ἐφάψατ' ὧν ἔπεσι. τὸν μὲν ἀγάλλων θεὸς
ἔδωκεν δίφρον τε χρύσεον πτεροῖσίν τ' ἀκάμαντας ἵππους·
ἕλεν δ' Οἰνομάου βίαν παρθένον τε σύνευνον.

PINDARVS

THE STORY OF IAMUS AND HOW THE GIFT OF PROPHECY WAS CONFERRED ON HIM

Ἦλθεν δ' ὑπὸ σπλάγχνων ὑπ' ὠδῖνός τ' ἐρατᾶς Ἴαμος
ἐς φάος αὐτίκα. τὸν μὲν κνιζομένα
λεῖπε χαμαί· δύο δὲ γλαυκῶπες αὐτὸν
δαιμόνων βουλαῖσιν ἐθρέψαντο δράκοντες ἀμεμφεῖ
ἰῷ μελισσᾶν καδόμενοι. βασιλεὺς δ' ἐπεὶ
πετραέσσας ἐλαύνων ἵκετ' ἐκ Πυθῶνος, ἅπαντας ἐν οἴκῳ
εἴρετο παῖδα, τὸν Εὐάδνα τέκοι· Φοίβου γὰρ αὐτὸν φᾶ γεγάκειν
πατρός, περὶ θνατῶν δ' ἔσεσθαι μάντιν ἐπιχθονίοις
ἔξοχον, οὐδέ ποτ' ἐκλείψειν γενεάν.
ὣς ἄρα μάννε. τοὶ δ' οὔτ' ὦν ἀκοῦσαι
οὔτ' ἰδεῖν εὔχοντο πεμπταῖον γεγενημένον. ἀλλ' ἐν
κέκρυπτο γὰρ σχοίνῳ βατίᾳ τ' ἐν ἀπειράτῳ,
ἴων ξανθαῖσι καὶ παμπορφύροις ἀκτῖσι βεβρεγμένος ἁβρὸν
σῶμα· τὸ καὶ κατεφάμιξεν καλεῖσθαί μιν χρόνῳ σύμπαντι μάτηρ
τοῦτ' ὄνυμ' ἀθάνατον. τερπνᾶς δ' ἐπεὶ χρυσοστεφάνοιο λάβεν
καρπὸν Ἥβας, Ἀλφεῷ μέσσῳ καταβὰς ἐκάλεσσε Ποσειδᾶν' εὐρυβίαν,
ὃν πρόγονον, καὶ τοξοφόρον Δάλου θεοδμάτας σκοπόν,
αἰτέων λαοτρόφον τιμάν τιν' ἑᾷ κεφαλᾷ,
νυκτὸς ὑπαίθριος· ἀντεφθέγξατο δ' ἀρτιεπὴς

13—2

πατρία ὅσσα, μετάλλασέν τέ μιν· Ὄρσο, τέκνοι,
δεῦρο πάγκοινον ἐς χώραν ἴμεν φάμας ὄπισθεν.

PINDARVS

412   THE DISTAFF

Γλαύκας ὦ φιλέριθ᾽ ἀλακάτα δῶρον Ἀθανάας
γύναιξιν, νόος οἰκωφελίας αἷσιν ἐπάβολος,
θάρσεισ᾽ ἄμμιν ὑμάρτη πόλιν ἐς Νείλεω ἀγλάαν,
ὅππυι Κύπριδος ἶρον καλάμῳ χλῶρον ὑπασσάλῳ.
τυῖδε γὰρ πλόον εὐάνεμον αἰτήμεθα πὰρ Διός,
ὅππως ξέννον ἔμον τέρψομ᾽ ἰδὼν κἀντιφίλησ᾽ ἐῶ,
Νικίαν, Χαρίτων ἰμεροφώνων ἱερὸν φύτον,
καὶ σὲ τὰν ἐλέφαντος πολυμόχθω γεγενημέναν
δῶρον Νικιάας εἰς ἀλόχω χέρρας ὀπάσσομεν,
σὺν τᾷ πόλλα μὲν ἔργ᾽ ἐκτελέσεις ἀνδρείοις πέπλοις,
πόλλα δ᾽ οἷα γύναικες φορέοισ᾽ ὑδάτινα βράκη,
δὶς γὰρ μάτερες ἄρνων μαλάκοις ἐν βοτάνᾳ πόκοις
πέξαιντ᾽ αὐτοένει, Θευγένιδός γ᾽ ἔννεκ᾽ εὐσφύρω·
οὕτως ἀνυσίεργος, φιλέει δ᾽ ὅσσα σαόφρονες.
οὐ γὰρ εἰς ἀκίδρας οὐδ᾽ ἐς ἀέργω κεν ἐβολλόμαν
ὕπασσαί σε δόμοις ἀμμετέρας ἔσσαν ἀπὺ χθόνος.
καὶ γάρ τοι πάτρις, ἃν ὦξ Ἐφύρας κτίσσε ποτ᾽ Ἀρχίας
νάσω Τρινακρίας μύελον, ἀνδρῶν δοκίμων πόλιν·
νῦν μὰν οἶκον ἔχοισ᾽ ἄνερος, ὃς πολλ᾽ ἐδάη σόφα
ἀνθρώποισι νόσοις φύρμακα λύγραις ἀπαλακέμεν,
οἰκήσεις κατὰ Μίλλατον ἐράνναν πεδ᾽ Ἰαόνων,
ὡς εὐαλάκατος Θεύγενις ἐν δαμότισιν πέλη,
καὶ οἱ μνᾶστιν ἄει τῶ φιλαοίδω παρέχῃς ξένω.
κῆνο γάρ τις ἐρεῖ τὤπος ἰδών σ᾽· ἦ μεγάλα χάρις
δώρῳ σὺν ὀλίγῳ· πάντα δὲ τίματα τὰ πὰρ φίλων.

THEOCRITVS

413   THE SPOILS OF WAR

Μαρμαίρει δὲ μέγας δόμος χάλκῳ· παῖσα δ᾽ Ἄρῃ κε-
    κόσμηται στέγα
λάμπραισιν κυνίαισι, κατ τᾶν λεῦκοι καθίπερθεν ἵππιοι
    λόφοι
νεύοισιν, κεφάλαισιν ἄνδρων ἀγάλματα, χάλκιαι δὲ
    πασσάλοις

κρύπτοισιν περικείμεναι λάμπραι κνάμιδες, ἄρκος ἰσχύ-
ρω βέλευς,
θώρακές τε νέω λίνω κώϊλαί τε κατ' ἄσπιδες βεβλή-
μεναι·
πὰρ δὲ Χαλκίδικαι σπάθαι, πὺρ δὲ ζώματα πολλὰ
καὶ κυπάσσιδες·
τῶν οὐκ ἔστι λάθεσθ', ἐπειδὴ πρώτιστ' ὑπὰ ἔργον
ἔσταμεν τόδε.

ALCÆVS

414 *ODE SUNG BY THE CHORUS OF THEBANS BEFORE
THE DISCOVERY OF LAIUS' MURDERER*

Τίς ὅντιν' ἁ θεσπιέπεια Δελφὶς εἶπε πέτρα
ἄρρητ' ἀρρήτων τελέσαντα φοινίαισι χερσίν;
ὥρα νιν ἀελλάδων
ἵππων σθεναρώτερον
φυγᾷ πόδα νωμᾶν.
ἔνοπλος γὰρ ἐπ' αὐτὸν ἐπενθρώσκει
πυρὶ καὶ στεροπαῖς ὁ Διὸς γενέτας,
δειναὶ δ' ἅμ' ἕπονται
Κῆρες ἀναπλάκητοι·
ἔλαμψε γὰρ τοῦ νιφόεντος ἀρτίως φανεῖσα
φάμα Παρνασοῦ τὸν ἄδηλον ἄνδρα πάντ' ἰχνεύειν·
φοιτᾷ γὰρ ὑπ' ἀγρίαν
ὕλαν ἀνά τ' ἄντρα καὶ
πέτρας ἅτε ταῦρος,
μέλεος μελέῳ ποδὶ χηρεύων,
τὰ μεσόμφαλα γᾶς ἀπονοσφίζων
μαντεῖα· τὰ δ' ἀεὶ
ζῶντα περιποτᾶται.

SOPHOCLES

415 *THE CONTEST FOR THE HAND OF DEIANIRA*

Μέγα τι σθένος ἁ Κύπρις ἐκφέρεται νίκας ἀεί.
καὶ τὰ μὲν θεῶν
παρέβαν, καὶ ὅπως Κρονίδαν ἀπάτασεν οὐ λέγω,
οὐδὲ τὸν ἔννυχον Ἅιδαν,
ἢ Ποσειδάωνα τινάκτορα γαίας·

ἀλλ' ἐπὶ τάνδ' ἄρ' ἄκοιτιν
τίνες ἀμφίγυοι κατέβαν πρὸ γάμων, τίνες
πάμπληκτα παγκόνιτά τ' ἐξῆλθον ἆεθλ' ἀγώνων.
ὁ μὲν ἦν ποταμοῦ σθένος, ὑψίκερω τετραόρου
φάσμα ταύρου,
Ἀχελῷος ἀπ' Οἰνιαδᾶν, ὁ δὲ Βακχείας ἄπο
ἦλθε παλίντονα Θήβας
τόξα καὶ λόγχας ῥόπαλόν τε τινάσσων,
παῖς Διός· οἳ τότ' ἀολλεῖς
ἴσαν ἐς μέσον ἱέμενοι λεχέων· μόνα δ'
εὔλεκτρος ἐν μέσῳ Κύπρις ῥαβδονόμει ξυνοῦσα.
τότ' ἦν χερός, ἦν δὲ τόξων πάταγος,
ταυρείων τ' ἀνάμιγδα κεράτων·
ἦν δ' ἀμφίπλεκτοι
κλίμακες, ἦν δὲ μετώπων ὀλόεντα
πλήγματα καὶ στόνος ἀμφοῖν.
ἁ δ' εὐῶπις ἁβρὰ
τηλαυγεῖ παρ' ὄχθῳ
ἦστο, τὸν ὃν προσμένουσ' ἀκοίταν.

SOPHOCLES

416 *THE UNFAILING DOOM OF SIN*

Τεάν, Ζεῦ, δύνασιν τίς ἀνδρῶν
ὑπερβασία κατάσχοι;
τὰν οὔθ' ὕπνος αἱρεῖ ποθ' ὁ παντογήρως
οὔτ' ἀκάματοι θεῶν
μῆνες· ἀγήρῳ δὲ χρόνῳ δυνάστας
κατέχεις Ὀλύμπου
μαρμαρόεσσαν αἴγλαν.
τό τ' ἔπειτα, καὶ τὸ μέλλον
καὶ τὸ πρὶν ἐπαρκέσει
νόμος ὅδ', οὐδὲν ἕρπειν
θνατῶν βιότῳ πάμπολύ γ' ἐκτὸς ἄτας.
ἁ γὰρ δὴ πολύπλαγκτος ἐλπὶς
πολλοῖς μὲν ὄνασις ἀνδρῶν,
πολλοῖς δ' ἀπάτα κουφονόων ἐρώτων·
εἰδότι δ' οὐδὲν ἕρπει,

πρὶν πυρὶ θερμῷ πόδα τις προσαύρῃ·
σοφίᾳ γὰρ ἔκ του
κλεινὸν ἔπος πέφανται,
τὸ κακὸν δοκεῖν ποτ' ἐσθλὸν
τῷδ' ἔμμεν, ὅτῳ φρένας
θεὸς ἄγει πρὸς ἄταν·
πράσσει δ' ὀλιγοστὸν χρόνον ἐκτὸς ἄτας.

SOPHOCLES

417   *THE LAMENT OF ELECTRA*

Ὦ φάος ἁγνὸν
καὶ γῆς ἰσόμοιρ' ἀήρ, ὥς μοι
πολλὰς μὲν θρήνων ᾠδάς,
πολλὰς δ' ἀντήρεις ᾔσθου
στέρνων πλαγὰς αἱμασσομένων,
ὁπόταν δνοφερὰ νὺξ ὑπολειφθῇ·
τὰ δὲ παννυχίδων ἤδη στυγεραὶ
ξυνίσασ' εὐναὶ μογερῶν οἴκων,
ὅσα τὸν δύστηνον ἐμὸν θρηνῶ
πατέρ', ὃν κατὰ μὲν βάρβαρον αἶαν
φοίνιος Ἄρης οὐκ ἐξένισεν,
μήτηρ δ' ἡμὴ χὠ κοινολεχὴς
Αἴγισθος, ὅπως δρῦν ὑλοτόμοι,
σχίζουσι κάρα φονίῳ πελέκει.
κοὐδεὶς τούτων οἶκτος ἀπ' ἄλλης
ἢ 'μοῦ φέρεται, σοί, πάτερ, οὕτως
αἰκῶς οἰκτρῶς τε θανόντος.
ἀλλ' οὐ μὲν δὴ
λήξω θρήνων στυγερῶν τε γόων,
ἔς τ' ἂν παμφεγγεῖς ἄστρων
ῥιπάς, λεύσσω δὲ τόδ' ἦμαρ,
μὴ οὐ τεκνολέτειρ' ὥς τις ἀηδὼν
ἐπὶ κωκυτῷ τῶνδε πατρῴων
πρὸ θυρῶν ἠχὼ πᾶσι προφωνεῖν.

SOPHOCLES

418   *THE REVENGE OF DEMETER FOR THE LOSS
              OF HER DAUGHTER*

Δρομαίων δ' ὅτε πολυπλανήτων
μάτηρ ἔπαυσε πόνων,

ματεύουσ' ἀπόρους
θυγατρὸς ἁρπαγὰς δολίους,
χιονοθρέμμονας δ' ἐπέρασ'
Ἰδαίαν Νυμφᾶν σκοπιάς·
ῥίπτει δ' ἐν πένθει
πέτρινα κατὰ δρία πολυνιφέα·
βροτοῖσι δ' ἄχλοα πεδία γᾶς
οὐ καρπίζουσ' ἀρότοις
λαῶν φθείρει γενεάν·
ποίμναις δ' οὐχ ἵει θαλερὰς
βοσκὰς εὐφύλλων ἑλίκων·
πολέων δ' ἀπέλειπε βίος,
οὐδ' ἦσαν θεῶν θυσίαι,
βωμοῖς τ' ἄφλεκτοι πέλανοι·
πηγάς τ' ἀμπαύει δροσερὰς
λευκῶν ἐκβάλλειν ὑδάτων
πένθει παιδὸς ἀλάστῳ.

EVRIPIDES

419 *THE WISDOM OF SELF-CONTROL AND EVIL
CONSEQUENCES OF PRIDE*

Ἀχαλίνων στομάτων
ἀνόμου τ' ἀφροσύνας
τὸ τέλος δυστυχία·
ὁ δὲ τᾶς ἡσυχίας
βίοτος καὶ τὸ φρονεῖν
ἀσάλευτόν τε μένει
καὶ συνέχει δώματα· πόρ-
σω γὰρ ὅμως αἰθέρα ναί-
οντες ὁρῶσιν τὰ βροτῶν Οὐρανίδαι·
τὸ σόφον δ' οὐ σοφία,
τό τε μὴ θνατὰ φρονεῖν.
βραχὺς αἰών· ἐπὶ τούτου
δέ τις ἂν μεγάλα διώκων
τὰ πάροντ' οὐχὶ φέροι·
μαινομένων οἵδε τρόποι
καὶ κακοβούλων παρ' ἔμοιγε φωτῶν.

EVRIPIDES

420   THE EVILS OF UNCONTROLLED LOVE

Ἔρωτες ὑπὲρ μὲν ἄγαν
ἐλθόντες οὐκ εὐδοξίαν
οὐδ' ἀρετὰν παρέδωκαν ἀνδράσιν. εἰ δ' ἅλις ἔλθοι
Κύπρις, οὐκ ἄλλα θεὸς
εὔχαρις οὕτω.
μήποτ', ὦ δέσποιν', ἐπ' ἐμοὶ
χρυσέων τόξων ἐφείης
ἱμέρῳ χρίσασ' ἄφυκτον οἰστόν.
στέργοι δέ με σωφροσύνα,
δώρημα κάλλιστον θεῶν.
μηδέ ποτ' ἀμφιλόγους ὀργὰς ἀκόρεστά τε νείκη
θυμὸν ἐκπλήξασ' ἑτέ-
ροις ἐπὶ λέκτροις,
προσβάλοι δεινὰ Κύπρις, ἀ-
πτολέμους δ' εὐνὰς σεβίζουσ',
ὀξύφρων κρίνοι λέχη γυναικῶν.
ὦ πατρίς, ὦ δῶμά τ' ἐμόν,
μὴ δῆτ' ἄπολις γενοίμαν
τὸν ἀμαχανίας ἔχουσα
δυσπέρατον αἰῶν'
οἰκτροτάτων ἀχέων.
θανάτῳ θανάτῳ πάρος δαμείην
ἁμέραν τάνδ' ἐξανύσασα· μόχθων δ'
οὐκ ἄλλος ὕπερθεν
ἢ γᾶς πατρίας στέρεσθαι.

EVRIPIDES

421   ION'S MORNING SONG

Ἅρματα μὲν τάδε λαμπρὰ τεθρίππων
  ἥλιος ἤδη κάμπτει κατὰ γῆν,
ἄστρα δὲ φεύγει πῦρ τόδ' ἀπ' αἰθέρος
  ἐς νύχθ' ἱεράν,
Παρνησιάδες δ' ἄβατοι κορυφαὶ
καταλαμπόμεναι τὴν ἡμερίαν
  ἁψῖδα βρυτοῖσι δέχονται.
σμύρνης δ' ἀνύδρου καπνὸς εἰς ὀρόφους

Φοίβου πέτεται,
θάσσει δὲ γυνὴ τρίποδα ζάθεον
Δελφίς, ἀείδουσ' Ἕλλησι βοάς,
ἃς ἂν Ἀπόλλων κελαδήσῃ.
ἀλλ', ὦ Φοίβου Δελφοὶ θέραπες,
τὰς Κασταλίας ἀργυροειδεῖς
βαίνετε δίνας, καθαραῖς δὲ δρόσοις
ἀφυδρανάμενοι στείχετε ναούς·
στόμα τ' εὔφημον φρουρεῖν ἀγαθόν,
φήμας τ' ἀγαθὰς τοῖς ἐθέλουσιν
μαντεύεσθαι
γλώσσης ἰδίας ἀποφαίνειν.
ἡμεῖς δέ, πόνους οὓς ἐκ παιδὸς
μοχθοῦμεν ἀεί, πτόρθοισι δάφνης
στέφεσίν θ' ἱεροῖς ἐσόδους Φοίβου
καθαρὰς θήσομεν ὑγραῖς τε πέδον
ῥανίσιν νοτερόν, πτηνῶν τ' ἀγέλας,
αἳ βλάπτουσιν
σέμν' ἀναθήματα, τόξοισιν ἐμοῖς
φυγάδας θήσομεν· ὡς γὰρ ἀμήτωρ
ἀπάτωρ τε γεγὼς τοὺς θρέψαντας
Φοίβου ναοὺς θεραπεύω.

EVRIPIDES

422 *DIRGE ON ALCESTIS ADDRESSED TO ADMETUS*

Ἐγὼ καὶ διὰ μούσας
καὶ μετάρσιος ᾖξα, καὶ
πλείστων ἁψάμενος λόγων
κρεῖσσον οὐδὲν ἀνάγκας
ηὗρον, οὐδέ τι φάρμακον
Θρῄσσαις ἐν σανίσιν, τὰς
Ὀρφεία κατέγραψεν
γῆρυς, οὐδ' ὅσα Φοῖβος Ἀσκληπιάδαις ἔδωκε
φάρμακα πολυπόνοις ἀντιτεμὼν βροτοῖσιν.
μόνας δ' οὔτ' ἐπὶ βωμοὺς
ἐλθεῖν οὔτε βρέτας θεᾶς
ἔστιν, οὐ σφαγίων κλύει.
μή μοι, πότνια, μείζων

ἔλθοις ἢ τὸ πρὶν ἐν βίῳ.
καὶ γὰρ Ζεὺς ὅ τι νεύσῃ,
 σὺν σοὶ τοῦτο τελευτᾷ.
καὶ τὸν ἐν Χαλύβοις δαμάζεις σὺ βίᾳ σίδαρον,
οὐδέ τις ἀποτόμου λήματός ἐστιν αἰδώς.
καὶ σ' ἐν ἀφύκτοισι χερῶν εἷλε θεὰ δεσμοῖς·
τόλμα δ'· οὐ γὰρ ἀνάξεις ποτ' ἔνερθεν
 κλαίων τοὺς φθιμένους ἄνω.
καὶ θεῶν σκότιοι φθίνουσι
 παῖδες ἐν θανάτῳ.
φίλα μὲν ὅτ' ἦν μεθ' ἡμῶν,
φίλα δ' ἔτι καὶ θανοῦσα·
γενναιοτάταν δὲ πασᾶν
ἐζεύξω κλισίαις ἄκοιτιν.
μηδὲ νεκρῶν ὡς φθιμένων χῶμα νομιζέτθω
τύμβος σᾶς ἀλόχου, θεοῖσι δ' ὁμοίως
 τιμάσθω, σέβας ἐμπόρων.
 καί τις δοχμίαν κέλευθον
 ἐμβαίνων τόδ' ἐρεῖ·
Αὕτα ποτὲ προὔθαν' ἀνδρός,
νῦν δ' ἐστὶ μάκαιρα δαίμων,
χαῖρ', ὦ πότνι', εὖ δὲ δοίης.—
Τοῖαί νιν προσεροῦσι φᾶμαι.

EVRIPIDES

423 *ODE SUNG BY CAPTIVE TROJAN WOMEN ON THEIR WAY TO HELLAS*

Ἐγὼ δὲ πλόκαμον ἀναδέτοις
μίτραισιν ἐρρυθμιζόμαν
 χρυσέων ἐνόπτρων
λεύσσουσ' ἀτέρμονας εἰς αὐγάς,
ἐπιδέμνιος ὡς πέσοιμ' ἐς εὐνάν.
 ἀνὰ δὲ κέλαδος ἔμολε πόλιν·
κέλευσμα δ' ἦν κατ' ἄστυ Τροίας τόδ'· ὦ
παῖδες Ἑλλάνων πότε δὴ πότε τὰν
Ἰλιάδα σκοπιὰν πέρσαντες ἥξετ' οἴκους;
 λέχη δὲ φίλια μονόπεπλος
 λιποῦσα, Δωρὶς ὡς κόρα,

σεμνὰν προσίζουσ'·
οὐκ ἤνυσ' Ἄρτεμιν ἁ τλάμων·
ἄγομαι δὲ θανόντ' ἰδοῦσ' ἀκοίταν
  τὸν ἐμὸν ἅλιον ἐπὶ πέλαγος,
πόλιν τ' ἀποσκοποῦσ', ἐπεὶ νόστιμον
ναῦς ἐκίνησεν πόδα καί μ' ἀπὸ γᾶς
ὥρισεν Ἰλιάδος, τάλαιν', ἀπεῖπον ἄλγει,
τὰν τοῖν Διοσκόροιν Ἑλέναν κάσιν Ἰδαῖόν τε βούταν
αἰνόπαριν κατάρᾳ διδοῦσ', ἐπεί με γᾶς
  ἐκ πατρῴας ἀπώλεσεν
  ἐξῴκισέν τ' οἴκων γάμος, οὐ γάμος, ἀλλ' ἀλάστορός
  τις οἰζύς·
ἂν μήτε πέλαγος ἅλιον ἀπαγάγοι πάλιν,
μήτε πατρῷον ἵκοιτ' ἐς οἶκον.
                              EVRIPIDES

424 *THE JUDGMENT OF PARIS AND ITS DISASTROUS
                CONSEQUENCES*

Ταὶ δ' ἐπεὶ ὑλόκομον νάπος ἤλυθον, οὑρειᾶν
πιδάκων νίψαν αἰγλᾶντα σώματ' ἐν ῥοαῖς·
  ἔβαν δὲ Πριαμίδαν ὑπερ-
  βολαῖς λόγων δυσφρόνων
παραβαλλόμεναι. Κύπρις εἷλε λόγοισι δολίοις,
  τερπνοῖς μὲν ἀκοῦσαι,
πικρὰν δὲ σύγχυσιν βίου Φρυγῶν πόλει
  ταλαίνᾳ περγάμοις τε Τροίας.
εἴθε δ' ὑπὲρ κεφαλᾶς ἔβαλεν κακὸν
  ἁ τεκοῦσά νιν μόρον
  πρὶν Ἰδαῖον κατοικίσαι λέπας,
ὅτε νιν παρὰ θεσπεσίῳ δάφνᾳ
βόασε Κασσάνδρα κτανεῖν,
μεγάλαν Πριάμου πόλεως λώβαν.
τίν' οὐκ ἐπῆλθε, ποῖον οὐκ ἐλίσσετο
  δαμογερόντων βρέφος φονεύειν;
οὔτ' ἂν ἐπ' Ἰλιάσι ζυγὸν ἤλυθε
  δούλιον, σύ τ' ἄν, γύναι,
τυράννων ἔσχεθες δόμων ἕδρας·

παρέλυσε δ' ἂν Ἑλλάδος ἀλγεινοὺς
πόνους, ὅτ' ἀμφὶ Τρωΐαν
δεκέτεις ἀλάληντο νέοι λόγχαις·
λέχη τ' ἔρημ' ἂν οὔποτ' ἐξελείπετο,
καὶ τεκέων ὀρφανοὶ γέροντες.

EVRIPIDES

425   THE LOVE OF GOD SUPREME

Τί γὰρ ἀλκά, τί δὲ κάλλος,
τί δὲ χρύσος, τί δὲ φάμα,
βασιλήϊοί τε τιμαί,
παρὰ τὰς Θεοῦ μερίμνας;
ὁ μὲν ἵππον εὖ διώκοι,
ὁ δὲ τόξον εὖ τιταίνοι,
ὁ δὲ θημῶνας φυλάσσοι
κτεάνων, χρύσειον ὄλβον·
ἑτέρῳ δ' ἄγαλμα χαίτῃ
καταειμένη τενόντων,
πυλύϋμνος δέ κεν εἴη
παρὰ κούροις, παρὰ κούραις,
ἀμαρύγμασι προσώπων·
ἐμὲ δ' ἀψόφητον εἴη
βιοτὰν ἄσημον ἕλκειν,
τὰ μὲν ἐς ἄλλους ἄσημον,
τὰ δὲ πρὸς Θεὸν εἰδότα.
σοφία δέ μοι παρείη
ἀγαθὰ μὲν νεότατα,
ἀγαθὰ δὲ γῆρας ἕλκειν,
ἀγαθὰ δ' ἄνασσα πλούτου.
πενίαν δ' ἄμοχθος οἴσει
σοφία γελῶσα, πικραῖς
ἄβατον βίου μερίμναις·
μόνον εἰ τόσον παρείη
ὅσον ἄρκιον καλιῆς
ἀπὸ γειτόνων ἐρύκειν,
ἵνα μὴ χρεώ με κάμπτοι
ἐπὶ φροντίδας μελαίνας.

SYNESIVS

426 *THE TRIUMPH OF JUSTICE*

WITH joy, with joy now, sacred Thebes, resound,
   feast and dance shall revel round:
  fortune fav'ring now appears,
  dries the bitter fount of tears,
  and bids the exulting song arise,
for low in dust the mighty tyrant lies.
  Beyond our hopes from those dark shores,
  where Acheron's sad torrent roars,
   comes our chief, and holds again
    the glories of his reign.

The gods, the gods hear when the pious calls;
   and the guilty tyrant falls.
  Gold and fortune's wanton ray
  blinded mortals leads away,
  lets wisdom's voice be heard no more,
and draws the pageant pomp of lawless power.
  Yet shall the gods at length look down,
  to justice give her radiant crown,
   kind in virtue's cause declare,
   and crush wealth's dazzling car.

427 *THE RESTORATION OF KING CHARLES II*

AS, when the new-born phœnix takes his way
  his rich paternal regions to survey,
of airy choristers a numerous train
attend his wondrous progress o'er the plain;
so, rising from his father's urn,
so glorious did our Charles return;
the officious Muses came along,
a gay harmonious quire like angels ever young:
the Muse that mourns him now his happy triumph sung.
Even they could thrive in his auspicious reign;
and such a plenteous crop they bore
of purest and well-winnowed grain,
as Britain never knew before.
Though little was their hire, and light their gain,
yet somewhat to their share he threw;
fed from his hand they sung and flew,
like birds of paradise that lived on morning dew.

                  J. DRYDEN

428   *THE FUTURE STATE OF THE GOOD AND
           THE EVIL*

FOR whoso holds in righteousness the throne,
   he in his heart hath known
how the foul spirits of the guiltie dead,
   in chambers dark and dread,
of nether earth abide, and penal flame;
   where he whom none may name
lays bare the soul by stern necessity;
   seated in judgment high.

*   *   *   *   *

But who the thrice-renewed probation
   of either world may well endure;
and keep with righteous destination
   the soul from all transgression pure;
to such and such alone is given,
   to walk the rainbow paths of heaven,
to that tall city of allmighty time,
   where Ocean's balmy breezes play,
and flashing to the western day
the gorgeous blossoms of such blessed clime
now in the happy isles are seen
sparkling through the groves of green;
and now, all glorious to behold,
   tinge the wave with floating gold.
Hence are their garlands woven; hence their hands
filled with triumphant boughs,—the righteous doom
of Rhadamanthus.

429   *DREAM OF HUMAN PRAISE*

I SUNG the joyful Pæan clear,
   and, sitting, burnished without fear
the brand, the buckler, and the spear—

waiting to strive a happy strife,
to war with falsehood to the knife,
and not to lose the good of life—

at least, not rotting like a weed,
but, having sown some generous seed,
fruitful of further thought and deed,

to pass, when life her light withdraws,
not void of righteous self-applause,
nor in a merely selfish cause—

in some good cause, not in mine own,
to perish, wept for, honour'd, known,
and like a warrior overthrown;

whose eyes are dim with glorious tears,
when, soil'd with noble dust, he hears
his country's war-song thrill his ears;

then dying of a mortal stroke,
what time the foeman's line is broke,
and all the war is rolled in smoke.

A. TENNYSON

430   *HYMN TO THE SUN*

GIVER of glowing light
though but a god of other days,
   the kings and sages
   of wiser ages
still live and gladden in thy genial rays!

   King of the tuneful lyre,
still poets' hymns to thee belong;
   though lips are cold
   whereon of old
thy beams all turn'd to worshipping and song!

   Lord of the dreadful bow,
none triumph now for Python's death;
   but thou dost save
   from hungry grave
the life that hangs upon a summer breath.

   Father of rosy day,
no more thy clouds of incense rise;
   but waking flowers
   at morning hours
give out their sweets to meet thee in the skies.

   God of the Delphic fane,
no more thou listenest to hymns sublime;
   but they will leave
   on winds at eve
a solemn echo to the end of time.

T. HOOD

431   TO THE NAUTILUS

WHERE Ausonian summers glowing
   warm the deep to life and joyance,
and gentle zephyrs, nimbly blowing,
wanton with the waves that flowing
by many a land of ancient glory,
and many an isle renown'd in story,
leap along with gladsome buoyance,
      there, Marinere,
      dost thou appear,
in faery pinnace gaily flashing,
through the white foam proudly dashing,
the joyous playmate of the buxom breeze,
the fearless fondling of the mighty seas.

Thou the light sail boldly spre[a]dest,
o'er the furrow'd waters gliding,
thou nor wreck nor foeman dreadest,
thou nor helm nor compass needest,
while the sun is bright above thee,
while the bounding surges love thee,
in their deepening bosoms hiding,
      thou canst not fear,
      small Marinere,
for though the tides, with restless motion,
bear thee to the desert ocean,
far as the ocean stretches to the sky,
'tis all thy own, 'tis all thy empery.

                              H. COLERIDGE

432   THE VANITY OF FAME

HE that thirsts for glory's prize,
   thinking that the top of all,
let him view the expansed skies
   and the earth's contracted ball,
'twill shame him then, the name he wan
fills not the short walk of one man.

O why vainly strive you then
   to shake off the bands of fate,
though fame through the world of men
   should in all tongues your names relate,
and with proud titles swell that story,
the dark grave scorns your brightest glory.

There with nobles beggars sway,
   and kings with commons share one dust,
what news of Brutus at this day,
   or Fabricius the just?
Some rude verse cut in stone or lead
keeps up the names, but they are dead.

So shall you one day, past reprieve,
   lie perhaps without a name,
but if dead you think to live
   by this air of human fame,
know, when time stops that posthume breath,
you must endure a second death.

H. VAUGHAN

433   SOLIS ANIMI BONIS NOS BELLUIS PRÆSTARE

'TIS not rich furniture and gems
   with cedar-roofs and ancient stems,
nor yet a plenteous lasting flood
of gold, that makes man truly good.
Leave to enquire in what fair fields
a river runs which much gold yields,
virtue alone is the rich prize
can purchase stars and buy the skies.
Let others build with adamant,
or pillars of carved marble plant,
which rude and rough sometimes did dwell
far under earth and near to hell.
But richer much (from death released)
shines in the fresh groves of the east
the Phœnix or those fish that dwell
with silvered scales in Hiddekel.
Let others with rare various pearls
their garments dress and in forced curls
bind up their locks, look big and high,
and shine in robes of scarlet dye.
But in my thoughts more glorious far
those native stars and speckles are
which birds wear or the spots which we
in leopards dispersèd see.
Virtue alone and nought else can
a difference make 'twixt beast and man,

and on her wings above the spheres
to the true light his spirit bears.
H. VAUGHAN

434   ON THE UNCERTAINTY OF FORTUNE

LEAVE off unfit complaints and clear
from sighs your breast, and from black clouds
your brow,
when the sun shines not with his wonted cheer,
and fortune throws an averse cast for you.
That sea, which vext with Notus is,
the merry west-winds will to-morrow kiss.

The sun to-day rides drousily,
to-morrow 'twill put on a look more fair,
laughter and groaning do alternately
return, and tears sport's nearest neighbours are.
'Tis by the gods appointed so,
that good fate should with mingled dangers flow.

Who drave his oxen yesterday
doth now over the noblest Romans reign,
and on the Gabii and the Cures lay
the yoke which from the oxen he had ta'en.
Whom Hesperus saw poor and low
this morning's eye beholds him greatest now.

If fortune knit amongst her play
but seriousness; he shall again go home
to his old country-farm of yesterday,
to scoffing people no mean jest become:
and with the crowned axe, which he
had ruled the world, go back and prune some tree;
nay, if he want the fuel cold requires,
with his own fasces he shall make him fires.
A. COWLEY

435   TO SAXHAM

THOUGH frost and snow lock'd from mine eyes
that beauty which without door lies,
the gardens, orchards, walks, that so
I might not all thy pleasures know;
yet, Saxham, thou, within thy gate,
art of thyself so delicate,

so full of native sweets, that bless
thy roof with inward happiness;
as neither from, nor to thy store,
winter takes aught, or spring adds more.
The stranger's welcome each man there
stamped on his cheerful brow doth wear;
nor doth this welcome, or his cheer,
grow less, 'cause he stays longer here.
There's none observes, much less repines,
how often this man sups or dines.
Thou hast no porter at the door
t' examine or keep back the poor;
nor locks nor bolts; thy gates have been
made only to let strangers in:
untaught to shut, they do not fear
to stand wide open all the year;
careless who enters, for they know
thou never didst deserve a foe;
and as for thieves, thy bounty's such,
they cannot steal, thou giv'st so much.
T. CAREW

436   THE LONE ROCK

THERE is a single stone   above yon wave,
    a rocky islet lone—   where tempests rave.
What doth it there?—The sea restless and deep,
breaks round it mournfully,   and knows no sleep.

The sea hath hung it round   with its wild weed,
no place can *there* be found   for better seed.
Storm-beaten rock! no change 'tis thine to know,
only the water's range   of ebb and flow.

The happy sounds of earth   are not for thee,
the voice of human mirth,   of children's glee:
no song of birds is thine,   no crown of flowers!
say, dost thou not repine   through long lone
                                     hours?

Yet stars for thee are bright   in midnight skies,
and tranquil worlds of light   around thee rise:
they smoothe thine ocean-bed, its heavings cease,
while they, from o'er thy head, breathe on thee peace.

The wearied man of grief
to whom comes no relief

No human ties are left,

he dwells, a thing bereft—

Yet o'er him from above
and He whose name is Love,
and thus he thankful learns
and trusting, peaceful, turns

like thee I deem,
through life's dark dream.

earth's hopes are gone;

blighted—alone.

bright spirits bend,
calls him His friend;
why grief was given,
to God in Heaven.

T. V. FOSBERY

437   *THE SATYR CARRYING ALEXIS*

SOFTLY gliding as I go
with this burden full of woe,
through still silence of the night,
guided by the glow-worm's light,
hither am I come at last.
Many a thicket have I past;
not a twig that durst deny me
not a bush that durst descry me,
to the little bird that sleeps
on the tender spray; nor creeps
that hardy worm with pointed tail,
but if I be under sail,
flying faster than the wind,
leaving all the clouds behind,
but doth hide her tender head
in some hollow tree, or bed
of seeded nettles; not a hare
can be started from his fare
by my footing; nor a wish
is more sudden, nor a fish
can be found with greater ease
cut the vast unbounded seas,
leaving neither print nor sound,
than I, when nimbly on the ground
I measure many a league an hour.

J. FLETCHER

438 LOVELY nymph, with eye serene,
dimpled smile, and frolic mien ;
come, with airy step advancing,
come, with blooming Hebe dancing:
o'er the meads I see thee straying—
Youth and Sport around thee playing—
gay Content, thy sister fair,
twines a garland round thy hair.
Thine the lips of roseate dye;
thine the pleasure-sparkling eye ;
thine the cheek that softly glows,
brighter than the blushing rose!
guide me to thy favourite bowers,
to deck thy rural shrine with flowers.
In thy lowly, sylvan cell,
Peace and Virtue love to dwell ;
ever let me own thy sway,
still to thee my tribute pay
when Zephyr waves his balmy wing,
   to kiss the sweets of May ;
when the soft melodies of spring
   resound from every spray;
with thee, sweet maid! I'll rove along,
   and tread the morning dews;
to hear the wood-lark's early song,
   to court the laughing muse.

                      F. HEMANS

439   *TO VENICE*

SUN-GIRT City! thou hast been
Ocean's child, and then his queen ;
now is come a darker day,
and thou soon must be his prey,
if the power that raised thee here
hallow so thy watery bier.
A less drear ruin then than now
with thy conquest-branded brow
stooping to the slave of slaves
from thy throne among the waves,
wilt thou be,—when the sea-mew
flies, as once before it flew,

o'er thine isles depopulate,
and all is in its ancient state,
save where many a palace-gate
with green sea-flowers overgrown,
like a rock of ocean's own,
topples o'er the abandon'd sea
as the tides change sullenly.
The fisher on his watery way
wandering at the close of day,
will spread his sail and seize his oar
till he pass the gloomy shore,
lest thy dead should, from their sleep
bursting o'er the starlight deep,
lead a rapid masque of death
o'er the waters of his path.
P. B. SHELLEY

440 YES, I remember well
    the land of many hues,
whose charms what praise can tell,
   whose praise what heart refuse?
Sublime, but neither bleak nor bare,
nor misty are the mountains there,—
softly sublime, profusely fair!
up to their summits clothed in green,
and fruitful as the vales between,
    they lightly rise
    and scale the skies,
and groves and gardens still abound;
   for where no shoot
   could else take root,
the peaks are shelved and terraced round;
earthward appear, in mingled growth,
   the mulberry and maize,—above
the trellised vine extends to both
   the leafy shade they love.
Looks out the white-walled cottage here,
the lowly chapel rises near;
far down the foot must roam to reach
the lovely lake and bending beach;
whilst chestnut green and olive grey
chequer the steep and winding way.

441 MARIUS AMID THE RUINS OF CARTHAGE

CARTHAGE! I love thee—thou hast run
    as I, a warlike race!
and now thy glory's radiant sun
    hath veil'd in clouds his face:
thy days of pride—as mine—depart;
thy Gods desert thee, and thou art,
    a thing as nobly base
as he whose sullen footstep falls
to-night around thy crumbling walls.

And Rome hath heap'd her woes and pains
    alike on me and thee,
and thou dost sit in servile chains,—
    but mine they shall not be!
though fiercely o'er this aged head
the wrath of angry Jove is shed,
    Marius shall still be free,
free—in the pride that scorns his foe,
and bares the head to meet the blow.

I wear not yet thy slavery's vest,
    as desolate I roam;
and though the sword were at my breast,
    the torches in my home,
still—still, for orison and vow,
I'd fling them back my curse; as now
    I scorn, I hate thee—Rome!
my voice is weak to word and threat—
my arm is strong to battle yet!

                      W. M. PRAED

442 THE POWER OF MUSIC

NOW strike the golden lyre again:
    a louder yet, and yet a louder strain!
Break his bands of sleep asunder
and rouse him like a rattling peal of thunder.
Hark, hark! the horrid sound
has raised up his head:
as awaked from the dead
and amazed he stares around.

Revenge, revenge, Timotheus cries,
see the Furies arise!
see the snakes that they rear
how they hiss in their hair,
and the sparkles that flash from their eyes!
Behold a ghastly band
each a torch in his hand!
these are Grecian ghosts, that in battle were slain
and unburied remain
inglorious on the plain:
give the vengeance due
to the valiant crew!
Behold how they toss their torches on high,
how they point to the Persian abodes
and glittering temples of their hostile gods.
—The princes applaud with a furious joy;
and the King seized a flambeau with zeal to destroy;
Thais led the way,
to light him to his prey,
and, like another Helen, fired another Troy!

J. DRYDEN

443   *RULE BRITANNIA*

WHEN Britain first at Heaven's command
    arose from out the azure main,
this was the charter of her land,
    and guardian angels sung the strain:
rule Britannia! Britannia rules the waves!
    Britons never shall be slaves.

The nations not so blest as thee
    must in their turn to tyrants fall,
whilst thou shalt flourish great and free
    the dread and envy of them all.

Still more majestic shalt thou rise,
    more dreadful from each foreign stroke;
as the loud blast that tears the skies
    serves but to root thy native oak.

Thee haughty tyrants ne'er shall tame;
    all their attempts to bend thee down
will but arouse thy generous flame,
    and work their woe and thy renown.

To thee belongs the rural reign;
   thy cities shall with commerce shine;
all thine shall be the subject main,
   and every shore it circles thine!

The Muses, still with Freedom found,
   shall to thy happy coast repair;
blest isle, with matchless beauty crown'd,
   and manly hearts to guard the fair:—
rule Britannia! Britannia rules the waves!
   Britons never shall be slaves!

J. THOMSON

444 *PRIMVM BONVM EST NON NASCI, SECVNDVM CITIVS MORI*

O NOT to be were best for man,
   or else in infancy
ere life hath well commenced its span
   to draw one breath—and die.

When life's faint flame begins to shine,
   to wane away to-night;
O, this were better than to pine
   through years of withering blight.

For soon as youth unfolds its years,
   each hour unfolds its care—
its pleasures, snatch'd mid grief and tears,
   are pleasures vain as air.

Then, too, the passions urge their sway,
   and gender countless woes—
wrath, envy, murder, wait their way,
   till manhood sees its close.

At length with sullen, tottering pace,
   comes solitary age,—
the last of all his fleeting race,
   life's last and dreariest stage.

Friendless, alone, and desolate—
   he wanders to the tomb,
all ills attend his wretched fate
   and centre in his doom.

445   *WELCOME, WELCOME!*

WELCOME, welcome do I sing,
  far more welcome than the spring;
he that parteth from you never
  shall enjoy a spring for ever.

Love that to your voice is near,
  breaking from your ivory pale,
need not walk abroad to hear
  the delightful nightingale.

Love that looks still on your eyes,
  though the winter have begun
to benumb our arteries,
  shall not want the summer's sun.

Love that still may see your cheeks,
  where all rareness still reposes,
is a fool if e'er he seeks
  other lilies, other roses.

Love, to whom your soft lip yields,
  and perceives your breath in kissing;
all the odours of the fields
  never, never, shall be missing.

Love that question would anew
  what fair Eden was of old,
let him rightly study you
  and a brief of that behold.
                                W. BROWNE

446   *REPINING*

GENTLE river! gentle river!
  wilt thou thus complain for ever?
Why, when nought obstructs thy flow,
dost thou sigh, and murmuring low
strike my ear with sounds of woe?
is it that some sandbank's force
for an instant stay'd thy course?
has some shoal or rugged rock
stemm'd thy waves with sudden shock?
wail no longer, gentle river!
these are past and gone for ever;
yonder is the wish'd-for sea,
home of rest and peace for thee!

Why does man, when all is shining,
dim the brightness by repining?
why, when no dark cloud hangs o'er him,
dreads he still some rock before him,
weeps o'er woes he long has past,
mourns his joys which did not last?
Weep no more, nor sigh, nor mourn,
yonder is the wish'd-for bourn,
home of peace and rest for thee,—
Death and Immortality!

SIR T. CROFT

447 *HORATIAN ODE UPON CROMWELL'S RETURN
FROM IRELAND*

So restless Cromwell could not cease
in the inglorious arts of peace,
   but through adventurous war
   urgèd his active star:

and like the three-fork'd lightning first,
breaking the clouds where it was nurst,
   did thorough his own side
   his fiery way divide:

Then burning through the air he went
and palaces and temples rent;
   and Cæsar's head at last
   did through his laurels blast.

'Tis madness to resist or blame
the face of angry heaven's flame;
   and if we would speak true,
   much to the Man is due

who, from his private gardens, where
he lived reservèd and austere
   (as if his highest plot
   to plant the bergamot)

could by industrious valour climb
to ruin the great work of time,
   and cast the Kingdoms old
   into another mould.

Though Justice against Fate complain,
and plead the ancient Rights in vain—
but those do hold or break
as men are strong or weak.
A. MARVELL.

448   *THE FIRST OF APRIL*

MINDFUL of disaster past,
and shrinking at the northern blast,
the sleety storm returning still,
the morning hoar, and evening chill,
reluctant comes the timid Spring.
Scarce a bee with airy ring
murmurs the blossom'd boughs around,
that clothe the garden's southern bound:
scarce a sickly straggling flower
decks the rough castle's rifted tower:
scarce the hardy primrose peeps
from the dark dell's entangled steeps:
o'er the field of waving broom
slowly shoots the golden bloom:
and, but by fits, the furze-clad dale
tinctures the transitory gale.
While from the shrubbery's naked maze,
where the vegetable blaze
of Flora's brightest 'broidery shone,
every chequered charm is flown.
The swallow, for a moment seen,
skims in haste the village green;
from the gray moor, on feeble wing,
the screaming plovers idly spring;
the butterfly gay-painted soon
explores awhile the tepid noon;
and fondly trusts its tender dyes
to fickle suns and flattering skies.
T. WARTON

449   *MODERN JERUSALEM*

FALL'N is thy throne, O Israel!
silence is o'er thy plains:
thy dwellings all lie desolate,
thy children weep in chains.

where are the dews that fed thee,
   on Etham's barren shore?
That fire from heaven, which led thee,
   now lights thy path no more.

Lord! thou didst love Jerusalem—
   once she was all Thy own:
her love Thy fairest heritage:
   her power Thy glory's throne:
till evil came, and blighted
   Thy long-loved olive-tree:—
and Salem's shrines were lighted
   for other gods than Thee.

Then sunk the star of Solyma,
   then pass'd her glory's day,
like heath that in the wilderness
   the wild wind whirls away.
Silent and waste her bowers,
   where once the mighty trod,
and sunk those guilty towers,
   where Baal reigned as God.

'Go'—said the Lord—'ye Conquerors,
   steep in her blood your swords:
and raze to earth her battlements,
   for they are not the Lord's!'

T. MOORE

450   TO A SKYLARK

HAIL to thee, blithe Spirit!
      bird thou never wert,
that from heaven, or near it
      pourest thy full heart
in profuse strains of unpremeditated art.

   Higher still and higher
      from the earth thou springest
   like a cloud of fire;
      the blue deep thou wingest,
and singing still dost soar, and soaring ever singest.

   In the golden lightning
      of the sunken sun
   o'er which clouds are brightening,
      thou dost float and run,
like an unbodied joy whose race is just begun.

The pale purple even
   melts around thy flight:
like a star of heaven
   in the broad day-light
thou art unseen, but yet I hear thy shrill delight:

keen as are the arrows
   of that silver sphere,
whose intense lamp narrows
   in the white dawn clear
until we hardly see, we feel that it is there.

451 All the earth and air
   when thy voice is loud,
as, when night is bare,
   from one lonely cloud
the moon rains out her beams, and heaven is overflowed.

What thou art we know not;
   what is most like thee?
from rainbow clouds there flow not
   drops so bright to see
as from thy presence showers a rain of melody.

With thy clear keen joyance
   languor cannot be:
shadow of annoyance
   never came near thee:
thou lovest; but ne'er knew love's sad satiety.

Better than all measures
   of delightful sound,
better than all treasures
   that in books are found,
thy skill to poet were, thou scorner of the ground!

Teach me half the gladness
   that thy brain must know,
such harmonious madness
   from my lips would flow
the world should listen then, as I am listening now!
P. B. SHELLEY

452   TO A SKYLARK

 UP with me! up with me into the clouds!
  for thy song, Lark, is strong;
up with me, up with me into the clouds!
  singing, singing,
with clouds and sky about thee ringing,
  lift me, guide me till I find
that spot which seems so to thy mind!

 I have walked through wildernesses dreary
and to-day my heart is weary;
had I now the wings of a Faery,
up to thee would I fly.
There is a madness about thee, and joy divine
in that song of thine;
lift me, guide me high and high
to thy banqueting-place in the sky.

  Joyous as morning,
thou art laughing and scorning:
thou hast a nest for thy love and thy rest:
and, though little troubled with sloth,
drunken Lark! thou would'st be loth
to be such a traveller as I.
Happy, happy Liver,
with a soul as strong as a mountain river
pouring out praise to the Almighty Giver,
  joy and jollity be with us both!

Alas! my journey, rugged and uneven,
through prickly moors or dusty ways must wind;
but hearing thee or others of thy kind,
as full of gladness and as free of heaven,
I, with my fate contented, will plod on,
and hope for higher raptures, when life's day is done.
      W. WORDSWORTH

453   CONSTAT GENITUM NIHIL

 WHEN the sun from his rosy bed
  the dawning light begins to shed,
the drowsy sky uncurtains round,
and the (but now bright) stars all drown'd

in one great light, look dull and tame,
and homage his victorious flame.
Thus, when the warm Etesian wind
the earth's seal'd bosom doth unbind,
straight she her various store discloses
and purples every grove with roses;
but if the South's tempestuous breath
breaks forth, those blushes pine to death.
Oft in a quiet sky the deep
with unmoved waves seems fast asleep,
and oft again the blust'ring North
in angry heaps provokes them forth.
If then this world, which holds all nations,
suffer itself such alterations,
that not this mighty, massy frame,
nor any part of it can claim
one certain course, why should man prate
or censure the designs of fate?
Why from frail honours, and goods lent,
should he expect things permanent?
since 'tis enacted by divine decree,
that nothing mortal shall eternal be.

H. VAUGHAN

454 *COMFORT FROM HIS MUSE IN PRISON*

THOUGH I miss the flowery fields
with those sweets the spring-tide yields;
though of all those pleasures past
nothing now remains at last,
but remembrance, poor relief,
that more makes than mends my grief;
she's my mind's companion still
maugre envy's evil will;
(whence she should be driven too,
wer't in mortal's power to do).
She doth tell me where to borrow
comfort in the midst of sorrow;
makes the desolatest place
to her presence be a grace;
and the blackest discontents
to be pleasing ornaments.
In my former days of bliss
her divine skill taught me this,

that from everything I saw
I could some invention draw,
and raise pleasure to her height
through the meanest object's sight.
By the murmur of a spring
or the least bough's rusteling;
by a daisy whose leaves spread
shut when Titan goes to bed,
or a shady bush or tree,
she could more infuse in me,
than all nature's beauties can
in some other wiser man.

G. WITHER

455 ELEGY ON CAPTAIN MATTHEW HENDERSON

MOURN, Spring, thou darling of the year!
 ilk cowslip cup shall kep a tear;
thou, Simmer, while each corny spear
    shoots up its head,
thy gay, green, flow'ry tresses shear
    for him that's dead!

Thou, Autumn, wi' thy yellow hair,
in grief thy sallow mantle tear!
Thou, Winter, hurling through the air
    the roaring blast,
wide o'er the naked world declare
    the worth we've lost!

Mourn him, thou Sun, great source of light!
mourn, Empress of the silent night;
and you, ye twinkling Starnies bright,
    my Matthew mourn;
for through your orbs he's ta'en his flight
    ne'er to return.

O Henderson! the man, the brother!
and art thou gone and gone for ever?
and hast thou crossed that unknown river,
    life's dreary bound!
Like thee, where shall I find another,
    the world around!

Go to your sculptured tombs, ye Great,
in a' the tinsel trash of state!

but by thy honest turf I'll wait,
    thou man of worth!
and weep the ae best fellow's fate
    e'er lay in earth.
R. BURNS

456 FROM THE ODE ON A DISTANT PROSPECT OF ETON COLLEGE

ALAS! regardless of their doom
    the little victims play!
no sense have they of ills to come,
    no care beyond to-day:
yet see how all around 'em wait
the ministers of human fate
and black Misfortune's baleful train!
Ah shew them where in ambush stand
to seize their prey, the murderous band!
    ah tell them they are men!

These shall the fury Passions tear,
    the vultures of the mind,
Disdainful Anger, pallid Fear,
    and Shame that sculks behind;
or pining Love shall waste their youth,
or Jealousy with rankling tooth
that inly gnaws the secret heart;
and Envy wan, and faded Care,
grim visaged comfortless Despair,
    and Sorrow's piercing dart.

Ambition this shall tempt to rise,
    then whirl the wretch from high
to bitter Scorn a sacrifice
    and grinning Infamy.
The stings of Falsehood those shall try,
and hard Unkindness' alter'd eye,
that mocks the tear it forc'd to flow;
and keen Remorse with blood defiled,
and moody Madness laughing wild
    amid severest woe.
T. GRAY

457   *HOHENLINDEN*

On Linden, when the sun was low,
  all bloodless lay th' untrodden snow;
and dark as winter was the flow
  of Iser, rolling rapidly.

But Linden saw another sight,
when the drum beat at dead of night
commanding fires of death to light
  the darkness of her scenery.

By torch and trumpet fast arrayed
each horseman drew his battle-blade,
and furious every charger neigh'd
  to join the dreadful revelry.

Then shook the hills with thunder riven;
then rush'd the steed, to battle driven;
and louder than the bolts of Heaven
  far flashed the red artillery.

But redder yet that light shall glow
on Linden's hills of stainèd snow,
and bloodier yet the torrent flow
  of Iser, rolling rapidly.

'Tis morn; but scarce yon level sun
can pierce the war-clouds, rolling dun,
where furious Frank and fiery Hun
  shout in their sulph'rous canopy.

The combat deepens. On, ye Brave,
who rush to glory, or the grave!
Wave, Munich, all thy banners wave,
  and charge with all thy chivalry!

Few, few shall part, where many meet!
the snow shall be their winding-sheet,
and every turf beneath their feet
  shall be a soldier's sepulchre.

                              T. CAMPBELL.

458   *ODE TO WINTER*

O Sire of storms! whose savage car
  the Lapland drum delights to hear,
when Frenzy with her bloodshot eye
implores thy dreadful deity—

archangel! Power of desolation!
fast descending as thou art,
say, hath mortal invocation
spells to touch thy stony heart:
then, sullen Winter! hear my prayer,
and gently rule the ruin'd year;
nor chill the wanderer's bosom bare
nor freeze the wretch's falling tear:
to shuddering Want's unmantled bed
   thy horror-breathing agues cease to lend,
and gently on the orphan head
   of Innocence descend.

But chiefly spare, O king of clouds:
the sailor on his airy shrouds,
when wrecks and beacons strew the steep
and spectres walk along the deep.
Milder yet thy snowy breezes
   pour on yonder tented shores
where the Rhine's broad billow freezes,
   or the dark-brown Danube roars.
O winds of Winter! list ye there
to many a deep and dying groan?
Or start, ye demons of the midnight air,
   at shrieks and thunders louder than your own?
Alas! e'en your unhallow'd breath
   may spare the victim fallen low;
but Man will ask no truce to death,
   no bounds to human woe.
T. CAMPBELL.

459   THE CONSTITUTION OF A STATE

WHAT constitutes a state?
   not high-raised battlement or laboured mound,
   thick wall or moated gate:
not cities proud, with spires and turrets crowned:
   not bays and broad-armed ports,
where, laughing at the storm, rich navies ride:
   not starred and spangled courts,
where low-bred baseness wafts perfume to pride.
   No: men, high-minded men,
with powers as far above dull brutes endued,
   in forest, brake, or den,
as beasts excel cold rocks and brambles rude:

  men who their duties know,
but know their rights; and knowing dare maintain,
  prevent the long-aim'd blow,
and crush the tyrant while they rend the chain.
  These constitute a state,
and sovereign Law, that state's collected will,
  o'er thrones and globes elate
sits empress, crowning good, repressing ill;
  smit by her sacred frown,
the fiend Discretion like a vapour sinks,
  and e'en the all-dazzling crown
hides his faint rays and at her bidding shrinks.
  Such was this heaven-loved isle,
than Lesbos fairer, and the Cretan shore!
  no more shall Freedom smile?
shall Britons languish, and be men no more?
  Since all must life resign,
those sweet rewards, which decorate the brave,
  'tis folly to decline,
and steal inglorious to a silent grave.
SIR W. JONES

460   *SONG*

SWEETEST love, I do not go
  for weariness of thee,
nor in hope the world can show
  a fitter love for me;
    but, since that I
at the last must part, 'tis best
thus to use myself in jest
  by feigned deaths to die.

Yesternight the sun went hence
  and yet is here to-day;
he hath no desire nor sense
  nor half so short a way:
    then fear not me,
but believe that I shall make
speedier journeys, since I take
  more wings and spurs than he.

O how feeble is man's power,
  that, if good fortune fall,
cannot add another hour
  nor a lost hour recall!

> But come bad chance,
> and we join to it our strength,
> and we teach it art and length
> itself or us t' advance.
>
> Let not thy divining heart
>   forethink me any ill;
> destiny may take thy part
>   and may thy fears fulfil;
>   but think that we
> are but turned aside to sleep;
> they who one another keep
>   alive ne'er parted be.
>
> J. DONNE

461 *WINTER*

> THEN let the chill Scirocco blow,
> and gird us round with hills of snow;
> or else go whistle to the shore,
> and make the hollow mountains roar.
>
> Whilst we together jovial sit
> careless, and crowned with mirth and wit,
> where, though bleak winds confine us home,
> our fancies round the world shall roam.
>
> We'll think of all the friends we know,
> and drink to all worth drinking to;
> when, having drunk all thine and mine,
> we rather shall want healths than wine.
>
> But where friends fail us, we'll supply
> our friendship with our charity;
> men that remote in sorrows live
> shall by our lusty brimmers thrive.
>
> We'll drink the wanting into wealth,
> and those that languish into health,
> th' afflicted into joy, th' opprest
> into security and rest.
>
> The worthy in disgrace shall find
> favour return again more kind,
> and in restraint who stifled lie
> shall taste the air of liberty.

The brave shall triumph in success,
the lovers shall have mistresses,
poor unregarded virtue praise,
and the neglected poet bays.

Thus shall our healths do others good,
whilst we ourselves do all we would,
for, freed from envy and from care,
what would we be, but what we are?

C. COTTON

462   THE GOLDEN AGE

HAPPY that first white age! when we
lived by the earth's mere charity;
no soft luxurious diet then
had effeminated men;
no other meat nor wine had any,
than the coarse mast, or simple honey;
and by the parents' care laid up
cheap berries did the children sup.
No pompous wear was in those days
of gummy silks or scarlet baise,
their beds were on some flow'ry brink,
and clear spring water was their drink.
The shady pine in the sun's heat
was their cool and known retreat,
for then 'twas not cut down, but stood
the youth and glory of the wood.
The daring sailor with his slaves
then had not cut the swelling waves,
nor for desire of foreign store
seen any but his native shore.
No stirring drum had scar'd that age,
nor the shrill trumpet's active rage;
no wounds by bitter hatred made
with warm blood soil'd the shining blade;
for how could hostile madness arm
an age of love to public harm?
when common justice none withstood,
nor sought rewards for spilling blood.
O that at length our age would raise
into the temper of those days!
But (worse than Ætna's fires!) debate
and avarice inflame our state.

Alas, who was it that first found
gold hid of purpose under ground ;
that sought out pearls and div'd to find
such precious perils for mankind?
H. VAUGHAN

463   ULYSSES AND THE SIREN

SIREN

COME, worthy Greeke, Ulysses, come,
 possesse these shores with me,
the windes and seas are troublesome,
 and here we may be free.
Here we may sit and view their toyle
 that travaile in the deepe,
enjoye the day in mirth the while,
 and spend the night in sleepe.

ULYSSES

Faire nymph, if fame or honour were
 to be attained with ease,
then would I come and rest with thee,
 and leave such toiles as these:
but here it dwels, and here must I
 with danger seeke it forth ;
to spend the time luxuriously
 becomes not men of worth.

SIREN

Ulysses, O be not deceived
 with that unreall name,
this honour is a thing conceived
 and rests on others' fame :
begotten only to molest
 our peace, and to beguile
(the best thing of our life) our rest
 and give us up to toyle.

ULYSSES

Delicious nymph, suppose there were
 nor honour nor report,
yet manlinesse would scorne to weare
 the time in idle sport :

for toyle doth give a better touch
to make us feele our joy;
and ease finds tediousness, as much
as labour yeelds annoy.

S. DANIEL

464 *EVENING SONG OF THE PRIEST OF PAN*

SHEPHERDS all, and maidens fair,
fold your flocks up, for the air
'gins to thicken, and the sun
already his great course hath run.
See the dew-drops how they kiss
ev'ry little flower that is,
hanging on their velvet heads,
like a rope of crystal beads:
see the heavy clouds low falling,
and bright Hesperus down calling
the dead night from under ground;
at whose rising mists unsound,
damps and vapours fly apace,
hovering o'er the wanton face
of these pastures, where they come,
striking dead both bud and bloom.
Therefore from such danger lock
ev'ry one his lovèd flock;
and let your dogs lie loose without,
lest the wolf come as a scout
from the mountain, and ere day
bear a lamb or kid away;
or the crafty thievish fox
break upon your simple flocks.
To secure yourselves from these,
be not too secure in ease;
let one eye his watches keep,
whilst the t'other eye doth sleep;
so you shall good shepherds prove,
and for ever hold the love
of our great god. Sweetest slumbers
and soft silence fall in numbers
on your eye-lids! so, farewell!
Thus I end my evening's knell.

J. FLETCHER

465   THE FIRST OF MAY

HAIL! sacred thou to hallowed joy,
   to mirth and wine, sweet First of May!
to sports, which no grave cares alloy,
   the sprightly dance, the festive play!
Hail! thou, of ever circling time
   that gracest still the ceaseless flow!
bright blossom of the season's prime,
   aye hastening on to winter's snow!
When first young Spring his angel face
   on earth unveiled and years of gold
gilt with pure ray man's guileless race,
   by law's stern terrors uncontrolled;
such was the soft and genial breeze
   mild Zephyr breathed on all around;
with graceful glee to airs like these
   yielded its wealth the unlaboured ground.
So fresh—so fragrant is the gale
   which o'er the islands of the blest
sweeps; where nor aches the limbs assail
   nor age's peevish pains infest.
Where thy hushed groves, Elysium, sleep,
   such winds with whispered murmurs blow;
so, where dull Lethe's waters creep,
   they heave, scarce heave the cypress bough.
And such, when heaven with penal flame
   shall purge the globe, that golden day
restoring, o'er man's brightened frame
   haply such gale again shall play.
Hail thou, the fleet year's pride and prime,
   hail! day, which fame should bid to bloom!
hail, image of primeval time!
   hail, sample of a world to come!
                    F. WRANGHAM

466   TO-MORROW

IN the downhill of life, when I find I'm declining,
   may my lot no less fortunate be
than a snug elbow-chair can afford for reclining,
   and a cot that o'erlooks the wide sea;

with an ambling pad-pony to pace o'er the lawn,
   while I carol away idle sorrow,
and blithe as the lark that each day hails the dawn
   look forward with hope for to-morrow.
With a porch at my door, both for shelter and shade
      too,
   as the sun-shine or rain may prevail;
and a small spot of ground for the use of the spade
      too,
   with a barn for the use of the flail:
a cow for my dairy, a dog for my game,
   and a purse when a friend wants to borrow;
I'll envy no nabob his riches or fame,
   nor what honours await him to-morrow.
From the bleak northern blast may my cot be completely
   secured by a neighbouring hill;
and at night may repose steal upon me more sweetly
   by the sound of a murmuring rill:
and while peace and plenty I find at my board,
   with a heart free from sickness and sorrow,
with my friends may I share what to-day may afford,
   and let them spread the table to-morrow.
And when I at last must throw off this frail covering
   which I've worn for three-score years and ten,
on the brink of the grave I'll not seek to keep hovering,
   nor my thread wish to spin o'er again:
but my face in the glass I'll serenely survey,
   and with smiles count each wrinkle and furrow;
as this old worn-out stuff, which is thread-bare to-day,
   may become everlasting to-morrow.
                                              COLLINS

467   *HYMN TO ADVERSITY*

DAUGHTER of Jove, relentless power,
      thou tamer of the human breast,
whose iron scourge and torturing hour
      the bad affright, afflict the best!
Bound in thy adamantine chain
the proud are taught to taste of pain,
and purple tyrants vainly groan
with pangs unfelt before, unpitied and alone.

When first thy Sire to send on earth
    Virtue, his darling child, design'd,
to thee he gave the heav'nly birth,
    and bade to form her infant mind.
Stern rugged nurse! thy rigid lore
with patience many a year she bore;
what sorrow was thou bad'st her know,
and from her own she learn'd to melt at others' woe.

O gently on thy suppliant's head,
    dread Goddess, lay thy chastening hand,
not in thy Gorgon terrors clad,
    not circled with the vengeful band
(as by the impious thou art seen)
with thundering voice and threatening mien,
with screaming Horror's funeral cry,
Despair, and fell Disease, and ghastly Poverty:

Thy form benign, O Goddess, wear,
    thy milder influence impart,
thy philosophic train be there
    to soften, not to wound my heart.
The generous spark extinct revive,
teach me to love and to forgive,
exact my own defects to scan,
what others are to feel, and know myself a Man.

                        T. GRAY

468   TRUE HAPPINESS

HE who is good is happy. Let the loud
   artillery of heaven break through a cloud,
and dart its thunder at him, he'll remain
unmoved, and nobler comfort entertain
in welcoming the approach of death, than vice
ere found in her fictitious Paradise.
Time mocks our youth and (while we number past
delights and raise our appetite to taste
ensuing) brings us to unflattered age:
where we are left to satisfy the rage
of threatening death; pomp, beauty, wealth, and all
our friendships, shrinking from the funeral.
The thought of this begets that brave disdain
with which thou view'st the world, and makes those
   vain

treasures of fancy serious fools so court
and sweat to purchase thy contempt or sport.
What should we covet here? why interpose
a cloud 'twixt us and heaven? Kind nature chose
man's soul the Exchequer where she'd hoard her
    wealth,
and lodge all her rich secrets; but by the stealth
of our own vanity, we are left so poor,
the creature merely sensual knows more.
The learned halcyon by her wisdom finds
a gentle season, when the seas and winds
are silenced by a calm, and then brings forth
the happy miracle of her rare birth,
leaving with wonder all our arts possest,
that view the architecture of her nest.
Pride raiseth us 'bove justice. We bestow
increase of knowledge on old minds, which grow
by age to dotage: while the sensitive
part of the world in its first strength doth live.
                                W. HABINGTON

469   *THE SATYR'S LEAVE-TAKING*

Satyr THOU divinest, fairest, brightest,
        thou most powerful maid and whitest,
    thou most virtuous and most blessèd,
    eyes of stars, and golden-tressèd
    like Apollo; tell me, sweetest,
    what new service now is meetest
    for the Satyr? Shall I stray
    in the middle air, and stay
    the sailing rack, or nimbly take
    hold by the moon, and gently make
    suit to the pale queen of night
    for a beam to give thee light?
    Shall I dive into the sea,
    and bring thee coral, making way
    through the rising waves that fall
    in snowy fleeces? Dearest, shall
    I catch thee wanton fawns, or flies
    whose woven wings the summer dyes

of many colours? get thee fruit,
or steal from heaven old Orpheus' lute?
all these I'll venture for, and more,
to do her service all these woods adore.

Holy Virgin, I will dance
round about these woods as quick
as the breaking light, and prick
down the lawns and down the vales
faster than the windmill-sails.
So I take my leave and pray
all the comforts of the day,
such as Phœbus' heat doth send
on the earth, may still befriend
thee and this arbour!
  Clorin And to thee
all thy master's love be free!
         J. FLETCHER

470   TO SOLITUDE

HAIL, old patrician trees, so great and good!
 Hail, ye plebeian underwood,
where the poetic birds rejoice,
and for their quiet nests and plenteous food
 pay with their grateful voice.

Here Nature does a house for me erect,
 Nature, the fairest architect,
who those fond artists does despise
that can the fair and living trees neglect,
 yet the dead timber prize.

Here let me, careless and unthoughtful lying,
 hear the soft winds above me flying
with all their wanton boughs dispute,
and the more tuneful birds to both replying,
 nor be myself too mute.

A silver stream shall roll his waters near,
 gilt with sun-beams here and there,
on whose enamelled bank I'll walk,
and see how prettily they smile, and hear
 how prettily they talk.

Ah! wretched and too solitary he,
    who loves not his own company!
  He'll feel the weight of 't many a day,
unless he calls in sin or vanity
    to help to bear 't away.
O solitude, first state of humankind,
    thou break'st and tam'st th' unruly mind,
  which else would know no settled pace,
making it move, well managed by thy art,
    with swiftness and with grace.
Thou the faint beams of reason's scatter'd light
    dost like a burning glass unite,
  dost multiply the feeble heat,
and fortify the strength, till thou dost bright
    and noble fires beget.

A. COWLEY

471   ODE TO LIBERTY

WHO shall awake the Spartan fife,
    and call in solemn sounds to life,
the youths, whose locks divinely spreading,
    like vernal hyacinths in sullen hue,
at once the breath of Fear and Virtue shedding,
    applauding Freedom loved of old to view?
What new Alcæus, fancy-blest,
shall sing the sword, in myrtles drest,
    at Wisdom's shrine awhile its flame concealing,
(what place so fit to seal a deed renowned?)
    till she her brightest lightnings round revealing,
it leap'd in glory forth, and dealt her prompted wound?
    O goddess, in that feeling hour,
        when most its sounds would court thy ears,
    let not my shell's misguided power
        e'er draw thy sad, thy mindful tears.
No, Freedom, no! I will not tell,
how Rome, before thy weeping face
with heaviest sound a giant-statue fell,
push'd by a wild and artless race
from off its wide ambitious base,
when Time his northern sons of spoil awoke,
        and all the blended work of strength and grace
        with many a rude repeated stroke
and many a barbarous yell to thousand fragments broke.

W. COLLINS

472 YET, even whene'er the least appeared,
the admiring world thy hand revered;
still 'midst the scattered states around,
some remnants of her strength were found;
they saw, by what escaped the storm,
how wondrous rose her perfect form;
how in the great, the laboured whole,
each mighty master poured his soul!
for sunny Florence, seat of art,
beneath her vines preserved a part,
till they, whom Science loved to name,
(O who could fear it?) quenched her flame.
And lo an humbler relic laid
in jealous Pisa's olive shade!
see small Marino joins the theme
though least, not last in thy esteem:
strike, louder strike the ennobling strings
to those, whose merchant sons were kings;
to him, who decked with pearly pride
in Adria weds his green-haired bride;
hail, port of glory, wealth and pleasure,
ne'er let me change this Lydian measure:
nor e'er her former pride relate,
to sad Liguria's bleeding state.
Ah no! more pleased thy haunts I seek,
on wild Helvetia's mountains bleak:
(where, when the favoured of thy choice
the daring archer heard thy voice,
forth from his eyrie roused in dread
the ravening eagle northward fled:)
or dwell in willowed meads more near,
with those to whom thy stork is dear:
those whom the rod of Alva bruised,
whose crown a British queen refused!
the magic works, thou feel'st the strains,
one holier name alone remains:
the perfect spell shall then avail,
hail nymph, adored by Britain, hail!

473 Beyond the measure vast of thought,
the work the wizard Time has wrought!
the Gaul, 'tis held of antique story,
saw Britain linked to his now adverse strand,

no sea between, nor cliff sublime and hoary,
he passed with unwet feet through all our land.
To the blown Baltic then, they say,
 the wild waves found another way,
where Orcas howls, his wolfish mountains rounding:
till all the banded west at once 'gan rise,
a wide wild storm even nature's self confounding,
 withering her giant sons with strange uncouth
 surprise.
 This pillared earth so firm and wide,
  by winds and inward labours torn,
 in thunders dread was pushed aside,
  and down the shouldering billows borne.
And see, like gems, her laughing train,
 the little isles on every side,
Mona, once hid from those who search the main,
 where thousand elfin shapes abide,
and Wight, who checks the western tide,
 for thee consenting Heaven has each bestowed,
a fair attendant on her sovereign pride:
 to thee this blest divorce she owed,
for thou hast made her vales thy loved, thy last
 abode!

W. COLLINS

474 *THE EXPOSTULATION*

IN doubtful twilight Nature sleeps
 within this silent grove:
love only his pale vigil keeps,
 and I, the slave of love.

Ah! cruel Julia, dare you brave
 the sea's engulfing tide?
Torn from me by the tossing wave,
 shall winds my hopes deride?

So your fond lover can you cheat,
 to all your vows untrue?
Yet dread th' avenging wind's deceit—
 know, seas are fickle too.

F. WRANGHAM

475   CHRISTIAN WARFARE

SOLDIER, go—but not to claim
 mouldering spoils of earth-born treasure,
not to build a vaunting name;
 not to dwell in tents of pleasure;
dream not that the way is smooth,
 hope not that the thorns are roses;
turn no wishful eye of youth
 where the sunny beam reposes:
  thou hast sterner work to do,
   hosts to cut thy passage through;
close behind thee gulfs are burning—
forward!—there is no returning.

Soldier, rest—but not for thee
 spreads the world her downy pillow;
on the rock thy couch must be,
 while around thee chafes the billow:
thine must be a watchful sleep,
 wearier than another's waking;
such a charge as thou dost keep
 brooks no moment of forsaking.
  Sleep, as on the battle-field,
   girded, grasping sword and shield:
those thou canst not name or number
steal upon thy broken slumber.

Soldier, rise—the war is done:
 lo, the hosts of hell are flying;
'twas thy Lord the battle won;
 Jesus vanquished them by dying.
Pass the stream—before thee lies
 all the conquered land of glory;
hark what songs of rapture rise;
 these proclaim the victor's story;
  soldier, lay thy weapons down,
   quit the sword, and take the crown;
triumph! all thy foes are banished,
death is slain, and earth has vanished.

       C. ELIZABETH

476   TO DEATH

THEN, Death, why should'st thou dreaded be
and shunn'd as some great misery,
that cur'st our woes and strife?
only because we're ill resolved,
and in dark error's clouds involved,
  think Death the end of Life;
    which most untrue,
    each place we view,
  gives testimonies rife.

The flowers that we behold each year
in chequer'd meads their heads to rear,
  new rising from their tomb;
the eglantines and honey-daisies,
and all those pretty smiling faces,
  that still in age grow young;
    even these do cry
    that though men die,
  yet life from death may come.

The towering cedars tall and strong
on Taurus and Mount Lebanon
  in time they all decay;
yet from their old and wasted roots
at length again grow up young shoots,
  that are as fresh and gay;
    then why should we
    thus fear to die,
  whose death brings life for aye?

The seed that in the earth we throw
doth putrify before it grow,
  corrupting in its urn;
but at the spring it flourisheth,
when Phœbus only cherisheth
  with life at his return.
    Doth Time's Sun this?
    Then sure it is
  Time's Lord can more perform.

                              J. HAGTHORPE

477   ON MAN'S MORTALITY

THE World's a bubble, and the life of Man
        less than a span;—
in his conception wretched, from the womb,
        so to the tomb;—
curst from his cradle, and brought up to years
        with cares and fears.
Who then to frail mortality shall trust
but limns on water, or but writes in dust.

Yet whilst with sorrow here we live opprest,
        what life is best?
Courts are but only superficial schools
        to dandle fools:
the rural parts are turned into a den
        of savage men:
and where's a city from foul vice so free,
but may be termed the worst of all the three?

Domestic cares afflict the husband's bed,
        or pain his head:
those that live single, take it for a curse,
        or do things worse:
these would have Children:—those that have them,
    moan
        or wish them gone:
what is it, then, to have or have no wife,
but single thraldom, or a double strife?

Our own affections still at home to please
        is a disease:
to cross the seas to any foreign soil,
        peril and toil:
wars with their noise affright us; when they cease,
        we are worse in peace;
what then remains, but that we still should cry
for being born, or, being born, to die?
                    FRANCIS LORD BACON

478 THE NYMPH COMPLAINING FOR THE DEATH
            OF HER FAUN

THE wanton troopers riding by
    have shot my faun and it will dye.

Ungentle men! They cannot thrive
to kill thee. Thou ne'er didst alive
them any harm: alas nor cou'd
thy death yet do them any good.

* * * *

It is a wond'rous thing, how fleet
'twas on those little silver feet:
with what a pretty skipping grace
it oft would challenge me the race:
and when 't had left me far away,
'twould stay, and run again, and stay:
for it was nimbler much than hindes;
and trod, as on the four winds.

* * * *

O help! O help! I see it faint!
and dye as calmely as a saint:
see how it weeps. The tears do come
sad, slowly dropping like a gumme.
So weeps the wounded balsome: so
the holy frankincense doth flow;
the brotherless Heliades
melt in such amber tears as these.
I in a golden vial will
keep these two crystal tears; and fill
it till it do o'erflow with mine;
then place it in Diana's shrine.
Now my sweet faun is vanish'd to
whither the swans and turtles go:
in fair Elysium to endure
with milk-white lambs and ermins pure.
O do not run too fast, for I
will but bespeak thy grave, and dye."

A. MARVELL.

479   *FAITH IN THE UNSEEN*

THERE are who, darkling and alone,
would wish the weary night were gone,
though dawning morn should only show
the secret of their unknown woe:
who pray for sharpest throbs of pain
to ease them of doubt's galling chain:
"only disperse the cloud," they cry,
"and if our fate be death, give light and let us die."

Unwise I deem them, Lord, unmeet
to profit by Thy chastenings sweet,
for Thou wouldst have us linger still
upon the verge of good or ill,
that on Thy guiding hand unseen
our undivided hearts may lean,
and thus our frail and foundering bark
glide in the narrow wake of Thy beloved ark.

'Tis so in war—the champion true
loves victory more when dim in view
he sees her glories gild afar
the dusty edge of stubborn war,
than if the untrodden bloodless field
the harvest of her laurels yield:
let not my bark in calm abide,
but win her fearless way against the chafing tide.
J. KEBLE.

480   TO THE NIGHT

SWIFTLY walk over the western wave,
        Spirit of Night!
out of the misty eastern cave
where all the long and lone daylight
thou wovest dreams of joy and fear
which make thee terrible and dear,—
        swift be thy flight!

Wrap thy form in a mantle gray
        star-inwrought!
Blind with thine hair the eyes of day,
kiss her until she be wearied out,
then wander o'er city, and sea, and land
touching all with thine opiate wand—
        come, long-sought!

When I arose and saw the dawn,
        I sigh'd for thee;
when light rode high, and the dew was gone,
and noon lay heavy on flower and tree,
and the weary Day turn'd to his rest
lingering like an unloved guest,
        I sigh'd for thee.

Thy brother Death came, and cried
    wouldst thou me?
Thy sweet child Sleep, the filmy-eyed,
murmur'd like a noon-tide bee
shall I nestle near thy side?
wouldst thou me?—And I replied,
    No, not thee!

Death will come when thou art dead,
    soon, too soon—
sleep will come when thou art fled;
of neither would I ask the boon
I ask of thee, belovéd Night—
swift be thine approaching flight,
    come soon, soon!
        P. B. SHELLEY

481   TO THE WEST WIND

O WILD West wind, thou breath of Autumn's
 being,
thou, from whose unseen presence the leaves dead
are driven, like ghosts from an enchanter fleeing,

yellow, and black, and pale, and hectic red,
pestilence-stricken multitudes: O thou,
who charioted to their dark wintry bed

the winged seeds, where they lie cold and low,
each like a corpse within its grave, until
thine azure sister of the Spring shall blow

her clarion o'er the dreaming earth, and fill
(driving sweet buds, like flocks, to feed in air)
with living hues and odours, plain and hill:

wild spirit, which art moving every where:
destroyer and preserver; hear, oh hear!

Make me thy lyre, even as the forest is:
what if my leaves are falling like its own!
the tumult of thy mighty harmonies

will take from both a deep autumnal tone,
sweet though in sadness. Be thou, spirit fierce,
my spirit! Be thou me, impetuous one!

Drive my dead thoughts over the universe
like withered leaves to quicken a new birth;
and, by the incantation of this verse,

scatter, as from an unextinguished hearth
ashes and sparks, my words among mankind!
be through my lips to unawakened earth
the trumpet of a prophecy! O wind
if Winter comes, can Spring be far behind!
P. B. SHELLEY

482   *TO THE RIVER BLYTH*

O THOU, that prattling on thy pebbled way
   through my paternal vale dost stray,
working thy shallow passage to the sea;
  O stream, thou speedest on
    the same as many seasons gone;
      but not, alas! to me
remain the feelings that beguiled
  my early road, when careless and content
  (losing the hours in pastimes innocent)
upon thy banks I strayed, a playful child;
  whether the pebbles that thy margin strew
  collecting heedlessly I threw;
  or loved in thy translucent wave
  my tender shrinking feet to lave;
  or else insnared your little fry,
  and thought how wondrous skilled was I!—
So passed my boyish days, unknown to pain,
days that will ne'er return again.
    It seems but yesterday
    I was a child—to-morrow to be grey!
So years succeeding years steal silently away.
Not fleeter thy own current, hurrying thee,
  rolls down to the great sea.
Thither O carry these sad thoughts—the deep
bury them;—thou meantime thy tenor keep,
and winding through the green-wood cheer,
as erst, my native peaceful pastures here.
W. L. BOWLES

483 THE LORD YOUR GOD HATH GIVEN YOU THIS LAND TO POSSESS IT

THERE is a land of pure delight
   where saints immortal reign;
infinite day excludes the night,
   and pleasures banish pain.

There everlasting Spring abides,
   and never-withering flowers;
death, like a narrow sea, divides
   this heavenly land from ours.

Sweet fields beyond the swelling flood
   stand dressed in living green;
so to the Jews old Canaan stood,
   while Jordan rolled between.

But timorous mortals start and shrink
   to cross this narrow sea,
and linger shivering on the brink,
   and fear to launch away.

O, could we make our doubts remove
   those gloomy doubts that rise,
and see the Canaan that we love
   with unbeclouded eyes!

could we but climb where Moses stood
   and view the landscape o'er,
not Jordan's stream, nor death's cold flood,
   should fright us from the shore.

                              I. WATTS

484 ORPHEUS AND THE SIRENS

THE bark divine, itself instinct with life,
   went forth and baffled ocean's rudest shocks,
escaping, though with pain and arduous strife,
   the huge encountering rocks;

and force and fraud o'ercome, and peril past,
   its hard-won trophy raised in open view,
through prosperous floods was bringing home at last
   its high heroic crew;

till now they cried (Æaea left behind,
   and the dead waters of the Cronian main),
"no peril more upon our path we find,
   safe haven soon we gain."

When, as they spake, sweet sounds upon the breeze
   came to them, melodies till now unknown,
and blended into one delight with these,
   sweet odours sweetly blown,—

sweet odours wafted from the flowery isle,
   sweet music breathéd by the Sirens three,
who there lie wait, all passers to beguile,
   fair monsters of the sea!

Fair monsters foul, that with their magic song
   and beauty to the shipman wandering
whose peril than disastrous whirlpools strong,
   or fierce sea-robbers bring.

485 Sometimes upon the diamond rocks they leant,
   sometimes they sat upon the flowery lea
that sloped toward the wave, and ever sent
   shrill music o'er the sea.

The winds, suspended by the charméd song,
   shed treacherous calm about that fatal isle;
the waves, as though the halcyon o'er its young
   were always brooding, smile;

and every one that listens, presently
   forgetteth home and wife and children dear,
all noble enterprise and purpose high,
   and turns his pinnace here.—

He cannot heed,—so sweet unto him seems
   to reap the harvest of the promised joy;
the wave-worn man of such secure rest dreams,
   so guiltless of annoy.

—The heroes and the kings, the wise, the strong,
   that won the fleece with cunning and with might,
their souls were taken in the net of song,
   snared in that false delight;

Till ever loathlier seemed all toil to be,
   and that small space they yet must travel o'er,
stretched, an immeasurable breadth of sea,
   their fainting hearts before.

486 "Let us turn hitherward our bark," they cried,
   "and, 'mid the blisses of this happy isle,
past toil forgetting and to come, abide
   in joyfulness awhile;

"and then, refreshed, our tasks resume again,
   if other tasks we yet are bound unto,
combing the hoary tresses of the main
   with sharp swift keel anew."

O heroes, that had once a nobler aim,
   O heroes sprung from many a godlike line,
what will ye do, unmindful of your fame,
   and of your race divine?

But they, by these prevailing voices now
   lured, evermore draw nearer to the land,
nor saw the wrecks of many a goodly prow,
   that strewed that fatal strand;

or seeing, feared not—warning taking none
   from the plain doom of all who went before,
whose bones lay bleaching in the wind and sun,
   and whitened all the shore.

And some impel through foaming billows now
   the hissing keel, and some tumultuous stand
upon the deck, or crowd about the prow,
   waiting to leap to land.

And them this fatal lodestar of delight
   had drawn to ruin wholly, but for one
of their own selves, who struck his lyre with might,
   Calliope's great son.

487 Of holier joy he sang, more true delight,
   in other happier isles for them reserved,
who, faithful here, from constancy and right
   and truth have never swerved;

How evermore the tempered ocean gales
   breathe round those hidden islands of the blest,
steeped in the glory spread, when daylight fails,
   far in the sacred West;

how unto them, beyond our mortal night,
   shines evermore in strength the golden day;
and meadows with purpureal roses bright
   bloom round their feet alway;

and how 'twas given thro' virtue to aspire
   to golden seats in ever-calm abodes;
of mortal men, admitted to the quire
   of high immortal Gods.

He says—a mighty melody divine,
   that woke deep echoes in the heart of each—
reminded whence they drew their royal line,
   and to what heights might reach.

And all the while they listened, them the speed
   bore forward still of favouring wind and tide,
that, when their ears were vacant to give heed
   to any sound beside,

the feeble echoes of that other lay,
   which held awhile their senses thralled and bound,
were in the distance fading quite away,
   a dull unheeded sound.

                        R. C. TRENCH

488   *TO A YOUNG LADY CURLING HER HAIR*

NO longer seek the needless aid
   of studious art, dear lovely Maid!
vainly from side to side, forbear
to shift thy glass, and braid each straggling hair.

As the gay flowers, which Nature yields
   spontaneous on the vernal fields,
     delight the fancy more than those
which gardens trim arrange in equal rows;

   as the pure rill, whose mazy train
   the prattling pebbles check in vain,

gives native pleasure, while it leads
its random waters, winding through the meads;

as birds, the groves and streams among,
in artless strains the vernal song
warbling, their wood-notes wild repeat,
and sooth the ear, irregularly sweet;

so simple dress and native grace
will best become thy lovely face!
for naked Cupid still suspects,
in artful ornaments concealed defects.

Cease then, with idly cruel care,
to torture thus the flowing hair;
O! cease with tasteless toil to shed
a cloud of scented dust around thy head.

Not Berenice's locks could boast
a grace like thine; among the host
of stars, though radiant now they rise,
and add new lustre to the spangled skies:

nor Venus, when her charms divine
improving in a form like thine
she gave her tresses unconfined
to play about her neck, and wanton in the wind.

W. DUNCOMBE.

489   *THE STORM*

CEASE, rude Boreas, blust'ring railer!
   list, ye landsmen, all to me!
messmates, hear a brother sailor
   sing the dangers of the sea;
from bounding billows, fast in motion,
   when the distant whirlwinds rise,
to the tempest-troubled ocean,
   where the seas contend with skies!

Hark! the boatswain hoarsely bawling,
   by topsail-sheets and haul-yards stand!
down top-gallants quick be hauling;
   down your stay-sails, hand, boys, hand!

Round us roars the tempest louder;
  think what fear our minds enthrals,
harder yet, it yet blows harder,
  now again the boatswain calls!

The top-sail yards point to the wind, boys,
  see all clear to reef each course;
let the fore-sheet go, don't mind, boys,
  though the weather should be worse.
Fore and aft the sprit-sail yard get,
  reef the mizen, see all clear;
hands up, each preventure-brace set,
  man the fore-yard, cheer, lads, cheer!

Now the dreadful thunder's roaring,
  peal on peal contending clash,
on our heads fierce rain falls pouring,
  in our eyes blue lightnings flash.
One wide water all around us,
  all above us one black sky,
different deaths at once surround us:
  hark! what means that dreadful cry?

O'er the lee-beam is the land, boys,
  let the guns o'erboard be thrown;
to the pump let every hand, boys;
  see! our mizen-mast is gone.
While o'er the ship wild waves are beating,
  we for wives or children mourn;
alas! from hence there's no retreating,
  alas! to them there's no return.

Still the leak is gaining on us;
  both chain-pumps are choked below—
Heaven have mercy here upon us!
  for only that can save us now.
—The leak we've found, it cannot pour fast,
  we've lightened her a foot or more;
up and rig a jury foremast,
  she rights, she rights! boys—we're off the shore.
                              G. A. STEVENS

490   *MAN'S MEDLEY*

HARK, how the birds do sing
    and woods do ring:
all creatures have their joy and man hath his.
    Yet, if we rightly measure,
        man's joy and pleasure
rather hereafter, than in present, is.
    To this life things of sense
        make their pretence:
in the other Angels have a right by birth:
    man ties them both alone,
        and makes them one,
with the one hand touching heaven, with the other
    earth.

    *   *   *   *   *

    But as his joys are double,
        so is his trouble:
he hath two winters, other things but one:
    both frosts and thoughts do nip:
        and bite his lip;
and he of all things fears two deaths alone.
    Yet even the greatest griefs
        may be reliefs,
could he but take them right, and in their ways.
    Happy is he, whose heart
        hath found the art
to turn his double pains to double praise.
                    G. HERBERT

491   *TO CONTEMPLATION*

OR lead me where amid the tranquil vale
    the broken stream flows on in silver light,
and I will linger where the gale
    o'er the bank of violets sighs,
listening to hear its softened sounds arise;
    and hearken the dull beetle's drowsy flight:
    and watch the horn-eyed snail
    creep o'er his long moon-glittering trail,
    and mark where radiant through the night
moves in the grass-green hedge the glow-worm's
        living light.
    Thee, meekest power! I love to meet,

as oft with even solitary pace
the scattered abbey's hallowed rounds I trace,
and listen to the echoings of my feet.
Or on the half-demolished tomb,
whose warning texts anticipate my doom,
mark the clear orb of night
cast through the storying glass a faintly-varied light.
  * * * *

But sweeter 'tis to wander wild
by melancholy dreams beguiled,
while the summer moon's pale ray
faintly guides me on my way
to the lone romantic glen
far from all the haunts of men,
where no noise of uproar rude
breaks the calm of solitude:
but soothing silence sleeps in all,
save the neighbouring waterfall,
whose hoarse waters falling near
load with hollow sounds the ear,
and with down-dasht torrent white
gleam hoary through the shades of night.
R. SOUTHEY

492 *THE PRAYER OF HABAKKUK THE PROPHET*

O Lord, I have heard thy speech, and was afraid:
O Lord, revive thy work in the midst of the years;
in wrath remember mercy.
God came from Teman,
and the Holy one from Mount Paran:
His glory covered the heavens,
and the earth was full of His praise.
Before Him went the pestilence,
and burning coals went forth at His feet:
and His brightness was as the light:
He had bright beams coming out of His side,
and there was the hiding of His power:
Thy bow was made quite naked.
I saw the tents of Cushan in affliction,
and the curtains of the land of Midian did tremble.
He stood and measured the earth:
He beheld, and drove asunder the nations;

and the everlasting mountains were scattered,
the perpetual hills did bow.
Thou didst cleave the earth with rivers:
Thou didst walk through the sea with Thine horses,
through the heap of great waters.
The mountains saw Thee and they trembled,
the stream of water overflowed:
the deep uttered his voice,
and lifted up his hands on high:
the sun and moon stood still in their habitation:
at the light of Thine arrows they went,
and at the shining of Thy glittering spear.
Was the Lord displeased against the rivers?
was Thy wrath against the sea,
that Thou didst ride upon Thine horses
and Thy chariots of salvation?
They came out as a whirlwind to scatter me:
their rejoicing was as to devour the poor secretly;
Thou didst march through the land in indignation,
Thou didst thresh the heathen in anger.
When I heard, my belly trembled:
my lips quivered at the voice:
rottenness entered into my bones,
and I trembled in myself,
that I might rest in the day of trouble:
when he cometh up unto the people,
he will invade them with his troops.
Although the fig-tree shall not blossom,
neither shall fruit be in the vines,
the labour of the olive shall fail,
and the fields shall yield no meat;
the flock shall be cut off from the fold,
and there shall be no herd in the stalls:
yet I will rejoice in the Lord,
I will joy in the God of my salvation.
The Lord God is my strength,
and He will make my feet like hinds' feet,
and He will make me to walk upon mine high places.

493   *PROPHECY OF THE DESTRUCTION OF TYRE*

Ezekiel xxvi. 2—21.

494 *DENUNCIATION OF GOD'S JUDGMENTS AGAINST THE JEWS*

Isaiah v.

495 *THANKSGIVING OF THE FAITHFUL FOR THE MERCIES OF GOD*

Isaiah xii.

496 *PREDICTION OF THE FALL OF BABYLON*

Isaiah xiv. 4—27.

497 *HEZEKIAH'S SONG OF THANKSGIVING*

Isaiah xxxviii. 9—20.

498 *DAVID'S LAMENTATION OVER SAUL AND JONATHAN*

II Samuel i. 17—27.

499 *MOSES' SONG*

Exodus xv. 1—19.

500 *MOSES' SONG*

Deuteronomy xxxii. 1—43.

501 *LAMENTATION OVER THE MISERY OF JERUSALEM*

Lamentations ii. 8—15.

502 *THE CALAMITIES OF THE FAITHFUL*

Lamentations iii. 1—9: 22—30.

503 *ZION BEWAILETH HER PITIFUL STATE*

Lamentations iv. 1—6.

504 *ZION'S PRAYER*

Lamentations v. 1—11.

505 *BALAAM'S PROPHECY*

Numbers xxiv. 5—9.

506 TO THE MEMORY OF THE FIRST LADY LYTTELTON

OFT would the Dryads of these woods rejoice
to hear her heavenly voice;
for her despising, when she deigned to sing,
the sweetest songsters of the spring:
the woodlark and the linnet pleased no more;
the nightingale was mute
and every shepherd's flute
was cast in silent scorn away,
while all attended to her sweeter lay.
Ye larks and linnets now resume your song,
and thou, melodious Philomel,
again this plaintive story tell;
for death has stopped that tuneful tongue,
whose music could alone your warbling notes excel.
In vain I look around,
o'er all the well-known ground,
my Lucy's wonted footsteps to descry;
where oft we us'd to walk,
where oft in tender talk
we saw the summer sun go down the sky;
nor by yon fountain's side,
nor where its waters glide
along the valley, can she now be found:
in all the wide-stretch'd prospect's ample bound
no more my mournful eye
can aught of her espy,
but the sad sacred earth where her dear relics lie.

507 So, where the silent streams of Liris glide,
in the soft bosom of Campania's vale,
when now the wintry tempests all are fled,
and genial Summer breathes her gentle gale,
the verdant orange lifts its beauteous head;
from every branch the balmy flowerets rise,
on every bough the golden fruits are seen;
with odours sweet it fills the smiling skies,
the wood-nymphs tend it, and th' Idalian queen:
but, in the midst of all its blooming pride,
a sudden blast from Apenninus blows,
cold with perpetual snows;
the tender-blighted plant shrinks up its leaves, and
dies.

O best of women! dearer far to me
  than when, in blooming life,
my lips first call'd thee wife;
how can my soul endure the loss of thee?
How in the world, to me a desert grown,
  abandon'd and alone,
without my sweet companion can I live?
  without thy lovely smile,
the dear reward of every virtuous toil,
what pleasures now can pall'd ambition give?
E'en the delightful sense of well-earn'd praise,
unshar'd by thee, no more my lifeless thoughts could
  raise.
                    GEORGE LORD LYTTELTON

508 *TO THE WORLD—THE PERFECTION OF LOVE*

YOU who are earth, and cannot rise
  above your sence,
boasting the envyed wealth which lyes
bright in your mistris' lips or eyes,
betray a pittyed eloquence.

That which doth joyne our soules, so light
  and quicke doth move,
that like the eagle in his flight,
it doth transcend all humane sight,
lost in the element of love.

You poets reach not this who sing
  the praise of dust
but kneaded, when by theft you bring
the rose and lilly from the spring
t' adorne the wrinckled face of lust.

When we speake love, nor art nor wit
  we glosse upon:
our soules engender, and beget
ideas, which you counterfeit
in your dull propagation.

While time seven ages shall disperse,
  wee'le talke of love,
and when our tongues hold no commerse,
our thoughts shall mutually converse;
and yet the blood no rebell prove.

And though we be of severall kind
  fit for offence;
yet are we so by love refined
from impure drosse, we are all mind.
Death could not more have conquer'd sence.

How suddenly those flames expire
  which scorch our clay!
Prometheus-like when we steale fire
from Heaven, tis endless and intire;
it may know age but not decay.

W. HABINGTON

509   *CHRIST IS RISEN*

AWAKE, thou wintry earth,
  fling off thy sadness;
fair vernal flowers, laugh forth
  your ancient gladness:
    Christ is risen.

Wave, woods, your blossoms all,
  grim death is dead;
ye weeping funeral trees,
  lift up your head:
    Christ is risen.

Come, see, the graves are green;
  it is light; let's go
where our loved ones rest
  in hope below:
    Christ is risen.

All is fresh and new;
  full of spring and light;
wintry heart, why wearest the hue
  of sleep and night?
    Christ is risen.

Leave thy cares beneath,
  leave thy worldly love;
begin the better life
  with God above:
    Christ is risen.

T. BLACKBURNE

510   *THE WISH*

THIS only grant me, that my means may lye
  too low for envy, for contempt too high;

some honour I would have,
not from great deeds, but good alone;
the unknown are better than ill known;
   rumour can ope the grave.
Acquaintance I would have, but when't depends
not on the number, but the choice of friends.
Books should, not business, entertain the light,
and sleep, as undisturbed as death, the night:
   my house a cottage more
than palace, and should fitting be
for all my use, not luxury:
   my garden painted o'er
with Nature's hand, not art's, that pleasures yield,
Horace might envy in his Sabine field.
Thus would I double my life's fading space,
for he that runs it well, twice runs his race:
   and in this true delight,
these unbought sports and happy state,
I would not fear, nor wish my fate,
   but boldly say each night;
To-morrow let my Sun his beams display,
or in clouds hide them: I have lived to-day.
                                        A. COWLEY

511   *CATO'S SOLILOQUY*

IT must be so—Plato, thou reason'st well!
   else whence this pleasing hope, this fond desire,
this longing after immortality?
Or whence this secret dread, and inward horrour
of falling into nought? why shrinks the Soul
back on herself, and startles at destruction?
'Tis the divinity that stirs within us;
'tis Heaven itself, that points out an hereafter,
and intimates eternity to man.
Eternity! thou pleasing, dreadful thought!
through what variety of untried being,
through what new scenes and changes must we pass!
the wide, the unbounded prospect, lies before me;
but shadows, clouds, and darkness rest upon it.
Here will I hold. If there's a Power above us,
(and that there is all Nature cries aloud
through all her works,) he must delight in virtue;
and that which he delights in must be happy.

But when! or where!—This world was made for
  Caesar.
I'm weary of conjectures—this must end 'em.
                [*Laying his hand on his sword.*
Thus am I doubly armed: My death and life,
my bane and antidote, are both before me:
this in a moment brings me to an end;
but this informs me I shall never die.
The soul secured in her existence smiles
at the drawn dagger, and defies its point:
the stars shall fade away, the sun himself
grow dim with age, and nature sink in years,
but thou shalt flourish in immortal youth,
unhurt amidst the war of elements,
the wrecks of matter, and the crush of worlds.
                                        J. ADDISON

512   *CONSTANCY*

WHO is the honest man?
    He that doth still and strongly good pursue,
to God, his neighbour, and himself most true;
  whom neither force nor fawning can
unpin or wrench from giving all their due.

  Whose honesty is not
so loose or easy, that a ruffling wind
can blow away, or glittering look it blind:
  who rides his sure and even trot,
while the world now rides by, now lags behind.

  Who when great trials come,
nor seeks nor shuns them; but doth calmly stay,
till he the thing and the example weigh;
  all being brought into a sum,
what place or person calls for, he doth pay.

  Whom none can work or woo,
to use in any thing a trick or sleight;
for above all things he abhors deceit;
  his words and works and fashion too
all of a piece and all are clear and straight.

  Whom nothing can procure
when the wide world runs bias, from his will
to writhe his limbs, and share, not mend the ill.
  This is the marksman, safe and sure,
who still is right, and prays to be so still.
                                        G. HERBERT

513   TO CONTEMPLATION

I WILL meet thee on the hill,
where with printless footsteps still
the morning in her buskin grey
springs upon her eastern way;
while the frolic zephyrs stir,
playing with the gossamer,
and on ruder pinions borne
shake the dew-drops from the thorn.
There, as o'er the fields we pass,
brushing with hasty feet the grass,
we will startle from her nest
the lively lark with speckled breast;
and hear the floating clouds among
her gale-transported matin-song;
or on the upland stile, embowered
with fragrant hawthorn snowy-flowered,
will sauntering sit, and listen still
to the herdsman's oaten quill,
wafted from the plain below,
or the heifer's frequent low.
Or, when the noontide heats oppress,
we will seek the dark recess,
where in the embowered translucent stream
the cattle shun the sultry beam;
and o'er us on the marge reclined
the drowsy fly her horn shall wind,
while Echo from her ancient oak
shall answer to the woodman's stroke;
or the little peasant's song
wandering lone the glens among.
                              H. K. WHITE.

514   FIELD FLOWERS

YE field flowers! the gardens eclipse you, 'tis true,
Yet, wildings of Nature, I doat upon you,
for ye waft me to summers of old,
when the earth teemed around me with fairy delight,
and when daisies and buttercups gladdened my sight,
like treasures of silver and gold.

I love you for lulling me back into dreams
of the blue Highland mountains and echoing
    streams,
and of birchen glades breathing their balm,
while the deer was seen glancing in sunshine remote,
and the deep mellow crush of the wood-pigeon's note
    made music that sweetened the calm.
Not a pastoral song has a pleasanter tune
than ye speak to my heart, little wildings of June:
    of old ruinous castles ye tell,
where I thought it delightful your beauties to find,
when the magic of Nature first breathed on my mind,
    and your blossoms were part of her spell.
Even now what affections the violet awakes;
what loved little islands, twice seen in their lakes,
    can the wild water-lily restore;
what landscapes I read in the primrose's looks,
and what pictures of pebbled and minnowy brooks,
    in the vetches that tangled their shore.
Earth's cultureless buds, to my heart ye were dear,
ere the fever of passion, or ague of fear
    had scathed my existence's bloom;
once I welcome you more, in life's passionless stage,
with the visions of youth to revisit my age,
    and I wish you to grow on my tomb.

                            T. CAMPBELL

515   *THE LAST MAN*

ALL worldly shapes shall melt in gloom,
    the Sun himself must die,
before this mortal shall assume
    its Immortality!
I saw a vision in my sleep,
that gave my spirit strength to sweep
    adown the gulf of Time!
I saw the last of human mould,
that shall Creation's death behold,
    as Adam saw her prime!
the Sun's eye had a sickly glare,
    the Earth with age was wan,
the skeletons of nations were
    around that lonely man!

Some had expired in fight,—the brands
still rusted in their bony hands;
　in plague and famine some!
Earth's cities had no sound nor tread;
and ships were drifting with the dead
　to shores where all was dumb!
Yet prophet-like that lone one stood
　with dauntless words and high,
that shook the sere leaves from the wood
　as if a storm passed by,
saying, We are twins in death, proud Sun,
thy face is cold, thy race is run,
　'tis Mercy bids thee go:
for thou ten thousand thousand years
hast seen the tide of human tears,
　that shall no longer flow.
　　　　　　　　　　T. CAMPBELL.

516　　　　*MODERN GREECE*

HE who hath bent him o'er the dead
　ere the first day of death is fled,
the first dark day of nothingness,
the last of danger and distress,
(before Decay's effacing fingers
have swept the lines where beauty lingers,)
and marked the mild angelic air,
the rapture of repose that's there,
the fixed yet tender traits that streak
the languor of the placid cheek,
and—but for that sad shrouded eye,
　that fires not, wins not, weeps not, now,
　and but for that chill, changeless brow,
where cold Obstruction's apathy
appals the gazing mourner's heart,
as if to him it could impart
the doom he dreads, yet dwells upon;
yes, but for these and these alone,
some moments, aye, one treacherous hour,
he still might doubt the tyrant's power;
so fair, so calm, so softly sealed,
the first, last look by death revealed!
Such is the aspect of this shore;
'tis Greece, but living Greece no more!
　　　　　　　　　　LORD BYRON

517   BEAUTY

AS rising on its purple wing
the insect-queen of eastern spring
o'er emerald meadows of Kashmeer
invites the young pursuer near,
and leads him on from flower to flower
a weary chase and wasted hour,
then leaves him, as it soars on high,
with panting heart and tearful eye:
so Beauty lures the full-grown child
with hue as bright and wing as wild;
a chase of idle hopes and fears,
begun in folly, closed in tears.
If won, to equal ills betrayed,
woe waits the insect and the maid:
a life of pain, the loss of peace,
from infant's play and man's caprice:
the lovely toy so fiercely sought
hath lost its charm by being caught,
for every touch that wooed its stay
hath brushed its brightest hues away,
till charm and hue and beauty gone,
'tis left to fly or fall alone.

      LORD BYRON

518   ODE TO EVENING

IF aught of oaten stop or pastoral song,
may hope, chaste Eve, to soothe thy modest ear
 (like thy own solemn springs,
  thy springs, and dying gales);
O nymph reserved,—while now the bright-haired sun
sits in yon western tent, whose cloudy skirts,
 with brede ethereal wove,
  o'erhang his wavy bed,
and air is hushed, save where the weak-eyed bat
with short shrill shriek flits by on leathern wing,
 or where the beetle winds
  his small but sullen horn,
as oft he rises 'midst the twilight path,
against the pilgrim borne in heedless hum,—
 Now teach me, maid composed,
  to breathe some softened strain,
whose numbers stealing through thy darkening vale,

may not unseemly with its stillness suit;
    as, musing slow, I hail
    thy genial, loved return!
for when thy folding-star arising shows
his paly circlet, at his warning lamp
    the fragrant Hours, and elves
    who slept in buds the day,
and many a nymph who wreathes her brows with sedge,
and sheds the fresh'ning dew, and, lovelier still,
    the pensive pleasures sweet,
    prepare thy shadowy car.
Then let me rove some wild and heathy scene;
or find some ruin, 'midst its dreary dells,
    whose walls more awful nod
    by thy religious gleams.
Or if chill blustering winds or driving rain
prevent my willing feet, be mine the hut
    that from the mountain's side
    views wilds, and swelling floods,
and hamlets brown, and dim-discovered spires,
and hears their simple bell, and marks o'er all
    thy dewy fingers draw
    the gradual dusky veil.
While Spring shall pour his showers, as oft he wont,
and bathe thy breathing tresses, meekest eve!
    while Summer loves to sport
    beneath thy lingering light;
while sallow Autumn fills thy lap with leaves;
or Winter, yelling through the troublous air,
    affrights thy shrinking train,
    and rudely rends thy robes;
so long regardful of thy quiet rule,
shall Fancy, Friendship, Science, smiling Peace,
    thy gentlest influence own,
    and love thy favourite name!
                      W. COLLINS

519   *TO PRIMROSES FILLED WITH MORNING DEW*

WHY do ye weep, sweet Babes? can tears
    speak grief in you,
    who were but born
    just as the modest morn
teemed her refreshing dew?

Alas, you have not known that shower
   that mars a flower;
   nor felt the unkind
   breath of a blasting wind;
   nor are ye worn with years;
   or warpt, as we,
   who think it strange to see
such pretty flowers, like to orphans young,
to speak by tears, before ye have a tongue.
Speak, whimpering younglings, and make known
   the reason why
   ye droop and weep;
   is it for want of sleep?
   or childish lullaby?
or that ye have not seen as yet
   the violet?
   Or brought a kiss
from that sweet-heart, to this?
No, no, this sorrow shown
   by your tears shed
would have this lecture read,
that things of greatest, so of meanest worth,
conceived with grief are and with tears brought
   forth.
R. HERRICK

520   *CORINNA'S GOING A MAYING*

GET up, get up for shame, the blooming morn
upon her wings presents the god unshorn.
See how Aurora throws her fair
fresh-quilted colours through the air:
get up, sweet slug-a-bed, and see
the dew-bespangling herb and tree.
Each flower has wept, and bowed towards the East,
above an hour since: yet you not drest,
   nay, not so much as out of bed?
   when all the birds have matins said,
   and sung their thankful hymns: 'tis sin;
   nay, profanation to keep in,
when as a thousand Virgins on this day
spring sooner then the lark to fetch in May.
Rise; and put on your foliage, and be seen
to come forth, like the spring-time, fresh and green;

and sweet as Flora. Take no care
for jewels for your gown or hair:
fear not: the leaves will strew
gems in abundance upon you:
besides, the childhood of the day has kept,
against you come, some orient pearls unwept:
  come and receive them while the light
  hangs on the dew-locks of the night:
  and Titan on the Eastern hill
  retires himself, or else stands still
till you come forth. Wash, dress, be brief in praying:
few beads are best, when once we go a Maying.

Come let us go, while we are in our prime;
and take the harmless folly of the time.
  We shall grow old apace, and die
  before we know our liberty.
  Our life is short; and our days run
  as fast away as does the sun:
and as a vapour, or a drop of rain
once lost, can ne'er be found again:
  so when or you or I are made
  a fable, song or fleeting shade;
  all love, all liking, all delight
  lies drowned with us in endless night.
Then while time serves, and we are but decaying;
Come, my Corinna, come, let's go a Maying.

R. HERRICK

HERMOTIMUS

VAINLY were the words of parting spoken;
  ever more must Charon turn from me.
Still my thread of life remains unbroken,
  and unbroken it must ever be;
    only they may rest
    whom the Fates' behest
from their mortal mansion setteth free.

I have seen the robes of Hermes glisten—
  seen him wave afar his serpent wand;
but to me the Herald would not listen—
  when the dead swept by at his command,
    not with that pale crew
    durst I venture too—
ever shut for me the quiet land.

Day and night before the dreary portal
  phantom-shapes, the guards of Hades, lie;
none of heavenly kind nor yet of mortal,
  may unchallenged pass the warders by.
    None that path may go,
    if he cannot show
  his last passport to eternity.

Cruel was the spirit-power thou gavest—
  fatal, O Apollo, was thy love!
Pythian! Archer! brightest God and bravest,
  hear, O hear me from thy throne above!
    Let me not, I pray,
    thus be cast away:
  Plead for me—thy slave—O plead to Jove!

I have heard thee with the Muses singing—
  heard that full melodious voice of thine,
silver-clear throughout the ether ringing—
  seen thy locks in golden clusters shine;
    and thine eye, so bright
    with its innate light,
  hath ere now been bent so low as mine.

Hast thou lost the wish—the will—to cherish
  those who trusted in thy godlike power?
Hyacinthus did not wholly perish!
  still he lives, the firstling of thy bower;
    still he feels thy rays,
    fondly meets thy gaze,
  though but now the spirit of a flower.

W. E. AYTOUN.

PASSAGES FOR TRANSLATION

INTO LATIN COMIC IAMBICS

1   SCENE FROM TWELFTH NIGHT

SIR ANDREW AGUE-CHEEK—SEBASTIAN—SIR TOBY BELCH
—CLOWN

Sir And. Now, sir, have I met you again? there's for you.
  [*striking Seb.*
Seb. Why, there's for thee, and there, and there: are all the people mad? [*draws, beating Sir A.*
Sir To. Hold, sir, or I'll throw your dagger o'er the house.
Clo. This will I tell my lady straight: I would not be in some of your coats for two-pence.
Sir To. Come on, sir; hold! [*holding Seb.*
Sir And. Nay, let him alone; I'll go another way to work with him; I'll have an action of battery against him, if there be any law in Illyria: though I struck him first, yet it's no matter for that.
Seb. Let go thy hand.
Sir To. Come, sir, I will not let you go. Come, my young soldier, put up your iron: you are well flesh'd; come on.
Seb. I will be free from thee. What wouldst thou now? If thou dar'st tempt me further, draw thy sword.
Sir To. What, what! Nay, then I must have an ounce or two of this malapert blood from you. [*draws*
                                       W. SHAKESPEARE

2   SCENE FROM MERRY WIVES OF WINDSOR

FALSTAFF—BARDOLPH

Fal. Bardolph, I say!
Bard. Here, sir.
Fal. Go, fetch me a quart of sack; put a toast in't. Have I lived to be carried in a basket, like a barrow of

butcher's offal; and to be thrown into the Thames? Well, if I be served such another trick, I'll have my brains ta'en out and buttered, and give them to a dog for a new-year's gift. The rogues slighted me into the river with as little remorse as they would have drowned a bitch's blind puppies, fifteen i' the litter; and you may know by my size, that I have a kind of alacrity in sinking; if the bottom were as deep as hell, I should down. I had been drowned, but that the shore was shelvy and shallow; a death that I abhor; for the water swells a man, and what a thing should I have been, when I had been swelled! I should have been a mountain of mummy.

W. SHAKESPEARE

3   SCENE FROM COMEDY OF ERRORS

ADRIANA—DROMIO—LUCIANA

Adr. Say, is your tardy master now at hand?
Drom. At hand! nay, he is at two hands with me, and that my two ears can witness.
Adr. Say, didst thou speak with him? know'st thou his mind?
Drom. Aye, aye, he told his mind upon mine ear: beshrew his hand, I scarce could understand it.
Luc. Spake he so doubtfully, thou could'st not feel his meaning?
Drom. Nay, he struck so plainly, I could too well feel his blows: and withal so doubtfully that I could scarce understand them.
Adr. But say, I pr'ythee, is he coming home? It seems, he hath great care to please his wife.

W. SHAKESPEARE

4 'Why,' exclaimed one of them to the aged dame, 'thou that art, like a corpse on the funeral pile, a disgrace to mortal life, and Pluto's abomination, dost thou make game of us that thou hast thus been sitting at home all day idle? What? at this late hour, after all our labours and perils hast thou nothing to give us for supper, and nought to think of but continually to pour wine down thy throat, into that greedy growling stomach of thine?'

'Brave, honourable young gentlemen, my masters,' replied the old woman, who seemed frightened out of her wits, 'all, all is ready, stewed meats, sweet and smoking, in rich gravy, wine in abundance, cups cleaned bright, and plenty of loaves of bread. The water too, for your hasty bath, is heated as usual.'

5   SCENE FROM MERRY WIVES OF WINDSOR

MR FORD—MR PAGE—MRS FORD

Ford. WELL, he's not here I seek for.
Page. No, nor no where else, but in your brain.
Ford. Help to search my house this one time: if I find not what I seek, show no colour for my extremity, let me for ever be your table-sport; let them say of me, As jealous as Ford, that searched a hollow walnut for his wife's leman. Satisfy me once more; once more search with me.
Mrs Ford. What, hoa, mistress Page! come you and the old woman down; my husband will come into the chamber.
Ford. Old woman! What old woman's that?
Mrs F. Why, it is my maid's aunt of Brentford.
Ford. A witch, a quean, an old cozening quean! Have I not forbid her my house! She comes of errands does she! We are simple men; we do not know what's brought to pass under the profession of fortune-telling. She works by charms, by spells, by the figure, and such daubery as this; beyond our element; we know nothing.——Come down, you witch, you hag, you; come down I say.
Mrs F. Nay, good, sweet husband; good gentlemen, let him not strike the old woman.
[*Enter Falstaff in woman's clothes, led by Mrs Page.*]
Mrs Page. Come, mother Prat, come give me your hand.
Ford. I'll prat her:——out of my door, you witch, you rag, you baggage, you polecat, you ronyon! out, out, I'll conjure you, I'll fortune-tell you.
[*exit Falstaff.*

6   SCENE FROM COMEDY OF ERRORS

ANTIPHOLUS OF SYRACUSE—DROMIO OF EPHESUS

Ant. Stop in your wind, sir; tell me this, I pray; where have you left the money that I gave you?

Drom. O,—sixpence, that I had o' Wednesday last:
to pay the saddler for my mistress' crupper;—
the saddler had it, sir, I kept it not.
Ant. I am not in a sportive humour now;
tell me and dally not, where is the money?
We being strangers here, how dar'st thou trust
so great a charge from thine own custody!
Drom. I pray you, jest, sir, as you sit at dinner:
I from my mistress come to you in post;
If I return, I shall be post indeed:
for she will score your fault upon my pate.
Ant. Come, Dromio, come, these jests are out of season;
reserve them till a merrier hour than this.
Where is the gold I gave in charge to thee?
Drom. To me, sir! why you gave no gold to me.
Ant. Come on, sir knave; have done your foolishness,
and tell me, how thou hast disposed thy charge.
Drom. My charge was but to fetch you from the mart
home to your house, the Phœnix, sir, to dinner;
my mistress and her sister stay for you.
Ant. Now, as I am a Christian, answer me,
in what safe place you have bestowed my money;
or I shall break that merry sconce of yours,
that stands on tricks when I am undisposed.

7 SCENE FROM COMEDY OF ERRORS

DROMIO OF SYRACUSE—ANTIPHOLUS OF SYRACUSE

Ant. How now, sir? is your merry humour altered?
as you love strokes, so jest with me again.
You know no Centaur? you received no gold?
your mistress sent to have me home to dinner?
my house was at the Phœnix? Wast thou mad,
that thus so madly thou didst answer me?
Drom. What answer, sir? when spake I such a word?
Ant. Even now, even here, not half an hour since.
Drom. I did not see you since you sent me hence
home to the Centaur, with the gold you gave me.
Ant. Villain, thou didst deny the gold's receipt;
and told'st me of a mistress and a dinner;
for which, I hope, thou felt'st I was displeased.
Drom. I am glad to see you in this merry vein:
what means this jest? I pray you, master, tell me.

Ant. Yea, dost thou jeer and flout me in the teeth?
Thinkest thou, I jest? Hold, take thou that and
that [*beating him*
Drom. Hold, sir, for God's sake: now your jest is earnest:
upon what bargain do you give it me?

8   SCENE FROM COMEDY OF ERRORS

ANTIPHOLUS—LUCIANA—ADRIANA—DROMIO

Ant. Plead you to me, fair dame? I know you not:
in Ephesus I am but two years old,
as strange unto your town, as to your talk;
who every word by all my wit being scanned
want wit in all one word to understand.
Luc. Fye, brother, how the world is changed with you:
When were you wont to use my sister thus?
She sent for you by Dromio home to dinner.
Ant. By Dromio?
Drom. By me?
Adr. By thee: and this thou didst return from him,—
that he did buffet thee and in his blows
denied my house for his, me for his wife.
Ant. Did you converse, sir, with this gentlewoman?
what is the course and drift of your compáct?
Drom. I, sir? I never saw her till this time.
Ant. Villain, thou liest: for even her very words
didst thou deliver to me on the mart.
Drom. I never spake to her in all my life.
Ant. How can she thus then call us by our names,
unless it be by inspiration!

9   SCENE FROM COMEDY OF ERRORS

ANTIPHOLUS OF EPHESUS BEFORE THE DUKE OF
EPHESUS

Ant. My liege, I am advised what I say;
Neither disturbed with the effect of wine,
nor heady-rash, provok'd with raging ire,
albeit, my wrongs might make one wiser mad.
This woman lock'd me out this day from dinner:
that goldsmith there, were he not pack'd with her,

could witness it, for he was with me then;
who parted with me to go fetch a chain,
promising to bring it to the Porcupine,
where Balthazar and I did dine together.
Our dinner done, and he not coming thither,
I went to seek him: in the street I met him;
and in his company, that gentleman,
there did this perjur'd goldsmith swear me down,
that I this day of him receiv'd the chain,
which, God he knows, I saw not: for the which,
he did arrest me with an officer.
I did obey; and sent my peasant home
for certain ducats: he with none return'd.
Then fairly I bespoke the officer,
to go in person with me to my house.
By the way we met
my wife, her sister, and a rabble more
of vile confederates; along with them
they brought one Pinch; a hungry lean-fac'd villain,
a mere anatomy, a mountebank,
a thread-bare juggler, and a fortune-teller;
a needy, hollow-ey'd, sharp-looking wretch,
a living dead man: this pernicious slave,
forsooth, took on him as a conjurer;
and, gazing in mine eyes, feeling my pulse,
and with no face, as 'twere, outfacing me,
cries out, I was possessed: then all together
they fell upon me, bound me, bore me thence;
and in a dark and dankish vault at home
there left me and my man, both bound together;
till gnawing with my teeth my bonds in sunder,
I gain'd my freedom, and immediately
ran hither to your grace; whom I beseech
to give me ample satisfaction
for these deep shames and great indignities.

10   SCENE FROM THE FOX

MOSCA, *the knavish parasite of* VOLPONE, *a rich and childless Venetian nobleman, persuades* VOLTORE, *an advocate, that he is, named for the inheritance of his master, who feigns himself to be dying.*

Volt. But am I sole heir?

Mos. Without a partner, sir; confirmed this morning;
the wax is warm yet, and the ink scarce dry
upon the parchment.
Volt. Happy, happy, me!
by what good chance, sweet Mosca?
Mos. Your desert, sir;
I know no second cause.
Volt. Thy modesty
is not to know it: well, we shall requite it.
Mos. He ever liked your course, sir: that first took him.
I oft have heard him say, how he admired
men of your large profession, that could speak
to every cause and things mere contraries,
till they were hoarse again, yet all be law;
that, with most quick agility could turn
and (re)-return; could make knots, and undo them:
give forkèd counsel; take provoking gold
on either hand and put it up: these men,
he knew, would thrive with their humility.
And, for his part, he thought he should be blest
to have his heir of such a suffering spirit,
so wise, so grave, of so perplexed a tongue,
and loud withal, that would not wag nor scarce
be still, without a fee; when every word
your worship but lets fall, is a chequin!

B. JONSON

11 SCENE FROM THE FOX

MOSCA—VOLPONE, *after practising upon the avarice of an old gentleman* CORBACCIO

Volp. [*leaping from his couch*] O, I shall burst!
let out my sides, let out my sides—
Mos. Contain
your flux of laughter, sir; you know this hope
is such a bait, it covers any hook.
Volp. O, but thy working and thy placing it!
I cannot hold; good rascal, let me kiss thee:
I never knew thee in so rare a humour.
Mos. Alas, sir, I but do, as I am taught;
follow your grave instructions; give them words;
pour oil into their ears, and send them hence.

Volp. Tis true tis true. What a rare punishment
is avarice to itself!
Mos. Ay, with our help, sir.
Volp. So many cares, so many maladies,
so many fears attending on old age,
yea, death so often called on, as no wish
can be more frequent with them, their limbs faint,
their senses dull, their seeing, hearing, going,
all dead before them; yea, their very teeth,
their instruments of eating, failing them:
yet this is reckoned life! nay, here was one
is now gone home, that wishes to live longer!
feels not his gout nor palsy; feigns himself
younger by scores of years, flatters his age
with confident belying it, hopes he may,
with charms, like Æson, have his youth restored:
and with these thoughts so battens, as if fate
would be as easily cheated on, as he,
and all turns air!

B. JONSON

12 SCENE FROM EVERY MAN IN HIS HUMOUR

WELL-BRED—CAPTAIN BOBADILL—E. KNOWELL

Wel. Captain Bobadill, why muse you so?
Know. He is melancholy too.
Bob. 'Faith, sir, I was thinking of a most honourable piece of service, was performed to-morrow, being St Mark's to-day, shall be some ten years now.
Know. In what place, captain?
Bob. Why, at the beleaguering of Strigonium, where no less than two hours, seven hundred resolute gentlemen, as any were in Europe, lost their lives upon the breach. I'll tell you, gentlemen, it was the first but the best leaguer that ever I beheld with these eyes, except the taking in of—what do you call it? last year—by the Genoways; but that of all other was the most fatal and dangerous exploit that ever I was ranged in, since I first bore arms before the face of the enemy, as I am a gentleman and a soldier!
Know. Then you were a servitor at both, it seems; at Strigonium, and what do you call 't?

Bob. By St George, I was the first man that entered the breach, and had I not effected it with resolution, I had been slain, if I had had a million of lives——observe me judicially, sweet sir : they had planted me three demi-culverins just in the mouth of the breach ; now, sir, as we were to give on, their master-gunner (a man of no mean skill and mark, you must think), confronts me with his linstock, ready to give fire ; I, spying his intendment, discharged my petronel in his bosom, and with these single arms, my poor rapier, ran violently upon the Moors that guarded the ordinance and put 'em pell-mell to the sword.

B. JONSON

13   SCENE FROM THE ALCHEMIST

FACE, *the house-keeper, in order to conceal what had been going on in his Master* LOVEWIT'S *house, during his absence, tries to persuade him that it was shut up on account of being visited by an apparition.*

Face. Good sir, come from the door.
Love. Why, what's the matter?
Face. Yet farther, you are too near yet.
Love. In the name of wonder,
    what means the fellow !
Face. The house, sir, has been visited.
Love. What with the plague? Stand thou then farther.
Face. No, sir, I had it not.
Love. Who had it then ? I left
    none else but thee in the house.
Face. Yes, sir, my fellow,
    the cat that kept the buttery, had it on her
    a week before I spied it ; but I got her
    conveyed away in the night : and so I shut
    the house up for a month—
Love. How !
Face. Purposing then, sir,
    t' have burnt rose-vinegar, treacle tar,
    and have made it sweet, that you should ne'er
       have known it ;
    because I knew the news would but afflict you, sir.

Love. Breathe less and farther off! why this is stranger:
the neighbours tell me all here that the doors
have still been open—
Face. How, sir!
Love. Gallants, they tell me, men and women,
and of all sorts, tag-rag, been seen to flock here—
Face. They did pass through the doors then,
or walls, I assure their eye-sights and their spec-
tacles;
for here, sir, are the keys, and here have been,
in this my pocket now above twenty days:
and for before, I kept the fort alone there.
                                               B. JONSON

14   SCENE FROM THE GUARDIAN

DURAZZO *reproved by* CAMILLO *for indulging the extrava-
gance of his nephew and ward.*

Dur. Tell me of his expenses! which of you
stands bound for a gazet? he spends his own;
and you impertinent fools or knaves, (make choice
of either title, which your signiorships please,)
to meddle in't.
Cam.   Your age gives privilege
to this harsh language.
Dur.   My age! do not use
that word again; if you do, I shall grow young
and swinge you soundly. I would have you know
though I write fifty odd, I do not carry
an almanack in my bones to predeclare
what weather we shall have; nor do I kneel
in adoration of the spring and fall
before my doctor.
Cam.   This is from the purpose
Dur. I cannot cut a caper, or groan like you
when I have done, nor run away so nimbly
out of the field: but bring me to a fence-school,
and crack a blade or two for exercise,
ride a barbed horse, or take a leap after me,
following my hounds or hawks, and you'll confess
I am in the May of my abilities
and you in your December.

Lent.   We are glad you bear
    your years so well.
Dur.   My years! no more of years;
    if you do, at your peril
Cam.   We desire not
    to prove your valour.
Dur.   'Tis your safest course
Cam. But, as friends to your fame and reputation,
    come to instruct you, your too much indulgence
    to the exorbitant waste of young Caldoro,
    your nephew and your ward, hath rendered you
    but a bad report among wise men in Naples.
Dur. Wise men!—in your opinion; but to me
    that understand myself and them, they are
    hide-bounded money-mongers: they would have me
    train up my ward a hopeful youth, to keep
    a merchant's book; or at the plough; clothe him
    in canvass or coarse cotton: let him know
    no more than how to cipher well or do
    his tricks by the square root; grant him no plea-
        sure
    but quoits and nine-pins: suffer him to converse
    with none but clowns and coblers.
                                        P. MASSINGER

15   THE PARASITE

WHAT art, vocation, trade or mystery
    can match with your fine parasite? — The
        Painter!
He! a mere dauber; A vile drudge the Farmer:
their business is to labour, ours to laugh,
to jeer, to quibble, faith sirs! and to drink,
aye, and to drink lustily. Is not this rare?
'Tis life, my life at least: the first of pleasures
were to be rich myself; but next to this
I hold it best to be a Parasite,
and feed upon the rich. Now mark me right!
you know my humour, not one spark of pride,
such and the same for ever to my friends:
if cudgell'd, molten iron to the hammer
is not so malleable; but if I cudgel,
bold as the thunder: is one to be blinded?
I am the lightning's flash: to be puff'd up?

I am the wind to blow him to the bursting:
choak'd, strangled? I can do't and save a halter:
would you break down his doors? Behold an earth-
 quake:
open and enter them? A battering ram:
will you sit down to supper? I'm your guest,
your very *Fly* to enter without bidding:
would you move off? You'll move a well as soon:
I'm for all work, and though the job were stabbing,
betraying, false-accusing, only say,
Do this! and it is done: I stick at nothing;
they call me Thunder-bolt for my dispatch;
friend of my friends am I: let actions speak me;
I'm much too modest to commend myself.
R. CUMBERLAND

16   THE RIGHT USE OF RICHES

WEAK is the vanity, that boasts of riches,
 for they are fleeting things; were they not such,
could they be yours to all succeeding time,
'twere wise to let none share in the possession:
but if whate'er you have is held of fortune,
and not of right inherent, why, my father,
why with such niggard jealousy engross
what the next hour may ravish from your grasp,
and cast into some worthless favourite's lap?
Snatch then the swift occasion while 'tis yours;
put this unstable boon to nobler uses;
foster the wants of men, impart your wealth
and purchase friends; 'twill be more lasting treasure,
and, when misfortune comes, your best resource.
R. CUMBERLAND

17   HOMO ES

IF you, O Trophimus, and you alone
 of all your mother's sons have Nature's charter
for privilege of pleasures uncontrolled,
with full exemption from the strokes of fortune,
and that some god hath ratified the grant,
you then with cause may vent your loud reproach,
for he hath broke your charter and betrayed you;

but, if you live and breathe the common air
on the same terms as we do, then I tell you,
and tell it in the tragic poet's words—
*of your philosophy you make no use,
if you give place to accidental evils.*—
The sum of which philosophy is this—
you are a man, and therefore Fortune's sport,
this hour exalted and the next abased:
you are a man, and, though by nature weak,
by nature arrogant, climbing to heights
that mock your reach and crush you in the fall:
nor was the blessing you have lost the best
of all life's blessings, nor is your misfortune
the worst of its afflictions; therefore, Trophimus,
make it not such by overstrained complaints,
but to your disappointment suit your sorrow.
R. CUMBERLAND

18   *PEACE—THE SOVEREIGN GOOD*

PHILOSOPHERS consume much time and pain,
to seek the sovereign good; nor is there one
who yet hath struck upon it: Virtue some,
and prudence some contend for, whilst the knot
grows harder by their struggle to untie it.
I, a mere clown, in turning up the soil
have dug the secret forth:—All-gracious Jove!
tis Peace, most lovely and of all beloved;
peace is the bounteous goddess, who bestows
weddings and holidays and joyous feasts,
relations, friends, wealth, plenty, social comforts
and pleasures, which alone make life a blessing.
R. CUMBERLAND

19   *RETORT FROM A MAN OF LOW BIRTH TO AN OLD
      WOMAN PRATING ABOUT HER ANCESTRY*

GOOD gossip, if you love me, prate no more;
what are your genealogies to me?
Away to those, who have more need of them!
let the degenerate wretches, if they can,
dig up dead honour from their fathers' tombs,
and boast it for their own—Vain empty boast!
when every common fellow, that they meet,
if accident have not cut off the scroll,
can shew a list of ancestry as long.

You call the Scythians barbarous, and despise them;
yet Anacharsis was a Scythian born;
and every man of a like noble nature,
tho' he were moulded from an Æthiop's loins,
is nobler than your pedigrees can make him.

R. CUMBERLAND

20 *VIRTUE ALONE IS TRUE NOBILITY*

TIS only title thou disdain'st in her, the which
I can build up. Strange is it, that our bloods,
of colour, weight and heat, poured all together,
would quite confound distinction, yet stand off
in differences so mighty: if she be
all that is virtuous, (save what thou dislik'st
a poor physician's daughter) thou dislik'st
of virtue for the name: but do not so:
from lowest place where virtuous things proceed,
the place is dignified by the doer's deed:
where great additions swell, and virtue none,
it is a dropsied honour: good alone
is good, without a name: vileness is so:
the property by what it is should go
not by the title. She is young, wise, fair;
in these to nature she's immediate heir;
and these breed honour: that is honour's scorn,
which challenges itself as honour's born,
and is not like the sire: Honours best thrive,
when rather from our acts we them derive
than our fore-goers: the mere word's a slave,
deboshed on every tomb, on every grave;
a lying trophy, and as oft is dumb,
where dust and damned oblivion is the tomb
of honoured bones indeed.

W. SHAKESPEARE

NOTES

§ 9 two stanzas from *the Fountain*, a Conversation.
§ 10 from *Old Mortality*.
§ 13 from lines composed at Grasmere; the Author having just read of the dissolution of Fox being hourly expected.
§ 19 from *Heart of Mid Lothian:* 1. 4, comp. Minucius Felix *Apolog.* l. 36, § 6: *ut qui viam terit, eo felicior, quo levior incedit, ita beatior in hoc itinere vivendi qui paupertate se sublevat, non sub divitiarum onere suspirat:* Lactantius, *Div. Inst.* VII. 1, § 20.
§ 29 written by Queen Elizabeth, while prisoner at Woodstock, with charcoal on a shutter See Percy's *Reliques*.
§ 35 '*Scripseram prius hoc de poesi morali caput,*' says Sir William Jones in his Lectures on Asiatic poetry, p. 350, '*quam scirem unde fabulam hanc quæ ab Addisono nostro etiam citatur sumsisset Chardinus: sed legi eam nuperrime in Sadii opere perfectissimo, quod* Bustan *seu* Hortus *inscribitur, et a Sadio ipso, poeta, si quis alius, ingenioso, inventam puto: ipsius itaque elegantes versus citabo cum mea qualiscunque sit versione:*' and after quoting the original with a literal Latin translation, he paraphrases thus:

*Rigante molles imbre campos Persidis
e nube in æquor lapsa pluviæ guttula est,
quæ, cum modestus eloqui sineret pudor,
'Quid hoc loci, inquit, quid rei misella sum?
quo me repente, ah! quo redactam sentio?'
Cum se verecundanti animulâ spernent,
illam recepit gemmeo concha in sinu;
tandemque tenuis aquula facta est unio:
nunc in coronâ lætâ Regis emicat
docens, sit humili quanta laus modestiæ.*

§ 70 from the *Saint's Tragedy*.
§ 92 from the *Cresphontes*.
§ 94 l. 3, an πείθει ποτὶ πλόον? l. 4, πολλὸς βυθοῖ Ahrens.

§ 98 l. 3, comp. Eurip. *Fr. apud Stobæum*, p. 185:
ὅταν δ' ἴδῃς πρὸς ὕψος ἠρμένον τινά,
λαμπρῷ τε πλούτῳ καὶ γένει γαυρούμενον
τούτου ταχεῖαν νέμεσιν εὐθὺς προσδόκα·
ἐπαίρεται γὰρ μεῖζον, ἵνα μεῖζον πέσῃ.

§ 106 l. 3, *the trew fayrn*, the true beauty: comp. PART I, § 203, l. 10: The indiscriminate use of substantives and adjectives was common in the older poetry: traces of it may be found in such colloquial expressions as *the dark* for *darkness*.

§ 107 l. 1, *culver*, dove.

§ 112 l. 8, *fondly*, foolishly: *prevent*, forestall.

§ 114 l. 6, *bill*, voice, note: l. 9, *bird of hate*, cuckoo.

§ 115 l. 10, *Emathian conqueror:* the story is told of Alexander the Great by Ælian *Var. Hist.* XIII. 7; and by Pliny *Nat. Hist.* VII. 29.

§ 119 l. 12, *to poison*, compared to poison.

§ 174 l. 3, *nae gowans glint*, no daisies peep out: l. 4, *cleeding*, clothing: l. 8, *burnie*, little rivulet: l. 9, *brae*, declivity: l. 12, *cranreuch*, hoar-frost.

§ 196 l. 1, *bravery*, finery.

§ 200 l. 17, lightning-gem, the precious stone, *ceraunium*, so called because it was supposed to be found where thunder had fallen.

§ 210 l. 1, *jo*, sweetheart: l. 4, *brent*, smooth: l. 7, *pow*, head: l. 10, *thegither*, together: l. 11, *cantie*, cheerful.

§ 215 on the Lady Mary Villiers, compare § 80.

§ 220 l. 3, *birks*, birches: l. 7, *siller saughs*, silver willows: l. 10, *breckans*, ferns: l. 13, *jouks*, runs low.

§ 224 l. 7, *maunds*, baskets.

§ 225 l. 15, *wonned*, lived.

§ 249 l. 11, *eild*, eld, old age: *buss*, bush: *bield*, shelter.

§ 280 Mrs Elizabeth Tollet, daughter of George Tollet, commissioner of the Navy in the reigns of King William and Queen Anne, and friend of Sir Isaac Newton, was authoress of a volume of poems, English and Latin, which were not published till after her death in 1754. See Nichols' *Select Collection*, vol. VI. p. 64.

§ 323 from *the Secular Masque:* l. 4, *wexing*, waxing.

§ 325 l. 9, *leal*, faithful: l. 23, *fain*, happy.

§ 327 the second stanza has been suppressed in the later editions of Wordsworth's poems. The first four verses in the earlier editions ran thus:
Though by a sickly taste betrayed
some may dispraise the lovely maid,
with fearless pride I say
that she is healthful, fleet and strong.

§ 328 from the *Paradise of Daintie Devices:* l. 8, *yelping*, or *yalping*, crying.

§ 329 from the *Spectator*, no. 366, where it is given as a translation from a song in Scheffer's *History of Lapland;* 'it will be necessary to imagine,' says the translator, 'that the author of this song, not having the liberty of seeing his mistress at her father's house, was in hopes of spying her at a distance in the fields.' Keble *Prælect. de poeticæ vi medicâ*, vol. 1, p. 74, remarks: '*omni melle dulciora sunt ea, quæ Lapponico cuidam amatori tribuuntur: quæ eo quidem magis placent, quod inter nives et pruinas, extremo orbis angulo, fiunt obvia.*'

§ 333 'The subject and simile,' in this beautiful Pindaric ode, 'are, as usual with Pindar, united. The various sources of poetry,' continues the Author, 'which give life and lustre to all it touches, are here described; its quiet majestic progress enriching every subject (otherwise dry and barren) with a pomp of diction and luxuriant harmony of numbers; and its more rapid and irresistible course, when swoln and hurried away by the conflict of tumultuous passions:' l. 13, power of harmony to calm the turbulent passions of the soul. The thoughts are borrowed from the first Pythian of Pindar. GRAY. See § 409.

§ 334 power of harmony to produce all the graces of motion in the body. GRAY: l. 17, Λάμπει δ' ἐπὶ πορφυρέῃσι παρείῃσι φῶς ἔρωτος, Phrynichus apud Athenæum. GRAY.

§ 343 *abused*, mistaken, deceived.

§ 344 The scene of the ode is supposed to lie on the Thames near Richmond: l. 6, *airy harp*, see note on § 264, *Fol. Silv.* PART I.; l. 19, *whitening spire*, Richmond Church, in which Thomson was buried, and in the neighbourhood of which he resided some time before his death.

§ 354 from the *Davideis*, Book i.

§ 355 Burke quotes this passage as a very fine example of the magnificence arising from a profusion of images, *on the Sublime and Beautiful*, Part ii. § 13: compare SIR W. JONES, *Poeseos Asiaticæ Comm.* p. 244.

§ 357 l. 6, *Corinthian*, the capitals of Corinthian pillars being decorated with leaves: l. 7, *twitter words*, the early chirping of birds in spring: l. 12, *echo lights*, reflected: so Byron, *Island* V.:

> the spars
> *echo* their dim light to the distant stars.

§ 359 from the *Discourse concerning the Government of Oliver Cromwell*.

§ 360 from the *Ode upon King Charles' restoration and return*.

§ 365 l. 3, *maun*, must, *stour*, dust: l. 9, *glinted*, peeped: l. 13, *wa's*, walls: l. 14, *bield*, shelter, comp. § 249: l. 16, *histie*, dry, barren.
§ 370 from *the Princess*.
§ 371 l. 7, *awful*, full of reverence: l. 12, *whist*, i.q. whisted, hushed: l. 19, *one way*, i.e. in one direction, towards where the infant Deity lay: l. 21, *for all*, notwithstanding all.
§ 372 l. 4, *than*, i.q. then: l. 5, *Pan*, used by Spenser and other poets as an epithet of the true GOD, the Lord of *all*: l. 14, *noise*, concert: l. 14, *as took*, so that it charmed: l. 18, *hollow round*, lunar sphere.
§ 376 Miss Ferrer was afterwards married to Dr Peckard, Master of Magdalen College, Cambridge, 1781—1797.
§ 380 from *Helga*.
§ 384 l. 9, *alate*, lately.
§ 400 The Hermias to whom the ode is addressed was τύραννος of the cities of Atarneus and Assus in Mysia; he invited Aristotle, for whom he entertained a warm attachment, to his Court, B.C. 347.
§ 401 l. 1, ἱστῶν παλιμβάμους ὁδοὺς, de mulieribus ἱστὸν ambientibus. Compare Jacob's *Del. Epigr. Anthol.* viii. 108.: where the weaver is spoken of as παριστίδιος δινευμένη; Hom. *Il.* i. 31, ἱστὸν ἐποιχομένη: l. 2, οἰκόριαι ἑταῖραι, *aequales quæ domi manent*: l. 6, τὸν δὲ σύγκοιτον *etc.*, *concubitorem autem suavem, modicum palpebris somnum consumens incumbentem* (in palpebras delapsum), h.e. puella tum demum, ubi tutas credebat pecudes, feris in lustra ante solis ortum regressis, somno vacabat paulisper. DISSEN. l. 10, ἐκ μεγάρων (sc. σεμνοῦ ἄντρου) προσέννεπε, 'called him out of his abode.'
§ 403 from the first Nemean ode: l. 1, ὑπὸ σπλάγχνων, *ex utero matris*, cf. § 411, l. 1: l. 14, βέλος, 'fear,' cf. Hom. *Il.* XI. 269.
§ 404 l. 8, παλίγγλωσσον, 'contradictory:' l. 19, ἐν σχερῷ, 'continually.'
§ 405 from the Second Olympian ode: l. 1, ἴσον—ἴσα, i.e. *noctu æque ac interdiu*: l. 2, ἀπονέστερον, *minus molestam (meliorem) quam mali vitam vident*: l. 3, ἐν χερὸς ἀκμᾷ, *vi manuum*: l. 5, κεινὰν παρὰ δίαιταν, *inopem propter victum*: l. 7, τοὶ δ' 'but the others, (i.e. the wicked, in opposition to the ἐσλοὶ οἵτινες ἔχαιρον εὐορκίαις, who are τίμιοι θεῶν, 'honoured of the gods,') endure a life too dreadful to look upon': l. 8, ἐστρὶς ἑκατέρωθι, 'thrice in this world and thrice in the spirit-world,' ἐτόλμασαν, *sustinuerunt*: l. 10, ἔτειλαν Διὸς ὁδὸν, *peragunt Jovis iter ad regiam Saturni*: Saturn is said to govern here, because the Golden Age was under his reign, from the resemblance of the condition of mankind then to that of the blessed now in the other world:

l. 11, νάσος Dorice pro νάσους. For this opinion of Pythagoras that souls passed from one body to another, till by length of time and many penances they had purged away all their imperfections, see Virgil *Æn.* VI. 638, *foll.*, Valerius Flaccus *Argon.* i. 84: 'The restriction of this to the third metempsychosis,' remarks Cowley, 'I do not remember anywhere else. It may be, thrice is taken indefinitely for several times.'

§ 406 from the *Agamemnon.*

§ 407 from the *Ajax.*

§ 408 The Ode to Rome, which is generally attributed to Erinna, has been ascribed by Welcker and others with better right to Melinno, an otherwise obscure poetess of the early part of the Roman period: l. 2, Dea urbis cognominis tutelaris in terrâ solio sceptrisque potitur, eique, ut diis Olympus, ita tellus est inconcussa sedes, ἄθραυστον, ἀεὶ ἀσφαλὲς ἕδος, Vide Homer *Odyss.* VI. 42: l. 5, πρέσβειρα, *veneranda*, i.q. πρέσβα: l. 9, σᾷ ὑπὸ σδεύγλᾳ λεπάδνων = ὑπὸ ζεύγλῃ τῶν σῶν λεπάδνων: l. 19, seges fortium virorum cum copia segetum comparatur, quæ proveniunt in agris. MOEBIUS. l. 20, καρπὸν ἀπ' ἀνδρῶν, i.q. καρπὸν ἀνδρῶν.

§ 409 from the First Pythian vv. 1—20, see § 333, l. 13, *note:* l. 2, σύνδικον *commune*: βάσις, *incessus saltantium*, a quo incipiebat comissatio; hinc ἀγλαΐας ἀρχὰ dicitur: l. 3, σάμασιν, *quum tu sonis tuis signum das*: l. 4, ἀμβολὰς τεύχῃς, i.q. ἀναβάλλῃ, *ordiaris:* Verte *simul ac choros regentia exordia cantuum tuorum suscitas et ordiris*. DISSEN. l. 8, γλεφάρων i.q. βλεφάρων: l. 9, 'but he in his slumber heaves his supple back, o'erpowered by thy vibrations' (ῥιπαῖσι, cf. § 417, l. 21): l. 12, κῆλα *tela cithanæ*: l. 13, ἀμφὶ σοφίᾳ, *per artem*: l. 17, Κιλίκων ἄντρον, Hom. *Il.* ii. 780: l. 20, χίονος ὀξείας, *gelu acutum*, Hor. *Od.* I. 9. 3.

§ 410 from the first Olympian: l. 1, πρός 'about the time of,' cf. § 401, l. 8: l. 2, ἔρεφον μέλαν, i.e. ὥστε μέλαν εἶναι: l. 9, ἐς χάριν τέλλεται, '*fuit aut tibi quidquam dulce meum*,' *Æn.* IV. 307: l. 10, πέδασον, *inhibe*, quum a tergo instans transfigeret certantes: l. 13, ὀλέσαις i.q. ὀλέσας: l. 15, ἕψοι γῆρας, *senectutem foveat omnium laudum expers*: l. 17, *sed ego non ero talis, mihi certum est subire hoc certamen; tu autem eventum da felicem*: l. 19, *neque vero* (ὧν pro οὖν) *irritas preces fecit*: l. 21, ἕλεν, *vicit Oenomaum, obtinuit virginem.*

§ 411 from the Sixth Olympian. Keble in a comparison between Horace's *Od.* iii. 4, *me fabulosæ Vulture in Appulo &c.* and this passage of Pindar, points out the superiority of the Greek poet to the Roman: he says Horace *agit, ut unus vicinorum; Pindarus vero* μάτηρ οἷα φράζει, *anxie quærit puerum, invento lætatur, Prælect.* V. p. 68: l. 1, ὑπὸ σπλάγχνων, *ex utero matris:* l. 13, βεβρεγμένος, cf. Lucret. ii. 820, *omnigenis perfusa coloribus;* v. 594, *lumen, quod terras omnes coelumque rigando compleat:* l. 14, τὸ καὶ κατεφάμιξεν *propterea faustum verbum pronuntiavit:* l. 18, λαοτρόφον τιμάν τωα, *dignitatem aliquam publicam, quæ augeat res populi.*

§ 412 'Suavissimum hoc poematium,' says JACOBS, 'scriptum est in commendationem coli eburneæ, quam poeta, Miletum vela facturus, Theugenidi, Niciæ Medici conjugi, donum destinavit. Dum ipsam colum, quam habitura sit dominam, docere videtur, honestissimam matronam ejusque maritum ingeniose et urbane laudat:' l. 3, θαρσεῦσ' ὑμάρτη, θαρσοῦσ' ὁμάρτει: πόλιν Νείλεω, Miletus, said to have been founded by *Nileus* or *Neleus*, son of Codrus, whence Apollonius Rhodius calls the inhabitants Νηλεῖδαι, *Argon.* i. 959: l. 4, ὑπασσαλῶ, vulgo ὑφ' ἁπαλῶ. Venus quæ Mileti imprimis colebatur, templum ibi habuit splendidum in arundineto extructum, unde ἡ ἐν καλάμοις sive ἡ ἐν ἕλει nomen accepit: l. 9, Νικιάας ἀλόχῳ, Νικίου ἀλόχου, i. e. Theugenis: l. 10, ἀνδρείοις πέπλοις = ἀνδρείους πέπλους: l. 11, βράκη, ῥάκη: ὑδάτινα, *thalassina* in reference to the colour, (*vide* Ovid. *A. A.* III. 177) or as others explain, *pellucida*, in reference to the texture: l. 12, δὶς πέξαιντ' αὐτοένει, (*si per Theugenidem esset), bis quotannis oves tonderi deberent:* l. 15, *non enim volebam te domo tribuere desidiosæ:* l. 17, ὣξ Εφύρας 'Αρχίας: Notum est Archia duce coloniam Corintho missam Syracusis dedisse originem, unde *Idyll.* xvi., Syracusæ appellantur 'Εφυραῖον ἄστυ, cf. Thucyd. vi. 3. 77. KIESSLING: l. 21, πεδά, μετά.

§ 414 from *Œdipus Rex*, v. 464.
§ 415 from *Trachiniæ*, v. 494: l. 16, *sola fausti tori largitrix* (*venustissima*, Wunder) *dea regebat certamen*, HERMANN. l. 20, κλίμακες, luctæ genus, de quo v. Ovid, *Metam.* IX. 51.
§ 416 from *Antigone*, v. 599.
§ 417 from *Electra*, v. 86: l. 21, ῥιπάς, cf. § 409, v. 9.
§ 418 from *Helena*, v. 1319.
§ 419 from *Bacchæ*, v. 382.
§ 420 from *Medea*, v. 628.
§ 421 from *Ion*, v. 82.
§ 422 from *Alcestis*, v. 962.
§ 423 from *Hecuba*, v. 925.
§ 424 from *Andromache*, v. 284.
§ 427 l. 1, imitated, according to J. Warton from G. Buchanan, *Genethliacon Jacobi Sexti*:

Sic ubi de patrio redivivus funere Phœnix
auroræ ad populos redit, et cunabula secum
ipse sua, et cineres patris inferiasque decoris

Notes

  fert humeris: quacunque citis adremigat alis,
  indigenæ comitantur aves, celebrantque canoro
  agmine: non illas species incognita tantum
  aut picturatæ capiunt spectacula pennæ:
So Sannazarius *de partu Virginis*, lib. ii. 415:
  Qualis nostrum cum tendit in orbem
  purpureis rutilat pennis nitidissima Phœnix,
  quam variæ circum volucres comitantur euntem:
  illa volans solem nativo provocat auro,
  fulva caput: stupet ipsa cohors, plausuque sonoro
  per sudum strepit innumeris exercitus alis.

§ 444 See Cicero, *Tusc. Disp.* I. c. xlviii.

§ 455 l. 2, *ilk*, each, *kep*, catch: l. 29, *ae*, one.

§ 457 at Hohenlinden (*High Lime-trees*) a forest near Munich, a French republican army, under Moreau, defeated the Austrians, Dec. 2, 1800.

§ 459 The sentiment is borrowed from the well-known fragment of Alcæus:

   οὐ λίθοι
 τείχεων εὖ δεδομαμένοι,
 ἀλλ' ἄνδρες πόλιος πύργος ἀρήϊοι.

§ 464 l. 32, *and soft silence*, i. q. with soft silence.

§ 471 The Scolion, ἐν μύρτου κλαδὶ τὸ ξίφος φορήσω, to which Collins refers, is not the composition of Alcæus but of Callistratus.

§ 472 l. 11, *they whom Science loved to name*, the family of the Medici: l. 18, *those whose merchant sons were kings*, the Venetians: the next line refers to the Doge of Venice: l. 4, *Liguria's state*, Genoa: l. 32, *those to whom thy stork is dear*, the Dutch: l. 33, *a British Queen*, Elizabeth.

§ 477 comp. the epigram of Poseidippus, *Fol. Silv.* PART I. § 75.

§ 520 l. 25, *beads*, prayers.

§ 521-2 Hermotimus, the hero of the ballad, from which this extract is taken, was a philosopher and prophet of Clazomenæ who possessed the faculty of effecting a voluntary separation between his soul and body: for the former could wander to any part of the universe, and even hold intercourse with supernatural beings, whilst the senseless frame remained at home. Before attempting any of these aerial flights, he took the precaution to warn his wife, lest, ere the return of his soul, the body should be rendered an unfit receptacle: but she one day committed his body to the flames, and effectually put a stop to his trances.

§ 6 l. 25 *sconce*, head.

§ 14 l. 2 *gazet*, a small Venetian coin.

INDEX OF SUBJECTS

The Numbers refer to the Sections

A

ADVERSITY, the school of heroism, 360: hymn to, 467
Affection, instability of, 337
Age, the golden age, 462
Alcestis, dirge on, 422
Alcæus, ode in imitation of, 459
Alps, the, at day-break, 190
AMPHION, 255
Anacreontic, 351
Angels, guardian, 91
Apollo, to, 324: canticle to, 2
April, to, 133: the first of, 443
Anon, 131, 255
Arion, 131
Arlinkow, the castle of, 341
Art and nature, 488
ASTROPHEL, the death of, 264
Autumn woods, 254

B

BABYLON, fall of, prophesied, 496
Balaam, the prophet, 84: prophecy of, 505
Bard, memory of the, 96
Beauty, 517: the true, 37, 106: the soul of, 241: and grief, 75
Bene qui latuit bene vixit, 308
Blindness, MILTON's sonnet on his own, 112
Blossoms, to, 270
Blyth, to the river, 482

Boy, the mountain-boy, 184: the Greek, 363
Bowl, the flowing, 167
Britannia, song to, 51, 443
BROWNE, WILLIAM, sonnet to, 33

C

Calm after a storm, description of, 200
Castara, the description of, 281
Cato's soliloquy, 511
Ceres, the revenge of, 418
Charity, 26
CHARLES II, king, the restoration of, 427
Cheerfulness, 28
Child, lines to a, embracing his mother, 157
Childhood, scenes of, revisited, 155: the poet's recollections of, 253
Chloris ill, 73
Christmas carol, 293
CHRIST, resurrection of, 510
Christian warfare, 475
Cicada, to the, 68
Clyde, to the, 43
COMFORTER, the, 209
Conqueror, the last, 206
Constancy, 22, 511
Consumption, sonnet to, 135
Contemplation, to, 45, 148, 364, 491
Content and rich, 38, 39, 40, 45
Content, sweet, 124
Contentment, 45: hymn to, 235, 236, 278

Index of Subjects 295

Contrast, the, 94
Coral insect, to the, 214
Corinna's going a Maying, 520
Cromwell's return from Ireland, 447
Culver, the, 107
CUMBERLAND, Lady Margaret, Countess of, 232, 233
Cypress, the wreath of, 336
CYRENE, 401

D

Daffodils, to, 181
Daisy, to the, 211, 212: to a mountain, 365, 366
DAVID's supplication to Michal, 150, 151: lamentation over Saul and Jonathan, 498
Day, the longest, 301
Death, to, 476: of the good, 13: emblem of, 86: invocation of, 138: nightpiece on, 144: of a son 182, of a young lady, 186—189: the weapons of, 206: memorials of, 291: the great leveller, 361, 362
Decease, release, 444
Deianira, the combat for, 415
Despondency, 165
Diana, hymn to, 267: song of, 323
Dirge, 288, 346: a mother's over her child, 204, 289: at sea, 287
Disappointment, on, 367
Distaff, the, 412
Dominus dominantium, 202
Doom, the common, 206
Drinking song, 69
Duty, the path of, 20

E

Earth, bounty of the, 63
Echo, song to, 146, 159: echoes, 260
Ecstasy, the, 389
ELECTRA, the lament of, 417
Elegy, 185: on Captain Henderson, 455
ELIZABETH's song, 70
Elysium, 227—229: description of, 405
Enchantment, the, 60
England, caution to, 85: lines addressed to, 145: complaint of the miseries of, 359
ENID's song, 67

Epitaph, on the Lady Mary Villiers, 80, 215: of the living author, 246
Eton College, ode on a distant prospect of, 456
Evening hymn, 5: the hour of, 169: evening repose, 180: expostulation, the, 474
Extreme of love or hate, 216

F

Falcon, the, 386
Fame, vanity of, 100, 101, 102, 103, 432: indifference to, 251
Fancy, ode to, 302
Farewell, a, 208
Farm, the poet on leaving his, 340
Field flowers, 514
Firmament, the, 393—4
Flowers from a Roman wall, 15
Fortune, to, 29: Enid's song to, 67: proof against, 235, 236: her spite quelled by patience, 284: the uncertainty of, 434

G

Gaiety, 82
GOD, love of, 425, insensibility to the mercies of, 244: address to, 339
Good, the, alone great, 321: their happiness in a future state, 405, 428: death of the, 13
Gratitude, its sweetness, 11, 428
Grace, native, 488
Grave, 234
Greece, modern, 263
Grief and beauty, 75

H

HALLAM, Arthur Henry, to the memory of, 305, 306, 307
Hamlet, the, 347, 348
Happiness, 308: true, 468
Heaven, 154, 265, 309, 483: in prospect, 242, 243
HEBER, Bishop, verses to his wife, 320
Hellas, the restoration of, 158, 275: sorrows of, for the loss of her heroes before Troy, 406

296 Index of Subjects

HENDERSON, elegy on Captain Matthew, 455
HERCULES, the birth and infancy of, 403, 404
HERMEAS of Atarnæ, ode to, 400
HERRICK, dialogue between, and Amaryllis, 224
HEZEKIAH'S song of thanksgiving, 497
Hohenlinden, 457
Home, 74
Hope, 137, 265
HORATIUS COCLES, 177
Humility, 23, 41
Hymn after foreign travels, 87: evening, 5

I

IAMUS, 411
Ideal, the pursuit of the, 229
Il penseroso, 180
Incarnation, the, 303, 304
Independence, 387
Infant, to a dying, 318
Ingratitude, 147
In memoriam, 205, 305—7
Insensibility, happy, 377
Invocation of the spirit of delight, 258, 259
ION, morning song of, 421
Iona, 269
Iser, the, 300
ISRAEL, lament for, 6: destruction of, 286: the exodus of, 354

J

JERUSALEM, modern, 449
Jew, song for the wandering, 199: God's judgment against the Jews, 286, 494
John Anderson, 210
Joys fly fast, 8: visions of departed, 21
Justice, the triumph of, 426

K

KEPLER, JOHN, prayer of, 311
King, the true, 358

L

LAIUS, the murderer of, 414
Lament, a, 183

Lamentations, 501—504
Land o' the leal, the, 325
Lapland love-song, 329
Lares, hymn to the, 231
LAWRENCE, MR, sonnet to, 113
LEICESTER, to my Lord of, 266
Liberty, ode to, 471—3
Life, the good, long, 30, 352—353: through death, 35: desire of long, 76: the shortness and uncertainty of, 153, 335: the means to attain a happy, 129: the winter of, 249: the character of a happy, 308: the shortness of and uncertainty of riches, 316, 317: the solitary, 319; the praise of a religious, 391, 392: the quiet, 319: the country, 343
Light, hymn to, 193—197
Lines on returning a blank book, 237, 238
Litany of the Holy Spirit, 209
Little is best, 19
LOFFT, CAPEL, sonnet to, 134
Loss, the, 176
London, 1802, 126
Lotos-eaters, the, 99
Louisa, 327
Love, true, 58: tyranny of, 61: universal rule of, 141: γλυκύπικρος, 97: and time, 110: and music, 179: philosophy of, 198: claim to, 226: young, 218: faithful, 280; immortality of, 310: love-song, 329, 330: immoderate, 420: mediocrity in, rejected, 216: the perfection of, 508
Lover, the desponding, 59, 274: the daybreak of the, 36: the injured, 52
LUCASTA, to, 262
Lucre, love of, 296
LUCY, 178
Lute, to his, 250
Lyrics for legacies, 1
LYTTELTON, monody to the memory of Lady, 506, 507

M

MAIDEN, song of the dying, 22
Man, shortsightedness of, 35: man's medley, 450
MARIUS amid the ruins of Carthage, 441
MARS, song of, 323

Index of Subjects   297

May, to, 379: the first of, 465
Melancholy, to, 180
Memnon's harp, 179
Memory, the pains of, 136: invocation of, 175: ode to, 299: a permanent blessing to the righteous, 295
Modern Greece, 263
Milton's House, 115
Misfortune, patience under, 284
Moon, sonnet to the, 105
Morning, the beauties of, 244: the melodies of, 272
Morpheus, 156
Mortality, on man's, 477
Moses, song of, 499, 500
Mourners, blessed, 350
Muse, the companionship of the, 454
Muses, a hymn to the, 83
Music, 3, 399: influence of, 47: power of, 255, 409, 442
Mutability, 191, 356

N

Nativity, ode on the, 371, 372, 373
Nature, the study of, brings not happiness, 66: the noble, 30: the education of, 282
Nautilus, to the, 431
Night, the lessons of, 393: to the, 480
Nightingale, the, 326: to the, 114
Nymph, the, complaining for the death of her fawn, 478

O

Oak, the, 230
October winds, 174
Ode to Evening, 518
Orpheus, 273: the prayer of, 65: and the Sirens, 484—7
Otter, to the river, 132

P

Pan, 95: song of the priest of, 201, 464: hymn of, 247
Parable, a, 89
Paris, Juno's offer to, 248; the judgment of, 424
Past and future, 221
Patience in adversity, 284

Patrick's purgatory, 257
Peace, to, 92, 374, 375, 385: the blessings of, 93: heavenly, 309
Pelops and Hippodamia, 410
Phillis, 279, 313
Piemont, on the massacre in, 116
Poesy, progress of, 239, 333, 334: address to, from prison, 454
Poet, obsequies of the, 96: house of the, when the assault was intended on the city of London, 115: trance of the, ended, 164: to his farm, 340
Poetry, his, his pillar, 342
Praise, dream of human, 429
Precepts, good, 32
Pride, 419
Primrose, the, 50: to an early, 322: to primroses filled with morning dew, 519
Proof to no purpose, 213
Proserpine, song of, 57
Prosperity, 98

R

Rainbow, the, 17
Redbreast, to the, 56
Redeem the past, 152
Reflections of an old man, 9
Regret, vanity of, 46, 446
Remembrance, 111
Requiescat, 203
Resurrection, ode on the, 16
Retirement, pleasures of, 119
Riches, the uncertainty of, 316, 317
Rivulet, the, 298
Rock, the lone, 436
Rome, to, 408
Rose, the, 122
Ross, on the death of Colonel Charles, in the action at Fontenoy, 332
Rule Britannia, 443

S

Sabrina, the spirit's address to, 256
Satyr, the, carrying Alexis, 437: leave-taking of the, 469
Saxham, to, 435
Scott, Sir W., on his departure from Scotland for Italy, 128
Sea, of the, 142: and land, 94: treasures of the, 276

Index of Subjects

Seamen, the song of the, 245
Seasons, the round of the, 192: a season for everything, 314
Self, dialogue between new and old, 331
September, 1815, 127
Serenade, 14
SIDNEY, Sir Philip, on the death of, 11
Simile, a, 7
SIMON, panegyric on the high priest, son of Onias, 355
Simplicity in dress, 488
Sin, the unfailing doom of, 416
Skylark, to a, 48, 450, 451, 452
Sleep, to, 123, 125
Soldier, the Christian, 395—6
Solitude, 368, 470: love of, 161, 162, 163
Song, Major Bellenden's, 10: a sad, 22: Fitz-Eustace's, 172, 173: drinking song, 300: Wolfram's, 81
Songstress, the, 222
Sorrows still pursue, 277
Sounds, midnight, 34: morning, 272
Spinning-wheel, song for the, 271
Spirit of delight, invocation of, 258, 259: the omnipresence of the great, 338: to the Almighty Spirit, 339
Spring, 170, 171, 376, 381: return of, 220, 378: northern, 380: ode on the, 397—8
ST JOHN the Evangelist, 104
Star, to a, 240: to the evening, 294
State, the constitution of a, 459
Storm, the, 489
Summer, on the departure of, 90, 357
Sun, hymn to the, 430: under eclipse, 402
Sympathy, blessing of, 77
Swallow, to the, 370

T

TEARS, vanity of, 25, 284
THALABA'S wanderings, 286
Thermopylæ, 166
The last man, 515
THOMSON, JAMES, ode on the death of, 344, 345
Timber, the, 349
Time, 223: breedeth change, 384: and love, 110
To-morrow, 466

Traitor, the, 173
Tranquillity, 71
Treasures of the deep, the, 276
Trojan women, lament of, on the downfall of Troy, 423
Troubles, on the folly of making, 54, 168, 388
TYRE, prophecy of destruction of, 493

V

VENICE, on the extinction of the republic of, 129: to, 439
VENUS, to, 369
Vicissitude, pleasure of, 382—3
Violet, to the, 42: to violets, 140
Virtue, beauty of, 62: man's surest stay, 328: alone makes difference between men and beasts, 433
Vita est benefactis extendenda, 352, 353

U

ULYSSES and the Siren, 463
Unseen, faith in the, 479
Urn, on a Grecian, 3.

W

War, the scourge of, 407: the spoils of, 413
Warfare, Christian, 472
Warrior, the, to his dead bride, 285: the falcon on the wrist of the, 386
Waterfall, the, 217
Welcome, 445
Winds, October, 174: ode to the west wind, 481
Winter, 461: the approach of, 139: on the winter solstice 1740, 149: the winter's evening, 261: the winter of life, 249: the pleasantness of, 297: ode, to, 458
Wish, a, 257: Cowley's, 160, 510
WOLFRAM'S song, 81
Woman, 290
World, the, 49: enmity with the, 161, 162, 163: world's wanderers, the, 44

Y

YEAR, the, 192
Youth, 283

INDEX OF FIRST LINES

A

	PAGE
A dew-drop, falling on the wild sea-wave	10
Ἀ μὲν οὔθ' ἱστῶν παλιμβάμους ἐφίλησεν ὁδούς	183
A power is passing from the earth	4
A slumber did my spirit seal	7
A trouble, not of clouds, or weeping rain	46
Abused mortals! did you know	153
Ἀχαλίνων στομάτων	200
Ἀκτὶς Ἀελίου, τί, πολύσκοπε	189
Again those sounds sweep on	10
Ah, fading joy, how quickly art thou past	17
Ah, happy Isle, how art thou chang'd and curst	163
Ah! who can tell how hard it is to climb	102
Alas! alas! thou turn'st in vain	91
Alas, how light a cause may move	149
Alas! regardless of their doom	227
All earthly charms, however dear	21
All the earth and air	223
All the world's bravery, that delights our eyes	77
All worldly shapes shall melt in gloom	266
Ἀλλ' ἐπεὶ σπλάγχνων ὕπο μάτερος	190
Almighty Spirit, thou that by	151
And said I that my limbs were old	52
And yet, as Angels in some brighter dreams	98
And what though winter will pinch severe	3
And when the sun begins to fling	69
Apollo!—king Apollo	141
Ἀρετὰ πολύμοχθε γένει βροτείῳ	188
Ἅρματα μὲν τάδε λαμπρὰ τεθρίππων	201
Art thou poor, yet hast thou golden slumbers	45
As an eagle, fed with morning	114
As rising on its purple wing	263
As when it happeneth that some lovely town	42
As, when the new-born phœnix takes his way	206
Ask me no more, my truth to prove	117
Ask me no more where Jove bestows	136
Ask me why I send you here	16
Ask not the cause why sullen Spring	17
At thy appearance, Grief itself is sad	76
Avenge, O Lord, thy slaughter'd saints, whose bones	42
Awake, awake, my Lyre	55
Awake, Aeolian lyre, awake	147
Awake, thou wintry earth	262

B

	PAGE
Bardolph! I say	273
Begin the song, and strike the living lyre	5
Beloved of God, to thee was given	37
Beneath a thick and silent shade	158
Beyond the Acherontian pool	91
Beyond the measure vast of thought	242
Blest youth, regardful of thy doom	146
Brightly, brightly hast thou fled	121
Bring me flowers all young and sweet	81
Brood not on things gone by	89
But, ah! what liveth long in happiness	3
But am I sole heir	278
But lately seen in gladsome green	101
But that immortall spirit, which was deckt	109
But thou who own'st that earthly bed	154
But when through all the infernal bounds	113
But who the melodies of morn can tell	113
By the streams that ever flow	22

C

Call it not vain:—they do not err	34
Calm is the morn without a sound	81
Can I cease to care	25
Can Love again o'er this sad breast	62
Captain Bodabill, why muse you so	280
Captain or Colonel, or Knight in arms	41
Care, thou canker of all joys	23
Care-charmer sleep, son of the sable Night	44
Χαῖρέ μοι, 'Ρώμα, θυγάτηρ 'Άρηος	193
Carthage! I love thee—thou hast run	216
Cease, rude Boreas, blust'ring railer	254
Child of the Spring! thou charming flower	13
Χρυσέα φόρμιγξ, Ἀπόλλωνος καὶ ἰοπλοκόμων	193
Cicada! thou who, tipsy with the dews	23
Come, gentle Venus, and assuage	169
Come, little infant, love me now	87
Come, peace of mind, delightful guest	172
Come take a woodland walk with me	93
Come, worthy Greeke, Ulysses, come	233
Consider ye and call for the mourning women	120

D

Daughter of Jove, relentless power	236
Dear mansion, once my father's home	151
Dear native brook! wild streamlet of the West	48
Doth then the world go thus, doth all thus move	44
Δρομαίων δ' ὅτε πολυπλανήτων	199
Dry those fair, those crystal eyes	25

E

Ἐγὼ καὶ διὰ μούσας	202
Ἐγὼ δὲ πλόκαμον ὐναδέτοις	203
Εἰ τὰ δάκρυ' ἡμῖν τῶν κακῶν ἦν φάρμακον	7
Εἰρήνα βαθύπλουτε καὶ	32
Εἰς ὄρος, μία δὲ βροτοῖς ἐστὶν εὐτυχίας ὁδός	8
Emblem of life, see changeful April sail	48
Ere, in the northern gale	104
Ἔρωτες ὑπὲρ μὲν ἄγαν ἐλθόντες	201
Every mortal, small or great	31
Ἦλθεν δ' ὑπὸ σπλάγχνων ὑπ' ὠδῖνός τ' ἐρατᾶς Ἴαμος	195

Index of First Lines 301

F

	PAGE
Fair Daffodils, we weep to see	69
Fair pledges of a fruitful tree	112
Fair ship, that from the Italian shore	131
Fair summer droops, droop men and beasts therefore	31
Fairest isle, all isles excelling	16
Fall'n is thy throne, O Israel	221
Farewell! on wings of sombre stain	161
Feathered lyric! warbling high	15
Few are my years, and yet I feel	60
First-born of Chaos, who so fair did'st come	75
Flow down, cold rivulet, to the sea	83
Fond words have oft been spoken to thee, Sleep	45
For lo the Sea that fleets about the land	52
For them the moon with cloudless ray	156
For Thou wert born of woman! Thou didst come	129
For whoso holds in righteousness the throne	207
Fortune, that with malicious joy	95
From life's superfluous cares enlarg'd	100

G

Gentle river! gentle river	219
Get up, get up for shame, the blooming morn	270
Give me more love or more disdain	86
Give pardon, blessed soul, to my bold cries	42
Giver of glowing light	208
Γλαυκᾶς ὦ φιλέριθ' ἀλακάτα δῶρον 'Αθανάας	196
Gloomy winter's now awa'	88
Go up and watch the new-born rill	126
God that madest earth and heaven	2
Goe find some whispering shade neare Arne or Poe	115
Gold I've none, for use or show	1
Gone are the glorious Greeks of old	165
Good gossip, if you love me	285
Good sir, come from the door	281

H

Had I a cave on some wild distant shore	17
Hail, Memory, hail! in thy exhaustless mine	125
Hail, old patrician trees, so great and good	239
Hail! sacred thou to hallowed joy	235
Hail to thee, blithe Spirit	222
Haply when from those eyes	96
Happy that first white age! when we	232
Happy the man, whose wish and care	138
Hark! hark! the lark at heaven's gate sings	4
Hark! how the birds do sing	256
Hark, how through many a melting note	142
Hark! whence that rushing sound	53
He is not moved with all the thunder-cracks	94
He that is down need fear no fall	6
He that loves a rosy cheek	11
He that of such a height hath built his mind	94
He that thirsts for glory's prize	209
He who hath bent him o'er the dead	267
He who is good is happy	237
Hear ye this word which I take up against you	2
Here, as to shame the temples decked	111
Here new-built towns, aspiring high	182
High on a rock, whose castled shade	152
How are thy servants blest, O Lord	30
How calm, how beautiful comes on	79
How dull! to hear the voice of those	61
How happy is he born and taught	132
How now, sir? is your merry humour altered	276

	PAGE
How short is Life's uncertain space	57
How sweet it were, hearing the downward stream	35
How sweet the answer Echo makes	107
How was he honoured in the midst of the people	160
Hues of the rich unfolding morn	99
Hush, sweet Lute, thy songs remind me	102

I

I 'm wearing awa', Jean	141
I did but look and love awhile	20
I envy not their hap	12
I feel no care for coin	12
I 've roamed through many a weary round	25
I leave mortality's low sphere	181
I love all that thou lovest	106
I met Louisa in the shade	143
I praised the Earth, in beauty seen	109
I saw a falling leaf soon strew	2
I sung the joyful Pæan clear	207
I travelled among unknown men	68
I view thee on the calmy shore	55
I wish I was by that dim Lake	105
I will meet thee on the hill	265
I would I were a careless child	60
If aught of oaten stop or pastoral song	268
If in the fight my arm was strong	119
If thou, my love, wert by my side	138
If to a rock from rains he fly	84
If to be absent were to be	108
If weeping eyes could wash away	119
If wine and music have the power	123
If you, O Trophimus, and you alone	284
Ill-busied man! why should'st thou take such care	26
In a drear-nighted December	174
In all thy need, be thou possest	9
In childhood, when with eager eyes	75
In doubtful twilight Nature sleeps	242
In glowing youth he stood beside	134
In the calm spring, when the earth bears	183
In the downhill of life, when I find I' m declining	235
In the hour of my distress	83
In time we see the silver drops	179
In vain with various arts they strive	36
In yonder grove a Druid lies	154
Ἴσον δὲ νύκτεσσιν αἰεί	191
It must be so—Plato, thou reason'st well	263
It is not Beauty I demand	90
It is not growing like a tree	9
It is not that my lot is low	169
It tells the conqueror	184
It was, and still my care is	93
It would less vex distressed man	159

J

John Anderson my jo, John	84

K

κείσθω δόρυ μοι μίτον· ἀμφιπλέκειν	8

L

Lay a garland on my hearse	7
Lawrence, of virtuous father virtuous son	40
Leave off unfit complaints and clear	211
Let ambition fire thy mind	101

Index of First Lines

	PAGE
Let not thy youth and false delights	118
Let us quit the leafy arbour	128
Let us turn hitherward our bark, they cried	252
Like the violet which alone	117
Liquid Peneus was flowing	100
Lo! where the rosy-bosom'd Hours	186
Lofft, unto thee one tributary song	49
Look as the flow'r which lingeringly doth fade	43
Look, Delia, how we esteem the half-blown Rose	44
Lord of the vale! astounding Flood	13
Love thy mother, little one	58
Lovely, lasting peace of mind	116
Lovely nymph, with eye serene	214
Lyke as the culver on the bared bough	38

M

Mark how, a thousand streams in one	87
Mark that swift arrow how it cuts the air	148
Μαρμαίρει δὲ μέγας δόμος χαλκῷ	166
Martial, the things that do attain	88
Μέγα τι σθένος ἁ Κύπρις ἐκφέρεται	197
Men call you fayre, and you doe credit it	38
Mild offspring of a dark and sullen sire	140
Milton, thou shouldst be living at this hour	46
Mindful of disaster past	221
Morpheus, the humble god that dwells	58
Mourn, Spring, thou darling of the year	226
Music the fiercest grief can charm	1
Music, when soft voices die	2
My conscience is my crown	11
My dear and only love, I pray	145
My dearest love, since thou wilt go	90
My eyes are dim with childish tears	3
My fortune might I form at will	7
My heart leaps up, when I behold	5
My liege, I am advised what I say	277
My soul, there is a country	132

N

No after-friendship e'er can raise	73
No bitter tears for thee be shed	122
No longer seek the needless aid	253
No nightingale did ever chant	89
No war, or battle's sound	171
Nor can it bliss you bring	22
Nor can the parted body know	53
Not faster yonder rowers' might	54
Not Love, not War, nor the tumultuous swell	47
Not marble, not the gilded monuments	39
Not once or twice in our rough island story	6
Not song, nor beauty, nor the wondrous power	48
Not that thy trees at Penshurst groan	110
Not yet enslaved, not wholly vile	53.
Now each creature joys the other	175
Now, sir, have I met you again	273
Now sober Cynthia spreads her lucid beam	50
Now strike the golden lyre again	216
Now that the winter's gone, the earth hath lost	177
Now the golden Morn aloft	177

O

O fair and goodly star, upon the brow of night	97
O for a sculptor's hand	29
O from thy kindred early torn	72
O, I shall burst	279

	PAGE
O lady, twine no wreath for me	149
O Lord, I have heard thy speech	257
O memory, celestial maid	66
O music, sphere-descended maid	187
O nightingale, that on yon bloomy spray	41
O not to be were best for man	218
O nymph! approach, while yet the temperate sun	64
Ω φάος άγνὸν	199
O Queen of numbers, once again	128
O sire of storms! whose savage ear	228
O snatch'd away in beauty's bloom	70
O Swallow, Swallow, flying, flying South	170
O thou by heaven ordained to be	122
O thou my lyre, awake, arise	55
O thou, that prattling on thy pebbled way	249
O thou! who bad'st thy turtles bear	173
O thou, who by the light of Nature dost enkindle	133
O voice divine, whose heavenly strain	166
O, weep not for the gathered rose	4
O wild West wind, thou breath of Autumn's being	248
O you, the Virgins nine	28
October winds, wi' biting breath	66
O'er the rolling waves we go	99
Of holier joy he sang, more true delight	252
Of power and honour the deceitful light	137
Oft on the troubled ocean's face	20
Oft with its fiery force	186
Oft would the Dryads of these woods rejoice	260
Oh, deem not they are blest alone	157
Oh, Fortune, how thy restless wavering state	8
Oh! from your sacred seats look down	28
Oh golden link connecting man with man	8
Oh, how hard it is to find	34
Oh! sacred Memory, tablet of the heart	127
Oh! that we two were maying	24
On Linden, when the sun was low	228
Once did She hold the gorgeous east in fee	47
Only a little more	153
Ὀφελε πρότερον αἰθέρα δῦναι μέγαν	192
Or lead me where amid the tranquil vale	256
Or when the winter torrent rolls	111
Orpheus with his lute made trees	15

P

Phillis is my only joy	116
Philosophers consume much time and pain	285
Phyllis! why should we delay	134
Play, Phœbus, on thy lute	1
Plead you to me, fair dame	277
Πρὸς εὐάνθεμον δ' ὅτε φυάν	194

Q

Queen and Huntress, chaste and fair	110
Queen of fresh flowers	176

R

Rarely, rarely, comest thou	106
Rest on your battle-fields, ye brave	155
Retire, and timely, from the world, if ever	24
Risest thou thus, dim dawn, again	131

S

Sacred Goddess, Mother Earth	19
Say, is your tardy master now at hand	274

Index of First Lines

	PAGE
Sees not my friend, what a deep snow	181
Servant of God! well done	185
She had left all on earth for him	21
She shall be sportive as the fawn	118
She sighs—like winds at eve	27
Shepherds all, and maidens fair	234
Shepherds, rise and shake off sleep	79
Short is our span; then why engage	14
Shout for the mighty men	62
Sing his praises that doth keep	33
Sleep, Ambition! Rage, expire!	179
Sleep!—we give thee to the wave	121
Sleep, little baby, sleep	137
Smiles on past Misfortune's brow	178
So much a stranger my severer Muse	10
So restless Cromwell could not cease	220
So, we'll go no more a roving	24
So, when the wisest poets seek	163
So, where the silent streams of Liris glide	260
Softly gliding as I go	213
Soldier, go—but not to claim	243
Sometimes upon the diamond rocks they leant	251
Star that bringest home the bee	124
Still is the toiling hand of Care	187
Stop in your wind, sir; tell me this	275
Strew on her roses, roses	80
Such is the fate of artless maid	167
Summer's last lingering rose is blown	51
Sun-girt City! thou hast been	214
Supreme Divinity! who yet	80
Sure thou didst flourish once	157
Sweet are the harmonies of Spring	126
Sweet daughter of a rough and stormy sire	64
Sweet Echo, sleeps thy vocal shell	59
Sweet Echo, sweetest nymph, that livest unseen	54
Sweet evening hour! sweet evening hour	64
Sweet Iser! were thy sunny realm	127
Sweet to the gay of heart is Summer's smile	49
Sweet warriour! when shall I have peace with you	38
Sweetest love, I do not go	230
Swift as light thoughts their empty career run	76
Swifter far than summer's flight	70
Swiftly turn the murmuring wheel	112
Swiftly walk over the western wave	247

T

	PAGE
Τὰ μὲν κατ' οἴκους ἐφ' ἑστίας ἄχη	191
Ταὶ δ' ἐπεὶ ὑλόκομον νάπος ἤλυθον, οὐρειᾶν	204
Τὸν ἅλα τὰν γλαυκὰν ὅταν ὤνεμος ἀτρέμα βάλλῃ	33
Τάχυ δὲ Καδμείων ἀγοὶ χαλκέοις	190
Take back the virgin page	96
Take these flowers, which purple waving	5
Τέαν, Ζεῦ, δύνασιν τίς ἀνδρῶν	198
Tell me not how fair she is	114
Tell me of his expenses! which of you	282
Tell me, thou Star, whose wings of light	13
The bark divine, itself instinct with life	250
The bright-haired sun with warmth benign	174
The dear illusions will not last	73
The Earth and Ocean were not hushed to hear	129
The Earth that in her genial breast	21
The Falcon is a noble bird	180
The fallen leaf repeats the mournful tale	30
The flower that smiles to-day	161
The fountains mingle with the river	78

F. S. II.   20

Index of First Lines

	PAGE
The Gift to king Amphion	104
The glories of our blood and state	164
The hinds how blest, who ne'er beguiled	156
The lady Mary Villiers lies	27
The lark now leaves his watery nest	11
The leaves around me falling	123
The low sweet tones of Nature's lyre	26
The merry waves dance up and down and play	18
The mountains huge, that seem to check the sky	12
The oracles are dumb	172
The peace of Heaven attend thy shade	72
The shape alone let others prize	98
The shepherds on the lawn	171
The snow, that crowns each mountain's brow	158
The solemn harmony	61
The sturdy rock, for all his strength	143
The sun is sinking in the fiery west	107
The sun-beams streak the azure skies	74
The time admits not flowers or leaves	130
The wanton troopers riding by	245
The warrior-chief in soft repose	92
The World's a bubble, and the life of Man	245
The world's great age begins anew	59
Thee the voice, the dance, obey	147
Thee Winter in the garland wears	84
Then, Death, why should'st thou dreaded be	244
Then feasted, to the flowery groves	183
Then let the chill Sirocco blow	231
There are who, darkling and alone	246
There be none of Beauty's daughters	103
There is a calm for those who weep	94
There is a land of pure delight	250
There is a single stone	212
There is a tongue in every leaf	150
There is no bound of time or place	92
They are all gone into the world of light	98
They sin who tell us Love can die	133
This little vault, this narrow room	86
This only grant me, that my means may lye	262
This world is all a fleeting show	57
Thou divinest, fairest, brightest	238
Thou rising sun, whose gladsome ray	144
Though frost and snow lock'd from mine eyes	211
Though I miss the flowery fields	225
Though rude winds usher thee, sweet day	124
Though the torrents from their fountains	78
Thrice happy he, who by some shady grove	43
Thus, while I ape the measure wild	103
Τί γὰρ ἀλκά, τί δὲ κάλλος	205
Τίκτει δέ τε θνατοῖσιν Εἰράνα μεγάλα	32
Time's an hand's-breadth; 'tis a tale	89
'Tis not rich furniture and gems	210
'Tis not wealth that makes a king	162
'Tis only title thou disdain'st in her	286
Τίς ὄντιν' ἁ θεσπιέπεια Δελφὶς εἶπε πέτρα	197
'Tis sweet to hear	5
'Tis vanished all—in hurried flight	56
To me the Sun is more delightful far	77
Toil on! toil on! ye ephemeral train	85
Too late I've stayed, forgive the crime	27
True love's the gift which God has given	19
Trust not, sweet soul, those curled waves of gold	82
Turn, Fortune, turn thy wheel	22
Tyrant of man! Imperious Fate	70
Tyre of the West, and glorying in the name	29

Index of First Lines 307

U

	PAGE
Under the greenwood tree	30
Unheard in summer's flaring ray	18
Unthinking, idle, wild and young	28
Up with me! up with me into the clouds	224

V

Vainly were the words of parting spoken	271
Victorious men of earth, no more	82
Virgin, daughter of Locrine	105

W

We are as clouds that veil the midnight moon	74
Weak is the vanity, that boasts of riches	284
Weak Lyre! thy virtue sure	56
Wee, modest, crimson-tipped flow'r	267
Welcome, maids of Honour	51
Welcome, welcome do I sing	219
Well, he's not here I seek for	275
Well, then, I now do plainly see	60
What art, vocation, trade or mystery	283
What constitutes a state	229
What hidest thou in thy treasure-caves and cells	115
What is grandeur, what is power	3
What is 't to me	95
What is this passing scene	168
What liberty so glad and gay	71
What man in his wits had not rather be poor	125
What time my heart unfolded its fresh leaves	50
What woke the buried sound that lay	68
When Britain first at Heaven's command	217
When I consider how my light is spent	40
When I have seen by Time's fell hand defaced	39
When I survay the bright	184
When Israel was from bondage led	160
When midnight o'er the moonless skies	6
When mirth is full and free	34
When riseth Lacedæmon's hardihood	108
When the crab's fierce constellation	135
When the oldest cask is opened	67
When the sun from his rosy bed	224
When the wearying cares of state	63
When to the sessions of sweet silent thought	40
When we meet as when we part	63
When winds the mountain oak assail	139
Where Ausonian summers glowing	209
Where is each boasted favourite of Fame	35
Where's now imperial Rome	36
Where old Euphrates winds his storied flood	36
Where shall the lover rest	65
Where shall the traitor rest	65
Where the angelic hosts adore Thee	32
Whether men do laugh or weep	15
While not a leaf seems faded; while the fields	46
Who are these coming to the sacrifice	9
Who is the honest man?	264
Who shall awake the Spartan fife	240
Whose calm soul in a settled state	180
Why art thou slow, thou rest of trouble, Death	50
Why dost thou heap up wealth, which thou must quit	136
Why do ye weep, sweet Babes? can tears	269
Why, exclaimed one of them	274
Why should man's aspiring mind	164

Index of First Lines

	PAGE
Why sittest thou on that sea-girt rock	145
Why so pale and wan, fond lover	19
Why, why repine, my pensive friend	14
With horns and with hounds, I waken the day	140
With lorn delight the scene I view'd	57
With how sad steps, O Moon, thou climb'st the skies	37
With joy, with joy now, sacred Thebes, resound	206
Woods, that wave o'er Delphi's steep	97

Y

Ye field flowers! the gardens eclipse you, 'tis true	265
Yes, I remember well	215
Yestreen the mountain's rugged brow	176
Yet ere I go	67
Yet, even whene'er the least appeared	241
You see this gentle stream that glides	85
You who are earth, and cannot rise	261

CAMBRIDGE PRINTED AT THE UNIVERSITY PRESS

www.ingramcontent.com/pod-product-compliance
Lightning Source LLC
Chambersburg PA
CBHW030017240426
43672CB00007B/987